The Fashionista Files

Additional Praise for *The Fashionista Files*

"*The Fashionista Files* is filled with the kind of advice that you get from your best girlfriends. It's all you need to look and feel amazing without looking like you actually tried."

—BOBBI BROWN, CEO, Bobbi Brown Cosmetics

"With the departure of *Sex and the City*, the fashion hungry obsessed need look no further than *The Fashionista Files*, an encyclopedia from A to Zegna on how to walk, talk, and look like a million bucks. Before it's in fashion, it's in *The Fashionista Files*."

—BONNIE FULLER, Chief Editorial Director, American Media Inc.

"Imagine a book that tells you not only what designers to wear, but how to pronounce them! Not only what time to arrive, but what to do once you get there! This is an indispensible guide to worshiping at the throne of fashion and fabulousness. *J'adore* it!"

—MICHAEL MUSTO, *The Village Voice*

"Melissa and Karen are the kind of terminally deranged fashionistas who give fashion a bad name . . . and I love them for it."

—SIMON DOONAN, author of *Wacky Chicks*

"The real princepessas Robinovitz and de la Cruz write the believe-it-or-not take on what's really going on behind the scenes of the ugly business of being beautiful. Wow! What a ride! I love this book."

—JANICE DICKINSON, "The World's First Supermodel"
and author of *No Lifeguard on Duty* and
Everything About Me Is Fake . . . and I'm Perfect!

Praise for *How to Become Famous in Two Weeks or Less* by Melissa de la Cruz and Karen Robinovitz

"For anyone who has ever stood before a bathroom mirror and secretly thanked The Academy, a hilarious guide to becoming 'It' in an age where the line between fame and infamy is as fine as a Manolo Blahnik stiletto heel." —BONNIE FULLER, former editor-in-chief, *US Magazine*

"Some are born famous, some achieve fame, and some have fame thrust upon them. For the rest of us, this book is essential reading."

—TOBY YOUNG, author of *How to Lose Friends and Alienate People*

"Let's face it, who doesn't want their fifteen minutes of fame? But the road to getting there can be as difficult as crawling over broken glass. Karen and Mel take you on an 'ouch-free' red carpet ride to the VIP room in this great read with lots of laughs along the way."
—ROSHUMBA WILLIAMS, supermodel and
correspondent for *Entertainment Tonight*

"Karen and Melissa capture the zeitgeist of American pop culture perfectly. Consider this 'the rules' to gaining popularity and fame for the generation raised on *The Real World*. Plus, it's a riot."
—MOLLY SIMS, MTV host, actress, supermodel

"[A] sassy and shamelessly shallow guide to landing in the limelight . . . [an] entertaining look at the often frightening world of fame."
—*Publisher's Weekly*

"A must-read for every aspiring A-lister, de la Cruz and Robinovitz's guidebook for pursuing fame and notoriety in New York high society has everything you'll need to hoist yourself above the hoi polloi; along with every reason not to bother."
—*Gotham* magazine

"Don't waste your time trying to make it on *American Idol*. All you need to propel yourself into the spotlight are the burning yearning for celebrity and a copy of this guffaw-inducing guidebook. Authors de la Cruz and Robinovitz created, then followed, a set of fame-focused rules which managed—for journalistic purposes—to launch them onto the most sparkling party pages and gossip columns. . . . The riotous read wittily illuminates the requirements of fame and consequently exposes why you probably don't want any part of it."
—*LA Confidential*

"Karen Robinovitz and Melissa de la Cruz will have you laughing on the red carpet in no time."
—*Marie Claire*

The Fashionista Files

Adventures in Four-inch Heels and Faux Pas

Melissa de la Cruz **and** Karen Robinovitz

Ballantine Books
New York

A Ballantine Book
Published by The Random House Publishing Group

Copyright © 2004 by Melissa de la Cruz and Karen Robinovitz

Ballantine and colophon are registered trademarks of Random House, Inc.

www.ballantinebooks.com

Library of Congress Control Number: 2004095332

ISBN 0-345-46328-5

Manufactured in the United States of America

First Edition: September 2004

4   6   8   9   7   5   3

Text design by Lee Fukui

This book is lovingly dedicated to our moms,

Ching de la Cruz and Judi Robinovitz,

the original fashionistas in four-inch heels,

who may regret teaching us so much about fashion

after reading our book/confessional.

Thank you for inspiring us to be all that we are—

and to look good doing it!

We would have nothing to wear

if it weren't for you!

Contents

The
Fashionista
Files

Fashion!
Don't Leave Home Without It

If you think fashionistas are that rare breed lucky enough to have been born in Paris and educated in Swiss boarding schools, are able to run in high heels and oversize sunglasses through airports, sip 1985 Château Lafite Rothschild with film directors in the Hamptons, edit fashion magazines, sit front-row at fashion shows, and own the latest outfit even before it hits the stores, you're right . . . but you're also wrong.

Today's fashionista is, as the Kinks put it, a dedicated follower of fashion. She is anyone who has rejected the tried-and-true, staid-and-sensible, matching-bag-and-shoes, no-white-after-Labor-Day rules to follow a fantasy of art-directed glory.

A fashionista is a teenage raver in all black, a drag queen with tearsheets of supermodels on her bedroom walls, a doctor who wears stilettos with her lab coat, a classics professor who revels in Prada, a twelve-year-old girl who reads Mommy's *Vogue* under the covers late at night and carefully plots what she'll wear to school at least twelve to fifteen hours in advance, and anyone and everyone whose world has been touched and inspired by fashion and who aspires to a life of whimsy, elegance, frivolity, and fabulousness.

You can recognize a fashionista by the pointy shoes she wears, her never-changing haircut, her affinity for French techno music, and her uncanny ability to get into nightclubs without waiting in line. She's the girl who can make a halter top from a T-shirt, knowingly guess what the starlets are wearing on Oscar night, and make Old Navy look like Chanel. She mixes cheap, no-name Kmart and thrift-store finds with high design. She puts herself together with ease—and daydreams about how to mix and match her clothing in new, innovative ways. She fancies accessories and understands that an outfit just isn't an outfit without the right pair of shoes.

Fashionistas are also not afraid to look slightly ridiculous. Just look at Betsey Johnson, who cartwheels down the fashion runway in all her kooky glory. Or Isabella Blow, the British muse of hat designer Philip Treacy, with her insane headgear. Like them, you have to be willing to take risks and slide into open-toe shoes in the winter. Stepping beyond the line is all part of the lifestyle. If a snide someone ever asks you if you're trying to look like an elfin hooker (as someone said to Karen when she wore a smashing emerald-green one-shouldered Alice Roi minidress with trailing chiffon shards to a party), or says, "Should I call you Pocahontas?" (as someone asked Mel when she had her hair done in Bo Derek braids way before J.Lo resurrected them in one of her videos), just take it in stride and don't let it bother you. Some people are intimidated by fashion. Don't be one of them!

Being a member of the fashion species is about more than just fashion. It is an entire way of being and living that includes an appreciation for all pop culture phenomena, from television and food to film and literature. It means going to trendy restaurants, or at least talking about them from an all-knowing point of view. A fashionista prides herself on the details—noticing everything from the lighting (flattering or not?), the curve of a table, the art on a wall, the hue of a shade of paint, the uniforms the waiters wear, the carb count of an Advantage bar.

Her vocabulary is stocked with fashion terms (utilitarian chic, empire waist, kick pleat). She has more black pants than you can imagine—and a reason behind why she needs each and every pair (they are so different from one another if you really think about it, you know). She drinks designer water (Evian, anyone?), and is obsessed with classic fifties cinema, guilty pleasures (fast food, disco, and celebrity gossip!), cell phones, lacy frills, spa moments, the pop art movement, British tabloids, car services (even if that means Mom dropping you off at the mall), and multicultural influences of all kinds. She can pull off the kind of crazy getups no one else could get away with. And she can make anything look stylish (all she needs is a pair of scissors, fabulous earrings, and a bit of imagination).

This book will show you how to embrace fashionistadom to the fullest, from how to maintain the treasures in your closet, to keeping your pocket Chihuahua safe in your Kelly bag while shopping, to ordering at restaurants, perfecting the double air-kiss, and loads of other tips for living large and loving every minute of it.

So if you are a fashionista (God bless!), or just want to look and talk like one (God bless!), then this is the book for you!

Like Mother, Like Daughter
✳ KAREN ✳

My mother is a fashionista. In all of the old pictures of her (posing, of course), she's wearing the best platform shoes, tight bell-bottom jeans, wide-brimmed hats, and lots of red suede. She was my style role model. And maybe my worst influence. When I was a child she carted me around when she went shopping, introducing me to designer names like Ungaro and Valentino. "These are the European greats," she once said, offering words of wisdom. I was probably eight at the time. And I remember watching her try things on and thinking that she was the most glamorous woman on Earth. Granted, it was the eighties, a time of excess, over-the-top fashion, shoulder pads, and vulgar indulgence. But to me, her day trips to stores seemed like theater. Fashion had a magical way of making people—or at least my mother and the other shoppers—happy. Mom emerged from the dressing room to find an eager gaggle of saleswomen applauding her, gushing, "Gorgeous! Beautiful! Smashing! Stunning!" I wanted to be all those things.

I learned valuable lessons from my mom on those excursions. She taught me that style is not about wearing expensive designer labels all at once, but putting them together in a way that reflects your personality. "Mix high fashion with jeans. Add shine, shimmer, and satin to cotton classics. Spice something up with a great hat. Have fun! Play," she said, encouraging me to try on her clothes and get creative with my own. She taught me that dressing is about fantasy, making up a character that fits a mood. And while it's not who you are at heart, it certainly can help you feel better. Even if it's just for a moment.

When she first married my father and they were struggling newlyweds saving to buy their first home, she would sneak to stores to buy boots without his permission. In 1968 she purchased $50 black leather knee-high boots that puckered down the front from a guy named Ivan Radowitz on Route 22 in Greenbrook, New Jersey. When she brought them home, excited and giddy to share her joy, my father went crazy. He yelled at her for being so frivolous. She cried and cried and begged to keep them. (She did and now she lives in Manolos. But she still has moments when she begs to keep certain fashion acquisitions that she picked up on a whim.)

In a way I was reared on fashion. It was my destiny. My mother was always very concerned with how I was dressed. There are tons of baby photos of me wearing her oversize Chanel sunglasses. She used to tape pink bows to my head when I had no hair. And she basically used me in order to indulge her own flights of fashion fancy. "Let's put her in this," she'd say, as if she were a mad scientist, mixing potions that could potentially explode. I was her doll. And I must have loved it, because the apple, much to my father's chagrin, does not fall far from the tree.

The evidence dates back to 1974. I was two and a half years old and my father was carrying me on his shoulders as he and my mom strolled Worth Avenue, the Rodeo Drive of Palm Beach, Florida. The sun rays poured onto storefronts like gleaming spotlights, beckoning passersby to enter and find the holy grail. We made our way up a small hill, and suddenly I saw it: the mother ship. It was gorgeous. A sleek black structure with crystal-clear glass and milky-white mannequins wearing disco confections of

My mom—chic in the
'60s, '70s, '80s, '90s,
and even on the ski
slopes!

velvet and fur. Epiphany struck! I swear, I thought I heard the *Star Wars* theme song as I proudly yelled at the top of my teeny lungs, "Look, Mommy! G-U-C-C-I! Gucci!" It was the first word I read. "We're in trouble," my father huffed. "Is it too late to return her?"

Forever Beautiful
✳ MELISSA ✳

I grew up in Manila, where my father headed his own investment bank and my mother was a well-photographed socialite. Her sizable walk-in closet had its own air conditioner. As a child I spent many afternoons there among her treasure trove of Yves Saint Laurent tunics, Oleg Cassini shifts, Valentino silk dresses, and Charles Jourdan shoes. My mother had women who visited her at home to give her facials, manicures, and pedicures, and a personal seamstress who masterfully re-created whatever outfit Jackie O was wearing that year (Mommy was big into Jackie O).

My mother never lets a day go by without wearing makeup. She is always impeccably coiffed and perfectly powdered. She revels in being feminine, and taught me it was my duty as a woman to always try to be pretty. (She still chastises my sister and me for not dressing up enough for when our husbands come home. We always complain she's so old-fashioned, but my husband said he would actually really appreciate it if I looked nice all the time.) She had an accounting degree and a successful career as a banker, but she never thought making it in a man's world meant giving up interest in your looks. In fact, she cultivated it. From my mom I learned to buy shoes I liked in every color (when you find a shape that fits you, invest!), and the power of a signature look. Friends and relatives from the Philippines still call capri pants "Ching's pants" because she always wore them in a variety of hues with four-inch heels.

She had a closet full of the best mules, and when I was twenty-one I was lucky enough to have been given a pair of her gold-heeled sexy strap sandals. (The sandals had two straps at the toe, and the ankle strap was a gold rubberized fabric that just looped around the ankle.) I never got as many compliments as I did when I wore those shoes. Men would fall at my feet. When the shoes broke in half, I took them to a cobbler to try to get them repaired. When I was told they were not salvageable, I felt like I had lost something special and irreplaceable. I'm still in mourning.

One of my fondest memories of our life in Manila is of my mother on her way out for the evening. She wafted down the staircase smelling of Diorrissimo, dripping with emerald and diamond jewelry. Her hair was perfectly set, and her high heels clicked on the marble floor. She was wearing a black silk blouse, a colorful tiered gypsy skirt, and a wide, elaborate, gold braided belt. I had some fifth-grade classmates over for a sleepover, and the group of girls stared at my mother as she came to kiss me good-bye. Manila society was very conservative back then—and my mother's outfit was one my friends had never seen before. I was apprehensive about their opinions.

"Wow" one of them breathed. "Your mom dresses soooo cool." The verdict was in. Fashion had won them over. And I've been trying to live up to that ever since.

Take it from us: A fashionista may be born, but she is also self-made. It has taken us years to develop our personal styles and find our fashionista niches. We've traded in our suburban past (yes, we both had a penchant for big hair, leg warmers, and acid-wash jeans) for fashionista sophistication (flatter hair, high heels, and dry-clean-only denim). To this day, we can accurately recount what we wore every first day of school. We curate our looks, right down to the "studied casual" sweats we wear when running out to get the dry cleaning. We catalog our memories and nights out by the ensembles we donned. ("Let's see . . . when did I meet him? Well, I was wearing a vintage strapless three-tiered ruffle minidress with a trailing scarf. So it must have been the summer of 2001.")

We still ransack our mothers' closets and have a sick habit of rationalizing our over-the-top, paycheck-busting purchases by saying, "It's for our daughters—someday." While we have both weathered (and endured) our fair share of ugly phases, too many "don'ts" to recall, overdoses of hairspray, and heavy black liquid eyeliner (!!!), we have always been enchanted by high fashion, fantastic indulgences, and the stylish trends by which the world turns. (Just ask our accountants!)

The moral of our stories: We have a weakness for style. All kinds of style: ladylike femme, power-suit-wearing mogul, masculine chic, edgy rocker chick, ghetto fabulous, nouveau hippie, contemporary cowgirl, space-age mod, grunge girl, prim preppy, bondage sexpot. We can't recall a single time we've hung out together without asking each other what we're wearing, where we bought it, and how soon we can borrow it. We've even discovered that we both own some of the same ridiculous things. We tear through magazines and fantasize about being able to have one piece from each different fashion spread—and we take this task so seriously, we even debate the advantages and disadvantages of each item. We even like to guess what we'd each want. We shop and put things on hold for each other and have been known to call each other at the eleventh hour before appointments, screeching, "What are you wearing? What should I wear? Should we both wear our white button-down Victorian shirts?"

We cherish fishnets and fedoras (such a chic combination), live beyond our means (ah, the life of a glamour girl), and own many, many pairs of shoes (you know the saying: You can never be too rich—or have too many pairs of shoes). We worship at the altars of Manolo Blahnik, Balenciaga, and Tom Ford, but are not afraid to go crazy in Tar-zjay (a.k.a. Target, but we like to use the French pronunciation) and Marshalls. Fashion. It is our passion. It is our obsession. It is our lives!

This tome will give you a fierce foray into the way of the fashionista. It's part memoir, full of our tales of fashion flops and feats, crashes and coups; and part self-help, packed with the kinds of tips that will help you to lead a life more fabulous. In our pages, you will find all the tools of the fashionista trade, everything you ever wanted to know about realizing your fashionista identity, building your closet from Gap to Gucci, shopping mantras to swear by, unleashing your inner couturier, beautifying to perfection, learning the proper jargon and vernacular, financing your haute habits, embracing the fashionista culture (icons, muses, designers of the past, films, books, and more—my, my, you have your work cut out for you), navigating the nightlife, and understanding the world of fashion shows and catwalk queens.

So strap on your stilettos and work it, girl.

CHAPTER 1

Êtes-Vous Fashionista?
Mais Oui!

If you have ever affected a British accent . . .

If you have ever spent a sleepless night worrying about the health of Marc Jacobs . . .

If you greet friends by kissing them on both cheeks (and you are not European) . . .

If you have ever sacrificed eating in order to shop . . .

If you have ever blown a paycheck on a pair of jeans . . .

If the only McCartney you are familiar with is Stella . . .

If your Visa bill is higher than your rent . . .

If you refer to designers by their first names in conversation (although you are not on a first-name basis with them) . . .

If you pester the mailman for your latest copy of *Vogue*, *Harper's Bazaar,* and *W* . . .

If you have absolutely nothing to wear (but your closet would heartily disagree) . . .

If you are usually late just because you just can't figure out what to put on your body . . .

Then you, my friend, are a fashionista. And there is no turning back now.

(Turn the page instead!)

LIFE IN THE "FASH" LANE

Welcome to the world of four-inch heels, four-ply cashmere, and four-dollar vintage dresses. Fashionistas will do anything to score the latest, the most obscure, the most absurd, the right-off-the-runway, the trendiest, the most expensive, the least expensive, the showstopper, the uniform, the marabou, the canvas, the nylon, the silk, the leather, the suede, the velvet, the tweed, the transparent, the ostrich feathers. We are a picky and difficult breed, with closets full of shredded tulle (but it's a Galliano!) and whalebone silk corsets (but it's a Gaultier!). We shop too much, eat too little, and sleep too late.

Our lives are often punctuated by sample sales and trunk shows, sometimes interrupted by phone calls from irate creditors, and always filled with overstuffed dry-cleaning bags on our living room floors. We experience dizziness when confronted by a supremely fabulous piece of clothing (it's called Balenciaga fever), and we have trouble sleeping if we don't have the right handbag for the season.

While we lust over the latest Parisian couture ball gowns, we also know the perils of head-to-toe designer, and we swoon when we see a well-dressed woman in a thrift-store jacket that may have served as the inspiration for Karl Lagerfeld's latest collection. We cheer when we score Dolce & Gabbana for 90 percent off! And sometimes we revel in retail (but shhhh, we're not proud of it). If it's impractical, theatrical, patterned, feathered, fur trimmed, and uncomfortable, you can bet it's hanging in our closet.

What we typically don't own: tailored classics, penny loafers, cable-knit sweaters (unless of course they've been shrunk, dyed, and somehow distressed, or are an intrinsic part of our ironic preppy phase). We live and die for our shoes. (They cost us a small fortune, after all.) And we'll take our favorite must-haves to our graves.

Some of you may scoff—huh, fashion is just so superficial. We have to say, it is. But it also isn't. Fashion is a part of life, something we need to protect our bodies from the cold and the radical agents that pollute the air (thank you, Alexander McQueen, for making such a mundane task look so damn good). It is also a form of art, self-expression, and a representation of more emotional roots. Fashion evokes a mental response from its appreciators. It can make us weep and make us feel empowered at once. It inspires thought, ideas, and creativity, and whether you shop Wal-Mart or Chanel, chances are we've all dealt with the same issues, moments, joys, and frustrations over fashion. Fashion. It does a life some good!

It's Not What You Can Do for Fashion; It's What Fashion Can Do for You

• It will cheer you up when you're feeling blue. Life is hard. Fashion is not. Wear red.

• It will transform your attitude and entire spirit. Nothing like a sleek pin-striped suit (with nothing under the jacket) or modern tuxedo with tall, tall heels and an envelope clutch to make you feel in charge. And trust us, you don't know power until you put on a pair of stiletto motorcycle boots and leather pants—or sexy until you slink into an Agent Provocateur slip and patent leather open-toe Betty Boop pumps.

• It will distinguish you from others. Who's going to forget the person who wears a gorgeous all-white suit with a black silk button-down shirt and striped black-and-white heels to an afternoon wedding, a lace dress and giant fedora to a luncheon, overalls rolled up with high, high heels and a teeny tank top and newsboy cap and great Chanel clutch for a casual Sunday brunch, or a fur jacket with a microminiskirt, knee-high boots, and a whole lot of attitude . . . for no reason at all?

• It will give you a reason to go out. What good will a hot little dress do for you if you're parked on the sofa, reading about what other people are wearing in a magazine and watching how celebrities dress on *E!* at the same time?

• When all else fails, it will give you something to fantasize about. Cavalli wishes and stiletto dreams for all!

• It makes you laugh. Just look through some of your old yearbooks for proof.

• It represents a moment in time. Proper day dresses with full skirts were fifties. Hippies were sixties. Bell-bottoms were seventies. Big shoulder pads were eighties. We're still trying to figure out the nineties. And it's too soon into the aughts to tell.

• It provides an excellent and organized way to catalog your memories. "Hmm, I can't remember when I dated Bryan. Wait. I was really into grunge then. Combat boots, three or four flannel shirts, skullcaps. So it was late 1993, early 1994."

• It helps the economy. Shopping is actually a charitable act in financially hard times. Give back, people!

This chapter will give you insight into our wacky world and break down our species into all the different types of fashionistas (choose a different one to be every day of the week), show you how to make over your mate (men often need so much help), teach you the importance of the almighty gay male best friend (who else will tell you when your butt looks fat without hurting your feelings or secretly being happy that it does?), and present the general rules we live by (rules, however, are made to be broken).

GENUS FASHIONISTA

Now that you're an acknowledged member of our tribe, figure out what kind of fashionista you are—or want to be. Here are the main subspecies of our breed—and what it takes to become each one:

The Fairy Godmother Fashionista

If your closet is an open house . . . if you share news about the latest sales . . . if you're always ready to help repair a hem, pick out a bridal gown, or lend your favorite cocktail dress to a friend in need, then you're everyone's favorite fashionista—the fairy godmother who expresses her love through fashion's magic. Your MO is to:

• Read Page Six's gossip in the *New York Post* (www.pagesix. com) religiously—celebrity gossip is now a vital part of your existence! Share choice tidbits with your inner circle.

• Make sure you put your psychic or astrologer at the top of your speed dial (if you don't have a mystic clairvoyant, get one, but please avoid hotlines with Dionne Warwick as a spokesperson).

• Bring your small, furry dog with you wherever you go. Consider naming it Jean-Claude.

• Become best friends with a flaming fashionista, who will love you when you're at your worst, find your beauty when you're broken out, and tell you when you're being crazy, high-maintenance, and incredibly cute in the same sentence.

• Laugh at your fashion follies and take risks with your style. The Fairy Godmother Fashionista is fun, bold, brazen, and brash inside and out; she is one of the brave few who can work it in short skirts, stilettos, and bobby socks without looking like a reject from a ZZ Top video.

• Live for bargain and thrift-store finds. If you see something your friends—or mom—would like, call them and ask if they'd like you to pick it up for them. You must do unto others, as the saying goes, as you'd like them to do unto you. And organize fashion sale field trips with the girls (and perhaps a pilgrimage to the Prada outlet outside Florence—even if it's on your honeymoon).

The Fashionista from "Across the Pond"

If you speak with a British accent, whether you grew up in Croydon (where Kate Moss was born on January 16, 1974) or in Michigan (like Madonna, who now speaks like the queen), call strangers "darling" and "love" as a matter of course, and date only shaggy-haired, questionably clean, wanna-be-rock-star types, you're a fash-ionista from the other side of the Atlantic. To perfect your schtick:

• Pair vintage concert T-shirts (Bowie, KISS, and the Rolling Stones are best—you adore glam rock) with sequins, crystals, and satin for evening.

• Revel in nightlife. Never come home before three in the morning. (You girls can sure par-tay.)

• Think of dinner as nothing more than a cigarette and a Diet Coke. Breakfast, however, can be hearty: steak and eggs.

• Avoid the torture of braces (you're secretly proud of your crooked teeth).

• Add vintage fur to your wardrobe. Wear with denim miniskirts.

• Don't fret over wine stains on your clothes (it only gives them character).

• Invest in a pony-hair handbag instead of a dog (animals are far too much work, as much as you love them). Consider naming it Jean-Claude.

The Boho Fashionista

You never use a blow-dryer. You own a passel of peasant shirts and djellabas. And you are a devout follower of Deepak Chopra, Ash-tanga yoga, and power Pilates. You're a flower-child fashionista! While you always shave your legs, you:

• Apply makeup in order to make it look like you don't. Make sure your lips are glossed at all times.

• Wear pigtails, low ponytails, and fresh flowers in your hair.

• Embrace Buddhism and say things like, "Oh, I must go home and 'sage' to clean off bad energy," after an encounter with frosty, snobby wicked-witch fashionistas.

- Mix expensive Marc Jacobs or Marni pieces with Kmart coups and Birkenstocks.

- Consider filmmaking as a career. Try getting Bill Murray to star in your second feature.

- Drink cranberry tea and warm water with lemon, and schedule a monthly colonic.

- Get a belly-button ring—and a tattoo of the "om" symbol on the small of your back.

- Always know when Mercury is in retrograde.

The Wicked-witch Fashionista

If you roll your eyes at knockoffs—even when you're secretly wearing one—and keep your sunglasses on at all times, even in elevators, you're the evil genius of the fashionista world. To keep your cold image going, you should:

- Hone your social-climbing skills by brushing up on the who's-who list of major socialites and royal players of your town. Befriend these women, if you can arrange it.

- Cultivate your ice-queen image by refraining from smiling in order to prevent laugh lines.

- Start saving for Botox. At the first sign of a forehead furrow, which can occur by twenty-five years of age, you *must* dash to your derm.

- Never eat in public (*quelle horreur!*). Work out—you want your arms to be a little *too* defined to incite the jealous gaze of your peers. Thrive on the envy of other women.

- Become legendary. Abuse your assistant. Make sure she takes down notes for the resultant tell-all best seller. Offer only gracious comments when it's published. You'll be even more admired.

- Ensure that you are well coiffed and manicured, including eyebrow, lip, and (eek!) chin waxing for all public appearances.

- Never leave home without a reservation. If by some foul chance you're made to wait, cause a stink by stomping your stiletto and name-dropping (make up fabulous-sounding names if need be).

The Quirky Fashionista

If you idolize Björk and think that the Marjan Pejoski swan dress she wore to the Oscars in 2000 was the *bomb,* wear black turtlenecks under white eyelet summer dresses, pile on smoky eye shadow and don Jeremy Scott's Venus on a Half Shell swimsuits (a swimsuit with an attached four-foot-tall foam clamshell on the butt), you're a fashionista on the cutting edge. You don't care what anyone thinks and you certainly march to the beat of your own drum. Your style:

• If you come from an upper-crust home, deny it. If you don't, act like you do—and *then* deny any wealthy, worldly beginnings.

• Perfect the vapid, blank gaze. (Note: You are above it, whatever *it* is.)

• Throw your mother's old prairie dress over jeans for a fresh look that's part Laura Ingalls Wilder and part Chloë Sevigny.

• Rent all films by Harmony Korine, Fellini, and Luis Buñuel of *Belle de Jour* fame.

• Read the works of Sylvia Plath and expatriate writers like George Sand.

• Date child prodigies who never went to college and built a lucrative career anyway; tortured artists with very pale skin and highly controversial bodies of work; former Ivy Leaguers turned actors who star in dark, eerie indie films, tend not to shave often, and wear tight polyester vintage pants. If those boys don't work out, former Ivy Leaguers turned middle-management admins are fine, too.

Sapphic Fashionista

Your uniform consists of smart loafers (Prada, if possible), small round glasses (rimless are preferable), man-style suits or low-slung trousers with a crease down the middle of the leg. Ellen is your hero. Rosie is not. You worship Hillary Swank's performance in *Boys Don't Cry*, but wish that the director had instructed her to let her armpit and leg hair grow. You're a lady-loving lady fashionista. You're here! You're queer! The world has no choice but to get used to it!

- Learn your way around a camera. Subscribe to *Vanity Fair.*

- Keep your hair on the shorter side of long.

- Develop an intense appreciation of twentieth-century and folk art.

- Pronounce your *S* sounds with a slight *lishp* (witnesh Melisha Etheridge).

- Dismiss all renegsbians (lesbians who become straight) from your Rolodex.

- Hang out with a circle of very creative types, including Madonna.

- Note: Being Sapphic does not mean you cannot embrace lipstick and dresses.

Sassy Teen Fashionista

You're artsy, moody, and gothic. People think you're angry, but really you're just misunderstood, and so what if you delight in slamming doors. You have a drawerful of vampy dark matte lipstick and a bit of a candle obsession. You're a teen fashionista with sass. To cultivate this persona:

- Make fishnet hose and combat boots part of your signature style.

- Disdain all forms of extravagance (so provincial!).

- Practice Wicca and design your own clothes (all it takes is a Hanes T-shirt and a pair of scissors, sweetheart).

- If you're not already publishing your own zine, start now.

- Acquire a wicked record collection from garage-sale vinyls.

- Never admit to liking those Lionel Richie love songs. (But it's okay. We all do!)

Mafia/Ghetto-fab Fashionista

If you're a label lover who speaks with a sharp Jersey/Brooklyn twang (i.e., "Whay-a are those Gooochie bags? Oh, they-a ov-a thay-a!"), who piles on large amounts of gold jewelry and liquid eyeliner, then just *fuhgeddaboudit*, you a fashionista, aiiight?

- Whether you hail from a rough neighborhood or from the better part of town, always keep up a tough appearance.

- Date street guys who ride Harleys.

- Get motorcycle boots—with stilettos.

- Keep your nails very long—and French manicured. Toes, too.

- Take crap from no one. Especially men. Slap them around if possible.

- Appreciate white fur, Lincoln Navigators, hip-hop music, and perhaps a good gun scandal here and there.

Mummy Fashionista

Soccer moms make your skin crawl. You can't bake a chocolate-chip cookie to save your life. You've named your offspring Philomena, Tuleh, and Tarquin. So start scheduling play dates in between trunk shows, manicures, and pedicures . . . you're the mother of all fashionistas!

- Learn how to get baby spit-up out of suede, leather, and goat-hair Gucci.

- Dress your child in chiffon, micro leather jackets, and funny little hats. Your baby (like your well-dressed husband, who, thanks to you, has become very aware of all the top designers and trends) is a glorified accessory, yet another extension of the image you project. She should dress like you, too (track pants with rainbow stripes and leopard slippers).

- Take photos of the little one when she wears her first La Perla. Label it as such. "Ya-elle, first La Perla!"

- Shop for your baby in cool locations or unexpected ones (boy clothing for girls, because little girls look the most adorable in killer cargo pants).

• Never let your baby go out in public with an outfit that has attached footsies (that's for bedtime only).

• Create a groovy nursery for your kid that would be the envy of all *your* friends.

• Messenger breast milk between shows during Fashion Week. Pumping up at the tents never felt so good.

Pop Tart Fashionista

Your pants barely cover your pubis and you regularly reveal at least twice the amount of skin most people would ever dream of exposing. You probably did some catalog modeling (or Mickey Mouse Club acting) as a child, but you're still waiting for your big record deal. In the meantime, you take karaoke spin classes at the gym. Hit everyone, baby, one more time, you're a fashionista pop princess in the making! Your deal is this:

• Tell people you're a virgin, even if you dress like a slut—and live with your boyfriend.

• Do five hundred sit-ups a day, a thousand if you're being good.

• Add very blond (peroxide!) highlights to your hair.

• Gravitate toward shoes with obnoxiously high platform soles.

• Dance at any opportunity.

• Add feather-trimmed coats, vinyl catsuits, and Daisy Dukes to your wardrobe rotation.

The Sisters Fashionista

Fashionistas are more powerful in numbers. So if you're any of the above and have a female sibling who's also any of the above, you fit this bill. Several examples of the type include:

• Jackie Onassis and Lee Radziwill: the original stylish sister pair. Jackie married a Kennedy and the richest man in the world; Lee married a count and was Truman Capote's best friend.

• The Miller sisters: Pia, Marie-Chantal, and Alexandra, heiresses to the duty-free fortune. They conquered the fashion and social universe in the early nineties, scoring a *Vanity Fair* profile and photo spread wherein they were depicted as nineteenth-century socialites. They once said the best advice their mother gave them was "don't bite your nails and don't get fat." Pia married and divorced a Getty; Alexandra married and divorced a von Furstenberg; Marie-Chantal married (and did not, at least at the time of publication, divorce) a prince of Greece and now designs a luxury line of (mostly cashmere) children's wear.

• Ashley and Mary-Kate Olsen: By the time they hit puberty, they had created a billion-dollar empire. They overcame their punch-line status to become formidable teen titans in girly embroidered minidresses and Range Rovers, with multi-million-dollar lofts in the West Village of New York.

• Paris and Nicky Hilton: Paris starred in a porno tape and her own hit reality TV show. Nicky is taller, younger, and has yet to hit the Internet most-wanted list. They both design handbags in Japan and wear head-to-toe serious designer duds at all times.

• Jane and Aerin Lauder: Heiresses to the Lauder fortune. Socialites and Oscar de la Renta, Carolina Herrera, Tuleh, Michael Kors, and J. Mendel mavens, they both work for the Lauder company and are often pictured in *Vogue, Bazaar,* and *Town & Country* in the most wonderful fashions.

MY FRIEND, THE FASHIONISTA
Karen, the Girl in "That Dress" at My Wedding
✳ MELISSA ✳

The church was a Gothic cathedral built in 1920, and I was kneeling in front of the sacristy, my soon-to-be-husband by my side. Everything was perfect. I had walked down the aisle without tripping on the voluminous tulle skirt of my Cinderella-meets-Grace-

Kelly gown, my dad had managed the handoff to Mike without a hitch, and Father O'Hare had quietly congratulated me on making a "spectacular entrance" and welcomed "all the beautiful fashionistas" to our wedding ceremony with genial charm. (Yes, he actually used that word! I was thrilled!)

Suddenly, there was a slight but audible gasp, a whispered ripple across the audience. I turned and saw my dear friend and writing partner Karen Robinovitz walking toward the reader's podium. She was wearing a completely backless beaded micromini Chloe dress that dipped so low in the back it practically grazed her bum.

And we were inside a Catholic church. (Luckily, she's Jewish.)

My relatives were scandalized. My friends, jaded New Yorkers all, looked just a tiny bit shocked. My parents nudged each other. Our *Marie Claire* editors in the pews took bets on the underwear situation (odds at five to one that she wasn't wearing any).

But I only smiled.

I had asked Karen to perform the first reading instead of relegating her to bridesmaid status and limiting her fashion choices for the evening. In fact, I had asked her to wear that specific dress to my wedding. "It's fantastic!" I told her. I knew it would cause a sensation, bring a hint of scandal, and give everyone something to talk about at the reception. A little bit of fashion fizz to add to the event.

Karen is the type of fashionista who thrives on "event" clothing. "If it doesn't scream 'Look at me!' then I don't want it," she has said, while trying on yet another ornately feathered, slashed-at-the-hip, cleavage-baring number. Her style is uniquely her own—a dash of super-high-end designer (think white fur chubbies by Alexander McQueen) over a pair of slim Levi's jeans (from the junior department), with signature skyscraper heels that add height to her tiny, four-foot-eleven-inch frame. She's unafraid of fashion and wears her clothing with utter confidence and a great sense of humor.

Everyone should have a fashionista friend like Karen. Not only does she own all these wonderful clothes—her closet serves as a communal source for her friends when we need to borrow some-

She has accepted Chloe as her personal savior! (You can't tell in this picture, but it's backless and revealing . . . trust me!)

thing a little outlandish, a little outrageous, for those extra-special occasions when a little black dress just won't do. Nothing to wear? Just pop over to Karen's and she'll find you the perfect thing.

We shop together, pore through magazines together, and conduct heated fashion play-by-plays on our outfits for the day. Her appetite for life is expressed in the vibrant way she dresses, and she's the first person I turn to for an opinion about a designer purchase. Her judgment is honest but never cruel. I look better because I have her in my life. She's taught me not to be afraid to be sexy, to stand out, and to claim the spotlight once in a while. My husband appreciates her influence as well—without her, I'd never wear the plunging V-neck tops that he adores (and that one insane Chloe barely-there T-shirt she got me as a gift when she came into a very large store credit after returning a present from her mother).

Later, at the reception, Karen apologized to Father O'Hare for her outfit. She felt a little guilty about her backless bravado.

"I'm sorry, I should have worn a sweater over my dress for the reading," she told him.

"My dear," Father O'Hare said, with a wink, "you were the best thing to happen to the altar!" Ahmen.

Sole Mates
✳ KAREN ✳

Melissa is not a fussy-clothes kind of girl. She is happiest in jeans and a little top of any kind, be it an Eley Kishimoto kimono, a tee from Target, a Marni hippie floral thing, or Gap button-downs (she has one in hot pink and one in turquoise, which she calls her "TV tops" because the colors pop on TV, should she have to make an appearance of any kind). Sure, she has a stable of hard-to-figure-out pieces that require a manual for wearing, dresses that have trains that may be hazardous to her health, and ruffled tops that don't quite stay buttoned (but they're Christian Dior!). But all in all, she's a laid-back fashionista who loves the fanciful, but is more often found in the casual. Down south is another story. Down south the girl is always equipped. She has a flawless shoe collection—four-inch-high turquoise Dolce & Gabbana heels with a fiercely pointy toe, vintage Vivienne Westwood platform sneaker clogs, gold pointy-toed numbers from the fifties, YSL sky-high stilettos with sassy polished prints across the toes, zipped-up Louboutins in denim . . . the list goes on and on. Even her sneakers are groovy—green-and-yellow suede Adidas slip-ons. Unfortunately, we are not the same shoe size.

I'll never forget the romantic evening in April of 2000, when we consummated our relationship (in fashionista speak, that means cocktails and seared scallops at a very trendy restaurant). We met at a party at the Chanel store before heading off to dinner at 60 Thompson, a posh hotel in Soho. Up until this time, our connection consisted of meeting once, writing incessant e-mails (often about fashion), and making a whole bunch of canceled plans. Upon first sight, I was smitten. A fresh breath of fashionista air was cast upon the dingy streets as Mel, a vision in midcalf, thong-toed Burberry high-heeled leather boots, emerged from a sullen yellow taxi. Three passersby stopped dead in their tracks to compliment her foot gear. And she modestly thanked them, adding that they were from last season and she had never actually worn them before.

She confessed that she christened the shoes for her night out with me. I was truly touched. Especially because I busted out my ridiculous Imitation of Christ eyelet top with prairie collar, worn untucked and cinched at the waist with a black leather braided fringe Bruce belt just for her! Fashionistas tend to express their love by dressing for one another. Before we made our way into the glazed doors of the Chanel store on Spring Street, we took a moment to ogle each other's styles. "A Marc Jacobs driving cap? Love!" "That Martine Sitbon ruched top? Hot!" I grabbed her arm as we marched onward and thought, *She's the one!*

At Chanel, we admired the same shoes, double air-kissed our way through the crowd, and played the "If you could have whatever you want in the store, what would it be" game while Rene, a good-looking DJ who typically does Tom Ford's and Diane von Furstenberg's runway shows, mixed up groovy down-tempo beats. After we had our fill (time it takes to really enjoy a fashion party: about ten minutes), we sashayed to the restaurant, showing up a cool fifteen minutes late for our reservation. And it was at our very glamorous dinner when we came up with the idea for this book. But the moment was so much bigger than that.

It was the beginning of a lifelong friendship, the kind of connection that can never be jeopardized by silly disagreements and cranky outbursts. We clicked on so many levels, talking about everything from losing our virginity, family upbringings, and our mutual affinity for science fiction, to outrageous hats, new restaurants, pop art, and repeats of television shows we both watched in high school (*Quantum Leap*). I appreciated everything about her— her wry and quirky sense of humor, her biting wit, her slightly repressed nature (she blames that on her religious background), the way she laughs and inhales instead of exhales, and, of course, her crazy shoes (I had coveted them when they came out and was on the waiting list. . . . Sadly, I never heard from the Burberry salesgirl about my acceptance, much like the admissions board of a university).

Leaving the fashion scene (we had numerous editor—and Chanel bag—sightings), I noticed something quite peculiar. Melissa was walking funny—and rather slowly. I knew it couldn't have been the wine. She had only one glass. I couldn't remember if she had this awkward walk—toe-heel, toe-heel instead of heel-toe, heel-toe—earlier. Her feet probably hurt, I thought, a typical (and overlookable) side effect of great shoes. Blisters. It happens all the time.

The following week bred another fabulous dinner. And again Mel had that odd walk. Toe-heel, toe-heel, toe-heel. She had the pace of an elderly woman with a hip problem and a walker. And her body was pitched forward ever so slightly. Like the Leaning Tower of Pisa. I asked her if she was okay. I wasn't sure if she was limping. "Shoes," she said, "I can't walk in heels." I explained that she should go heel-toe, heel-toe, and she shrugged her shoulders. "I know, I know. But I can't."

Such a defeatist attitude, I told her. "Of course you can! Try." We had a little lesson up Hudson Street in the West Village and lo and behold, Melissa was completely incapable of walking heel-toe, heel-toe when she wore a shoe with a heel that measured over two inches in height. And she has over a hundred pairs of stilettos! Such obstacles and risks of future posture and back problems, however, do not get in the way of her taste and zest for foot ornamentation. A true fashionista, the worse her walk gets, the more heels she buys. I have witnessed her try on many, many pairs of shoes that have killed what could be a beautiful gait. In her eyes, if she has trouble walking in them, they must be good! We have been late for meetings and we have missed grabbing at least a hundred taxis because of her shoe-stopping pace. She even admits her husband hates it when she wears heels for that very reason.

It's a small price to pay for glamour. And when she's sitting, she sure does look good.

They're Here! They're Queer! We're Used to It!

Fashionistas make the biggest fag hags. We herd the guys with the Flock of Seagulls haircuts. Our favorite designers are men who love men but adore women. After all, where would Amanda Harlech (a.k.a. Lady Harlech), who was once the muse of Karl Lagerfeld (damn, that woman must have the sickest wardrobe), be without Galliano? And what about Carine Roitfeld (editor of French *Vogue*) without Tom Ford? To fashionistas, gay men are vital accessories, an intrinsic part of our culture. They tell us the secrets to a man's mind—and take us dancing till all hours of the night (so what if they wind up ditching us at the bar to go home with a hunk in a tight white Hanes tee?). They understand our style, crazy quirks, and neuroses, and know how to meet our emotional needs better than any boyfriend. Plus, they have no problem escorting us out when we have no date—and letting us know when it's time to put down the fork at dinner ("No more carbs for you, missy!").

Friends of Dorothy

MELISSA

When I was eleven years old, my older cousin Maté was a slightly chubby fifteen-year-old guy who went everywhere with a small Spanish fan. He channeled Karl Lagerfeld in a country where machismo trumped Moschino any day. He was strange and unusual, and like Winona Ryder in *Beetlejuice,* I noticed him because I myself felt strange and unusual, too. I was infatuated with Maté. He had an outsize personality and constantly greeted relatives with two slobbering kisses on both cheeks. He screeched instead of giggled and called everyone "dahhhlink!" Maté and I both agreed that our uncle, *Tito* Ed (*Tito* means uncle in Tagalog), who had immigrated to the United States, was just the bomb.

Tito Ed had found success as a director in San Francisco. He staged full-blown, critically acclaimed productions of Broadway classics such as *Pippin* and *Oklahoma* in the Bay Area, as well as more unconventional fare like an all-male version of *Caligula.* When we picked up *Tito* Ed from the Manila airport in the early seventies, he walked out of the terminal wearing a bright orange jersey tank top, terry-cloth short-shorts, knee-high athletic socks, and platform flip-flops. His hair was teased into a bright red Afro and he was wearing huge, oversize sunglasses reminiscent of Elton John. Rather than denying entrance to his conservative homeland and targeting him as a freak, the security officer asked him, "Are you a star?"

"Of course!" *Tito* Ed replied, collecting his matching black leather luggage special-ordered from Spain.

My family soon joined *Tito* Ed in San Francisco, and my favorite memory of that time is when *Tito* Ed visited to take my sister and me shopping. His favorite store was Neiman Marcus. At twelve, he gifted me with my first grown-up watch (a crocodile-strap Anne Klein with fourteen-karat-gold trim) and introduced me to his favorite designers: Alexander Julian, Ralph Lauren, and Perry Ellis. *Tito* Ed would bounce into our house, a fifty-year-old man wearing his signature outfit—white cotton short-shorts, knee-high socks, and a Perry Ellis "America" T-shirt with the stars-and-stripes pattern emblazoned across his chest. Like all fashionistas, he was never afraid to look slightly ridiculous, and commanded a great deal of respect from the theater department at the university where he was a tenured professor.

When I went away for college, my best friend was Morgan, an Australian guy who had spent his formative years in Paris. He had a foppish haircut, a longish wave that gracefully swooped down over his left eye. (Morgan was called "the Guy with the Hair" in our dorm. Anyone who referred to him made a swishing motion on his head to symbolize the haircut.) Morgan and I spent orientation weekend bonding over our mutual love for Madonna. He was witty, sophisticated, and bitchy—everything I wanted to be, only male. It was love at first sight. We spent every weekend putting together outfits for "clubbing" and rejected the crunchy boho-granola aesthetic that was so popular at the time—Ecuadorian sweaters, Birkenstocks, flannel shirts. Ugh! At Morgan's suggestion, I wore velvet jackets, short denim cutoffs (a nod to *Tito* Ed), ropes of costume jewelry, and fishnet stockings with Doc Martens. We scoured the Fourth Street flea markets together, and discussed the merits of the Linda-Christy-Naomi supermodel trinity. He was a Christy guy; I was a Linda girl. We shared Naomi.

Six years later, when Morgan and I had our inevitable falling-out (you always do with your first love), I was the one who inherited our group of gay male friends. (I "won" them, just like in a real divorce.) They are my coterie, my clique, my most avid supporters, and my favorite group of people. Plus, they can match me drink for drink.

When my friends and I get together, I feel like I am living the high school experience I never had. We scream, titter, kiss one another pretentiously but with great enjoyment on both cheeks, make plans to see Margaret Cho concerts, dance on tables, throwing down vintage *Club MTV* dance moves (booty bumping, "the sandwich"—two people gyrating on one in the middle—and an exaggerated lambada).

They always notice my new outfits. Whenever I go out with "the gang," I have to make sure I am wearing something appropriately "fabulous" or I will not be forgiven for dressing down. The culture has come around to appreciating these men, and as a fashionista, I can only say, "Bravo!" (No pun intended!)

An Ideal Husband

KAREN

Love isn't always easy. No matter how great your significant other is, a straight man will never be capable of meeting all of your needs and understanding every twist and turn of your emotional self. Straight men are amazing, of course. They can make you feel safe, protected, adored. They'll hang your hats on hat hooks they've put up in your closet, figure out how to work your DVD player, and spoon you all night long. They'll carry your bags, pump the gas in your car, handle bug and vermin situations at home, and make you melt by kissing you just right. But, like all things in life, they have their limitations.

A straight man may not understand (or accept) a mental melt-down when it's "that time of the month." He doesn't always get the fact that you can't do anything for at least forty minutes after your manicure. When you complain about having nothing to wear—and can't deal with wearing the same jeans and black top again—he is not always sure how exactly to reassure you and val-idate your wary state of mind. On your fat and ugly days, his words of wisdom and consolation ("Don't be crazy") don't always do the trick.

You can tell things to a gay man that you wouldn't ordinarily tell to a straight man. You can angst about the size of your thighs with-out sounding like an annoying "do I look fat" girl. You can spend hours talking about hemlines, how your jeans fit, the cute waiter at your favorite Belgian boîte, and whether or not you really need that stitched YSL vest, which is only $500—on sale from $2,300! Gay men instinctively know how to dote on you in ways straight men don't. "I love your bag! Your thighs are so good in those jeans! That coat is divine! You look terrific. That lipstick is such a good color for you. Your skin is amazing. You are a goddess. You, you, you, you, you . . ."

That is why all women need a gay husband, a cheerleader, partner in crime, confidant, and best friend who will be at your beck and call at four A.M. when you return from a dastardly date, or go forty minutes out of his way to drop you off in a taxi first after a party just because you had a bad night. And if they ever piss you off—and trust me, they sometimes will—you can bluntly tell them, slam a door, hang up the phone, act like a brat, and trust that in fifteen minutes—or the next time figure skating is on TV and you want to share in the long program excitement—the whole thing will be forgotten.

Sam is my gay husband. I met him, a deliciously adorable five-foot-six-inch, broad-shouldered Russian with dyed red hair, a wardrobe of plaid, a perfect complexion, and baby-blue eyes, in 1995, and we have been attached at the hip ever since. He runs a restaurant PR firm and at the time I was writing about restaurants (I made the switch to fashion, where eating is a no-no, after packing on thirty pounds!). We had talked on the phone countless times before coming face-to-face. And I always loved his exuberant energy, his brash sense of humor, and his bluntness. Sam has an uncanny ability to say whatever it is he's thinking and never come off as offensive, rude, or judgmental. ("I can't talk to him for you," he once said, when I needed a quote from a restaurant manager for a story. "It's in my contract that we not speak because he's soooo annoying.")

He has seen me at my best (size two) and worst (size ten) and loved me just the same (though he has forbidden me from having dessert on more than one occasion. "You'll thank me later," he scolded when he pulled the fork—and soufflé—from my reach). We have traveled to London together—and I never had to worry about his making a move on me in bed (we shared a bed and often cuddled). I can pee in front of him, change without feeling the insecure need to hide my body, and try on all of my clothes and get an honest response about what works and what doesn't. ("Not so good for your shoulders, that top," he's said. "It makes you look like a linebacker, and you're going for ballerina, I'd guess.")

He has nursed me through many a bad breakup and come over to give me a hug at three A.M. when I called him, hysterical.

He has made me giggle like a high school girl on a first date more often than not. He has held my hand through scary movies and while walking down the cold city streets. He has saved my life by hooking me up with dinner reservations when I had nowhere to eat at nine P.M. on a Saturday night. He has escorted me to dozens of weddings and events where going stag would be unacceptable. And he has come home to my parents' house for holidays, where he fit right in . . . and managed to make the whole clan laugh when he asked my brother if he could convert him (to gayness) and got in on the family jokes about my dad's big hair (it's still feathered back and full, very Bee Gees, circa 1977).

I have accompanied him to his favorite gay bar (aptly named the Cock), served as the approval board for many of his boyfriends (very few men are good enough, I say), and babysat his darling pug, Sheila. The best thing about our relationship is that we never have to make apologies for our actions. Our love is purely unconditional. We can blow each other off and not take it personally. We can talk about our deepest, darkest secrets—and constipation problems—openly. We call each other a hundred times a day without seeming like stalkers. We have never argued. And I don't think we ever will.

I even put his sperm on hold, in case I turn forty and happen to be single and want a baby. (Don't worry. We'll turkey-baster it.) He promised to pay for private school and camp for our little one so I could use my disposable income for clothes. "You'll be the mommy to our baby," he's said. "Everything you say and do will leave an impression. You have to be a good fashion role model."

Oh, if only he were straight . . .

Flaming Fashionista

All your beautiful girlfriends are jealous of your perfect size-six figure. You screech when excited about the little things (terrier puppies, extra-long sleeves, women's shoes with a red sole—a tell-tale sign that they're designed by Christian Louboutin and hence, *très* fabulous) . . . you're a fashionista on fire! You and your posse of straight women friends gush over the same men, share jeans, and address one another by saying "girl" at the beginning of every sentence. *Queer Eye* has nothing on you!

• Adopt the Karl Lagerfeld "3-D" diet when your weight is up by at least 2.5 pounds. It is the insane regimen the designer went on with his doctor's support; he lost something like a hundred pounds on it.

• Wear many cashmere sweaters (and maybe even a cape) at once. Consider a walking stick like Andre Leon Talley, or an eye-patch, like John Galliano.

• Conquer at least three different bouts with addiction. Then fall off the wagon. Repeatedly.

• Be a charmer—this will help you flirt your way up to first class on airplanes.

• Sleep your way up the freebie ladder (bartenders, nightclub doormen, hairstylists).

• Wear cross-trainer sneakers with your good black pants.

• Carry a bag, which may affectionately be known as your man-purse (logos a must!).

The Flaming Fashionista subspecies also includes the following phyla:

Drag Queen Fashionista

If you get up in the morning and sing Ella Fitzgerald while blow-drying your Marilyn Monroe platinum-blond wig, pull on vintage Pucci housedresses for grocery shopping, wear a size-sixteen high-heel shoe, shave your armpits, legs, and mustache . . . you're fashionista royalty! Consider labeling yourself a "mactress."

• Adopt a signature persona, whether it's boozy sixty-year-old former socialite chanteuse, à la "Kiki" (Justin Bond's alter ego), or black glamazon supamodel (à la RuPaul).

• Host Tupperware parties. Wear white gloves as you display the goods.

• Perform. Learn to do Barbra, Bette, Liza, whatever tickles your fancy.

• Keep at least a dozen boas in your closet at all times, in case of emergency.

• Have a wig supplier.

• Exfoliate regularly. You have more products than a department store, sweetie.

Dandy Fashionista

If you wear four-piece tartan-colored Vivienne Westwood suits, never leave home without your bowler hat and a boutonnierre, and actually own a pair of spats . . . you're a fine-feathered fashionista.

• Put at least three hours into getting ready every morning.

• Makeup is a must. But stick to powder and eyebrow pencils. Faux beauty marks a plus.

• Iron your silk handkerchiefs.

• Befriend Bill Cunningham, the *New York Times*'s roving Styles photographer. He'll love you and constantly put you in his much-admired section depicting street fashion and trends.

• Spend rent money on bespoke Turnbull & Asser shirts.

• Carry a monogrammed cigarette case and lighter set. Even if you don't smoke.

- Get a business card that says, simply, "Dandy." While you're at it, use British words like "randy."

- Love Boy George.

PATRICK MCMULLAN

Patrick Macdonald, our favorite N.Y. dandy

TURNING FASHIONISTA MAKEOVERS FOR OUR MEN!
Constructing the Right Look
✳ MELISSA ✳

When people ask me what attracted me to my husband, the first thing that comes to mind isn't his beautiful blue-green eyes, his skinny, indie-rocker frame, or his honey-brown hair with natural blond highlights. It's not his goofy sense of humor, his sly wit, or his thoughtful and piercing intelligence. (God, do I sound like a contestant on *The Bachelor* or what?)

It was his shoes.

A pair of ragged Jack Purcell Converse All-Stars. Black canvas low-tops with a white plastic toe.

It was always a secret desire of mine to date someone who wore Jack Purcells. The coolest guys in high school and college always wore them—but they were way too cool for me. Back then I was still in my pleather-shoe phase. In college, the only guy I "dated" was my gay best friend, and he always wore slip-on Ferragamo loafers. Not exactly the weapons of mass seduction.

Mike was sitting cross-legged at a crowded party in Brooklyn, and the minute I spotted his shoes, I fell in love. I had to meet him.

To me, Jack Purcell sneakers are more than just footwear. They symbolize artistic, nonconformist aspiration. Jack Kerouac wore Jack Purcells. They are the shoes with the "sole" of a poet.

Back then, Mike was working a retro-fifties thrift-store look—spread-collared cotton shirts he'd pick up from vintage shops for eighty-nine cents with a wingspan from neck to shoulder, a beige polyester jacket, baggy 501s, and his trusty Jack Purcells. It took him from college to grad school to his first job as an architect. When we first met, he didn't know Dolce & Gabbana from Viktor & Rolf.

With my help, he's added high-fashion awareness to his wardrobe. Almost eight years later, the poly-cotton blends have given way to sleek Helmut Lang shirts, crisp Gucci suits, and trim Jil Sander pants. (He was crushed when Jil left her label—and like other fashionistos everywhere is eagerly anticipating her return.)

But when we moved to Los Angeles in late 2003, Mike was in a funk. "I need a new look," he said. He was tired of dressing like a typical New York architect, clad in minimal shades of charcoal and black. He wanted to look casually professional, like the other architects in his firm in a happier land where the sun often shines. These men wore designer T-shirts with Gucci jeans and interesting sneakers. Of course, we headed to my favorite place on earth: a designer outlet mall.

We started at the John Varvatos store, where he stocked up on fine-gauge knit T-shirts. Talk about high-end casual—they were a hundred bucks a pop, retail. Skeptics would scoff at such an expensive T-shirt, but buying designer does make a difference—the cut of the shirt was square, with a more flattering fit, and the finishes on the collar and sleeve seams were exquisite. Plus, they will last him a hell of a lot longer than any cotton variety. I also pulled a glen plaid sports coat, wool and cotton trousers, and he loved it all. At Prada he scored a pair of straight-leg jeans and two pairs of cotton pants. The pants were trim-cut with a slight, almost undetectable flare on the leg—a little David Bowie action that suited us just fine.

He picked out a checkered Ben Sherman broadcloth shirt with a matching tie in the same pattern by himself.

Mike as a scruffy slacker and then all duded up with a "Zoolander" expression

"This is the coolest shirt in the world!" he said.

"It's just like the one Ashton Kutcher was wearing in *US Weekly*!" I squealed in agreement.

Mike is now made over into a sleek, LA-style architect. Although he's now wearing Italian cashmere rather than vintage shirts from Sears, his feet are still shod in Jack Purcell sneakers. Of course, this time, they're limited-edition versions from John Varvatos.

Full-throttle Fashion
✳ KAREN ✳

The second I met Todd, I felt a connection so strong that I knew he would become my boyfriend. I can't explain it. I remember sitting with him, snuggled up on a banquette at a lounge, thinking, *Something feels really different about this.* I was so attracted to him—and not just because of what he looks like, which, admittedly, is gorgeous (the olive skin, the sexy dimples, the hazel-greenish-brown almond-shaped eyes, the long lashes, the goatee, the chiseled arms), but because of his warm, open energy, which was so inviting, I actually felt shy. He still makes fun of me for projecting the kind of body language that gave him no sign of whether I was into him. Yet the entire night I thought he was so yummy and amazing that I had to pull away. I was too scared to give him the green light.

He had a tempting tough-guy exterior, but such an air of sweetness. He made eye contact. He was full of compliments and said my shoes were sexy (black Louboutin sandals with four-inch heels and silver zippers instead of straps). He chivalrously opened all doors for me and made sure my glass of water was always full.

Between his harsh Brooklyn accent, his motorcycle racing, the Harley shop he used to own, the two (permanent) earrings in his left ear, the large tattoo that snakes up his left calf (I didn't see it on date one, but I heard about it), and the giant scar of a lion he had carved (yes, carved) into his back (that, I made him show me), Todd's image—not to mention his beat-up jeans, motorcycle boots, and black T-shirt with a red devil on it—was the complete opposite of every nice Jewish boy I had ever dated (and broken up with).

We came from such different worlds.

He's from Gravesend, a hard-core Brooklyn neighborhood with a heavy Catholic Italian population. He was, as he says, a street kid. He turned in his football helmet by the time he hit high school in exchange for a motorcycle helmet and a guitar (he gigged with a heavy-metal band and stayed out partying all night long). His dad split, and Todd, a smart kid with good grades and a bit of an antiauthority attitude, worked to put food on the table at the young age of fifteen, when he got his first tattoo.

Meanwhile, I'm from a mostly Jewish upper-middle-class suburb of New Jersey, where I attended a private school with a dress code and went on class ski trips to Austria. Mine was the life of summer sleepaway camp, a new car—with bow—on my seventeenth birthday, and SAT prep classes that began in eighth grade. At fifteen, I certainly wasn't getting tattoos and putting food on the table. I was the type who went to the library on weekends, never stayed out past curfew (okay, maybe once or twice), and used to make steak tartare and Caesar salads with my mom for dinner.

Back to our date: When I realized it was three minutes to midnight, I needed to go. I had a yoga class at nine A.M. and wanted my eight hours of sleep. Todd sweetly said, "I guess I have three minutes to kiss you before you turn into a pumpkin." (How irresistible.) After he tucked me into a cab, I watched him walk away and thought to myself, *If he turns his head around to look at me one last time, it means we'll fall in love and it's meant to be.* Two seconds later, he turned. And neither of us has looked back since.

I love everything about Todd, especially our differences. As hard as he is on the outside, is as soft as he is on the inside. He is the perfect fusion of a gentleman, a rebel, a knight in shining armor, a bad boy, a romantic, a responsibly wild child. He is a rock of stability and the best thing ever to happen to me. While we have the core, important things in common—our values, morals, life desires, psychological awareness, and senses of humor, as well as our need for adventure, weekend hikes, and lazy Sunday mornings—he once joked he's showing me the underworld (I am learning to play poker and ride a motorcycle), and I'm showing him the upperworld (he's learning yoga and taking trips to the Whitney Museum).

When we started dating, we went out for dinner and drinks three to four times a week. I'd always be dolled up (from Chloe jeans, chandelier earrings from Peru, and leather scarves to knee-high boots, classic pumps, and shrunken asymmetrical tops, he really appreciated my style and would take in every detail about my look) and he'd be laid-back cool with a Vanson Leathers jacket (a big motorcycle brand), a silver cross thumb ring, old-school Levi's, and Chrome Hearts tops that said "Fuck you" on them.

I happened to love his aesthetic—and still do. His clothes hang on him perfectly, revealing his defined, athletic body just right. And what he wears really suits him. Especially the motorcycle boots that make a heavy clunking noise when he walks, which, for some reason, always makes me feel that if we were walking down a dark alley and someone attacked us, I'd be in safe, able hands.

Then one day we were invited to a fashion party that required him to—gasp!—wear a suit. "Baby, I don't have a stylin' suit," he sheepishly confessed. I thought about it for a moment and said, "Who cares . . . just go in what you're comfortable with." But he didn't want to. "If I'm going to be by your side and you're so styled out, I want to be, too," he said.

Thus began his fashionisto conversion. We spent hours in and out of the best men's stores in the city, but everything we found was cut too loosely for him. We left each place empty-handed, Adidas shell-top sneakers notwithstanding. Todd wanted a more streamlined, sophisticated, European look. For that, there's only one place to go: Gucci. "Brace yourself," I warned, asking him to fork over his credit card.

I informed him that he would be spending a bit more money than he's used to, but that it would be worth it because we'd be investing in classic lifetime pieces that he'd wear forever. "You won't need a lot of dress clothes," I assured him, "just one pair of black pants. Maybe another in blue, gray, or tan, and a dress shirt or two. The rest you can mix and match with the clothes you already have.

Rough around the edges!

Nothing is hotter than slick Gucci pants with Adidas and an old T-shirt."

He tore through racks, holding up things I never imagined his liking—leather pants, cashmere waffle sweaters, long wool trench coats, three-button pin-striped suits, fitted pants with flared legs, and serious boots with a square toe and a chunky heel. I sat in the dressing room with him, lavishly doting, folding the pants under so they wouldn't look too long when he finally looked in the mirror, buttoning the cuffs of the shirts, and ensuring that everything, from the crease down the center of the pants to the neckline of a sweater, was perfect. "I like this no-pleats thing," he remarked. I even caught him turning around to catch a glimpse of his butt and giving himself a nod of approval. Furthermore, he didn't balk at the $560 price tag on the black wool trousers or the $250 one on the gray-black-and-white-striped shirt. "You're right about Gucci. If it looks this good, I don't mind spending," he admitted. We were treated to (designer) bottles of water and such impeccably good

ELIZABETH LIPPMAN

Streamlined and chic! So *GQ*!

service that Todd was impressed. "I should shop like this more often," he said. I was creating a monster!

At the end of the session, he left with three chic pairs of pants, a couple of sweaters, two beautiful button-down shirts, and the most outrageous suit I ever did see. Sadly, they didn't have the boots in his size . . . in any of the Gucci locations in the country. He asked the store to call—without my suggesting it, a move only a savvy fashionisto knows how to make. Clearly, he was born for this life!

Now when we go out, I find myself worrying that he looks better than I do! But he always whispers in my ear, "Nothing looks as good as you, my beauty." True or not, nothing sounds more delicious than that. Yet another reason I love him so.

This leads us to the last type of fashionista:

The Significant-other Fashionista (Sometimes Called the Fashionisto)

You thought Issey Miyake was a Japanese noodle, and Fendi a disease from the African sub-Sahara, but now you know better. You used to shop at the Gap and Banana Republic, but now you insist on Jil Sander suits and Helmut Lang overcoats. You've caught the bug—you're the fashionista's better half.

• Although you will begin to acquire more clothes than you ever deemed necessary, you will have to prepare to give up closet space. A lot of closet space. You can live out of a suitcase, right?

• Get promoted. You're going to need to make more money to support her shopping habit. And don't even think of balking at price tags or saying something like "Five hundred dollars for a pair of shoes?"

• Maintain your good looks. Hit the gym and slather on the Rogaine. She didn't marry you because you were balding and fat!

• Never put her jeans in the wash or be prepared for a bad scene. (They're dry-clean-only denim; you should know that by now.) The same goes for bras. Dryers warp them, mister, so let them air-dry over a rack in the bathroom.

• Cultivate your sense of humor and indulge her fashion fantasies. Never laugh at her outfits. *Unforgivable*.

• Learn the names of important designers and be able to spot them from a block away.

• Say *unflattering*, not *fat*. *Fat* should never be used to describe any part of your girl, or even in the presence of her, come to think of it. Not even if you're talking about meat or bacon.

Quick Tips for Making Over Your Man

• Do it gently. Rome wasn't built in a day, and neither was any self-respecting fashionisto.

• Stay true to who he is at heart. Work his new style around his needs. You're not trying to change him, just improve him. If you are trying to change him, it may be time to think about finding someone else.

• Begin by getting him new beauty products and work your way up from there. Once he sees the subtle differences lotion or hair gel can make, he will be more apt to try on the jeans you recommend.

• Ooh, ah, and compliment him to death. Changing a man's style is a lot like changing someone's grip on a tennis racket. It will be uncomfortable for him at first, but if he sees how positively you respond, he will get used to it—and realize how much better-off he is.

• Make sure he gets good shoes. Shoes are the most important part of anyone's look. Even if it's sneakers, they need to be the right sneakers (more of this in the closet chapter, which is next).

• Once you have new shoes, get to the jeans. His jeans should be relaxed and sitting on his hips, not his waist. Also, they should not, under any circumstances, taper at the bottom or be too baggy—or too tight—through the hip area. Introduce him to the bootleg cut. When you get them altered, if they need shortening, tell the tailor to keep the same kind of seam intact.

• Destroy all of his pleated pants. There is nothing worse than a cute guy in pleats. Invest in flat-front, flat-front, flat-front. We cannot stress that enough!

• Get him at least one crisp white button-down shirt, one shirt with French cuffs, and silver cuff links.

• If his hair needs a new look, take him to your place—your treat—and act like it's a gift, something you're doing just to be nice . . . which, of course, you are. You want him to look better. If that's not nice, what is?

THE UPS, THE DOWNS, THE GOOD, THE BAD, THE UGLY—THE CREEDS THAT GIVE US CRED

Like the Jews, the Hare Krishnas, and other minority groups, fashionistas have endured much persecution, i.e., magazine internships and multiple prom dress mishaps! It is because of our struggles of yesteryear that we are who we are today. Before you, as a fashionista, can enter a room in the drop-dead dress that causes a sensation, you must understand that the path to red-carpet glory is littered with the obstacles of fashion flops of the past. We are a people who relentlessly try the new, the daring, the impossible to explain. And therefore we have paid the consequences. We have found ourselves suffocating in the heat because we just had to wear our new leather motocross trousers . . . in August. We've been in the podiatrist's office, nursing ingrown toenails as a result of shoes that were too pointy and too small (but we had to have them anyway). And we're all the better because of it. Here's a look at some of our flops that made history.

A Hair-raising Tale
✳ MELISSA ✳

I am a survivor of an all-girl private high school in the snooty Pacific Heights area of San Francisco. As anyone can tell you, high school can be rough, but imagine if the only other people in your class were thirty-eight *debutantes*. Okay, maybe I'm exaggerating. There were only ten debutantes in our class that year; the other twenty-eight had to make do with their trust funds. Needless to say, nonconformity was not an option.

The girls I went to school with fit into three models: The first, in every sense of the word, were the gorgeous, slim-hipped, size-six (in my day, the popular girls weren't size zero yet—which is a really frightening prospect for teens these days), usually blonde, milk-and-cream-skinned goddesses; these girls were so frighteningly pretty that when they graduated they made a profession out of it, and not just by modeling. The prettiest girl in my high school went on to marry an heir to an oil fortune, and she now graces glossy magazines with riveting tales of how she stocks her closet. Still, she's not a fashionista. There's a difference between fashionista and just being rich enough to buy nice things. Real fashionistas have a joie de vivre, a certain wacky irrepressibility that keeps them just shy of overt materialism.

The other two types of girls at my school were the aspirational, snub-nosed, dark-haired girls who acted like ladies-in-waiting to the goddesses, while the third group was made up of everyone else: the misfits.

The misfits at my school included anyone who didn't wear a red Patagonia jacket over her uniform. To this day, I consider red (or blue) Patagonia jackets the uniform of the oppressor. I went to school wearing an ankle-length green army trench coat with epaulets and a beret. (The beret was a jaunty addition.) Other days I wore a gray fedora and an extra-long silk snakeprint scarf that I tied to my knee in homage to John Taylor of Duran Duran.

"What's up with the fedora?" I would hear the girls whisper.

"What's up with the scarf?"

"Why is it on her *knee?*"

I could have explained that I was working a skate-punk-hip-hop-quasi-alterno-new-wave-mall-rat look. But with my dyed-blond bangs, feathered hair, three-dollar Salvation Army blazer, and a best friend who dyed her long hair red with Kool-Aid and snorted when she laughed, I had no hope. On certain special Fridays, our school initi-

Mel at a really bad age. Her hair is bigger than the Xmas tree!

ated a "free dress" day, wherein students were allowed to wear whatever they wanted—within reason (i.e., no midriff-baring shirts or spandex leggings—as if!). Most of my classmates took the opportunity to bust out the Benetton, Esprit, Guess? jeans, cable-knit sweaters (the sweater of the oppressor!), and a colorful palette of pastels, plaids, or khakis.

I still remember my favorite free-dress outfit. It was a checkered minisuit (with mighty stiff shoulder pads), white tights, ruched boots, and my fake Louis Vuitton bucket bag. I still remember how much it cost—$19.99 from Foxmoor, a trendy store in the mall. It was my "New York" outfit. When I wore it, I dreamed I was dashing around the streets of Manhattan, a smart, successful, independent woman. I was sixteen then, and little did I know New Yorkers would never be caught dead in white tights and the hellacious perm I am sporting in this picture. But back then, this outfit was my rebellion against the cookie-cutter preppy wear of my peers. And even if I cringe when I see it, I'm still proud of the suburban girl who had big-city dreams bigger than her hair.

Bittersweet Sixteen
❋ KAREN ❋

When I was sixteen, I begged my parents to get me an oversize Dallas Cowboys fully sequined royal-blue football jersey—with shoulder pads and number on the back—to wear to my best friend's birthday party. It was expensive, so they said no. Not having it felt like such agony. I had no idea how I'd even get out of the house on the eve of her sixteenth year. Clearly no other ensemble would do. And one sweet day, my mother came home with it to surprise me (she got it through a friend, who knew a friend who worked in the showroom and was able to get it wholesale, which means half-price). It felt like a gift from the heavens. I was in a state of shock that I actually owned something so fabulous. The thought of wearing it was so exciting, I couldn't sleep for days. I wouldn't even put it in my closet. I left it hanging on the closet door, just so I could look at it at all times.

I wouldn't tell any of my friends what I'd be wearing to the party. I wanted to surprise people, as if it were a wedding dress. I turned up wearing it—with silver heels and a white sequined miniskirt (I opted to skip the matching sequined baseball hat, much to my mom's chagrin; even then I knew when to draw the fashion line!)—and thought I was the cat's meow. I danced all night and walked tall and proud in my shiny ensemble. "Some outfit" was the best compliment of the evening. They were just jealous, I told myself! I never wore it again—not because I didn't want to, but because I had no other place to wear it. Until one year later, when I was invited to another sweet sixteen in a different part of town, where the audience would be totally new. It's not the kind of look you can wear twice with the same crowd.

I pulled it out of my closet, slowly unzipped the garment bag, and took it out. But all of my giddy emotions of admiration had left the building. I felt a wave of sadness come over me. This wasn't so great. The shoulder pads were huge. And I didn't even really like the Cowboys. My dad happened to, but at the wise age of seventeen, I came to understand that it was probably just because of the cheerleaders.

I looked at this sparkling piece of fabric, thinking, *Huh . . . I remember it being much, much cuter.* I put it on, just to make sure. Suddenly I saw myself not as this cute little sylph in a daringly bold outfit, but a tiny little drag queen with a Bon Jovi haircut!

1-2-3 hike (this outfit out of the closet)!

I zipped the bag up and went with another dress—something simple and black with sequined straps. It was at that point that epiphany struck: The Cowboys outfit was a mistake. I hoped never to see it again.

Flash forward: I was twenty-one years old and I had to go to my cousin Bryan's bar mitzvah. I had gained twenty pounds during the first semester of college and none of my clothes fit. Not the dress I was originally supposed to wear. Not a suit, not a skirt, not even a blouse! I didn't want to go. There was no time to shop for something new. I got home from school on a Saturday morning and there were services to get to and a party to attend right away. I pleaded with my parents to let me stay home. But they wouldn't give in. They didn't understand that when fashionistas can't find the right clothes, leaving the house is simply not an option. Suddenly my mother emerged from the attic with the sequined football jersey, the largest piece of clothing in the house. "No! Not that! Anything but that," I screamed. The next thing I knew I was at the party, sitting (well, whining and moping) in the corner, stuffing myself with cake, in the midst of a miserable fashion moment. (Need I add that the skirt was my mother's—and I couldn't button or zip it, but the top was long enough to cover it up?)

All the waiters and valet attendants accosted me: "Hey, Dallas Cowboys fan!" "Hey, you like Troy Aikman?" "What about the cheerleaders?" I was mortified. My cousin's little friends yelled technical sports terms at me, like "Hike!" and "Touchdown!" No one knew I was secretly very stylish. To them I was just a dumpy Dallas Cowboys fan with very gaudy taste in clothing. I have yet to forgive my parents.

The Rules of the Game

In our years-long search for just the right outfit, we have compiled a few rules to get dressed by.

• Never do head-to-toe of the same designer. You'll look like a walking billboard. Always bring a bit of "you" to whatever you wear—a signature necklace, great earrings, your trusty old Levi's. Having a personal sense of style and injecting your personality into something is key.

• Mix high and low—ultraexpensive items along with cheap finds in order to project a careless, unsnobby image.

• Always have one ultraluxe item, like a handbag, a wallet, or a belt, or major jewelry to elevate your outfit. You can wear rags, but if you're carrying a Birkin, no one will ever know. One *New York Times* fashion critic likes to wear Wal-Mart with her five-hundred-dollar Celine platforms.

• Save supertrendy and easily identifiable items for five years after wearing them during their "it" season.

• Never wear more than one trend at once. Pick a focal point of your ensemble (a poncho!) and build your whole look around it (don't wear the poncho with high-heeled sneakers!).

• Own a trench coat. It's the one classic thing that will always look chic and fresh.

• Don't wear mid-calf-length skirts if you're short. It cuts the leg off.

- When in doubt, a white button-down shirt will always do. Just add great earrings, high heels, and anything from strands of pearls of different lengths to a groovy scarf, tied on the side or in the back so that the tails hang low in a seductive, exotic way.

- Walk with a purpose. If you look confident, people will think you are.

- Never look like you're trying too hard. Elegance should be effortless.

- Mix and match your clothes. Throw on suit jackets with jeans and tank tops with the pants—sans jacket.

- Wear a great bra at all times. Go to a lingerie store to find your right size, and before going out of the house lift your breasts in the bra to make sure that the nipples are centered and the "girls" look high and supported. Maidenform's One Fabulous Fit bra always does good things to the bust.

- Don't fear color. Embrace it. Just not too much of it!

- Avoid panty lines at all costs. They are wrong, wrong, wrong.

- Wear your clothes. Don't let them wear you. Know what works on your body and what doesn't and only buy something you love. Just because it's trendy doesn't always mean it's good.

Building the Fashionista Closet: The Eighth Wonder of the World— in Your Bedroom!

Fashionistas, contrary to popular belief, do not come in one size (size two). In fact, the shape of your body and size of your waist have nothing to do with the status of your fashionistadom. It's all about the closet, baby. And the beauty within. Whether your closet is a cavernous three-story walk-in or the size of a carry-on suitcase, what sets the fashionista closet apart from an ordinary closet is depth, versatility, and eclecticism. In the first chapter you discovered what kind of fashionista you are, but paradoxically, the fashionista is not limited to one "look," and she likes to experiment and play with tons of clothes, which she often considers costumes. The fashionista is a chameleon: ladylike in driving gloves and a sharp tweed suit one moment, a punk-rock chick in a dog collar and studded belt the next. She is a cross between a gypsy, a princess, and a diva. She's androgynous in the fall and hyperfeminine by the spring. She wears bohemian peasant blouses as well as conservative three-strand pearls. She's ready (and more than willing) to meet every direction of the trend weather vane.

More often than not, she's a pack rat, a collector, an obsessive-compulsive who can't let go of, say, a Hawaiian-tropic sarong in psychedelic colors even if she lives in New England (because who knows—she might jet off to Maui on a moment's notice, even if the nearest she usually gets to the beach is down by the Jersey shore to visit her cousin during Memorial Day weekend), or maybe she's still holding on to the polka-dot pleated halter dress she wore on her very first date with her husband (even if she doesn't fit into it anymore, she still remembers the look he gave her when he first saw her).

No matter what your style niche is, fashionistas the world over own essentially the same glamorous garments. You can bet each of us has just the perfect bias-cut cocktail dress, motorcycle boots, and classic trench coat. We are a tribe, a breed apart, after all. And we recognize one another by the small details of our clothing (a turned-up collar here, a peekaboo ruffle there) and the panache with which we wear them. So whether you're a boho, mummy, wicked witch, or fairy godmother, you'll need some essential fashionista ingredients to build your dream wardrobe. Just remember: Fashionista dressing is about confidence, individualism, and really, really, fabulous shoes. So let's get started. Here's your lesson on rifling through the racks, and while you're at it, welcome to a quick trip through our wardrobes. (If we find that it's winter in Narnia on the other end, God knows we'll be dressed for it!)

Here, a journey through what you'll need to achieve fashionista wardrobe status, from your toes to your head!

Must-have Fashionista Footwear

- Superpointy toes—The fashionista shoe has a pointy toe. We cannot stress this enough. While you might be tempted to go round-toed when this snub-nosed design comes around once every five years, the fashionista shoe is *always* pointy. So pointy they're almost elfin. Why pointy shoes? Because they scrunch the toe, narrow the foot, and give your look a certain dangerous edge. Round toes are just too, well, Minnie Mouse and cute, not sexy.

• Four-inch heels—Fashionistas cultivate a long-legged look, even if they're four-eleven (*especially* if they're four-eleven—Karen), and four-inch heels are best for achieving the proper skyscraper effect. Three-inchers are typically the fashionista's "sensible," even "comfortable" footgear. Three-inch is a day shoe. A work shoe. Four-inch heels spell nighttime drama. Five inches, and you're strutting in tranny hooker territory, which, depending on the occasion, is not such a bad thing.

• Wedgies—The wedge look goes in and out of style, but when it comes to poolside fashion, stilettos will make you look like you're trying too hard. So what's a girl who wants extra bathing suit appeal to do? Wear the wedgies, which are very easy to walk in and surprisingly comfy. They also work well with extra-long jeans that scrape along the floor as you walk, miniskirts, and shorts.

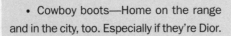

The wedge slide

• Cowboy boots—Home on the range and in the city, too. Especially if they're Dior.

• Thigh-high boots—For the sexy Julia-Roberts-in-*Pretty-Woman* look, without the streetwalker sensibility.

• Ankle boots—The basic boot for underneath pants and to make a statement with short skirts.

The High-high boot

• Knee-high boots—The standby for fall's knee-length skirts.

• Evening shoe—Night dressing calls for a little sparkly drama, a touch of satin,

The evening glamour

and decadent details like crystals, pearls, and a very slinky heel. Evening shoes also work well with jeans and tank tops. Very downtown-girl Kate Moss cool.

The mule

• Mules—Perfect for summer in Capri . . . or Connecticut. Just be wary: There is nothing that holds the shoe onto your heel, so sometimes you have to grip your toes to keep the shoe on your foot as you prance. Not good for the back, but what's life without a little struggle?

• Printed shoe—Embroidered tapestry is a well-heeled luxury. The rest of your ensemble can be plain as folk, and the shoes, the centerpiece, will make you stand out.

The tapestry platform

• Slingbacks—Much easier to wear than mules due to the strap that wraps around the back of the heel.

The slingback

• Strappy sandal—Foot bondage! Nothing like sexy, sexy straps to enhance the curves of the foot when you're stepping out in a slinky dress, a modern tuxedo, or cutesy short shorts.

• Sneakers—The fashionista sneaker is a very important part of the footwear collection. Even if we're tripping about in stilettos, at some point we have to run errands (dry cleaning, grocery store, taking

The strappy

Pierre, the mini-Yorkie, to the vet). For these instances, it is helpful to acquire the proper sneakers. Fashionista sneakers are either old-school (Adidas, Pumas, Tretorns, K-Swiss, even checkered Vans) or high-tech (Nike sneaker clogs or designer numbers by Samsonite, Yohji Yamamoto, Prada, or Jil Sander—all of which are reminiscent of bowling shoes), in interesting fabrics (leather, suede, denim) or unexpected colors (orange, silver, black patent). The fashionista sneaker is never one that could be mistaken for an early-eighties aerobic-class mainstay. (Unless you want to be postmodern and ironic, in which case, you might want to consider adding leg warmers!)

Note: Shoe upkeep and maintenance is key. Save all boxes and cloth or felt bags that come with designer shoes. Take Polaroids of the shoes and tape them to the outside of the boxes so that, when they're stacked in your closet, you know what is what. Go to a shoe service place and get tips put on the top portion of soles so you don't wear them down easily. Wash shoes after you've been in the rain or the snow, as moisture warps the leather. Treat all suede shoes to waterproof them. And get a suede brush for suede shoes, too. When not wearing shoes, keep the tissue paper inserted in them in order to preserve the shape of the shoe (otherwise you'll risk toe crushing). Search for a fantastic shoe healer who can cure all boo-boos. In Manhattan, everyone, from the Manolo store to Anna Wintour, relies on Shoe Service Plus in Midtown.

An Exception to Our Usual Four-inch-heel-only Rule: Gifts from the Land Down Under
✳ MELISSA AND KAREN ✳

In New York, the Ugg revolution came slowly, around 2002. As far as rustic hippie boots go, first we experienced the Minnetonka Moccasin renaissance, which popped up a while after the Birkenstock comeback, which occurred before the gardening-clog trend. The knee-high cowhide boots appeared on the shelves of froufrou boutiques in Nolita in 2000 and 2001, at the very same time that Native American–inspired boots by Marni were all the rage.

At $80 a pair (the Minnetonka versions), we couldn't resist bucking up. In the name of Pocahontas, we plunked down our maxed-out credit cards. We wore our mocs with denim miniskirts and rabbit-fur chubbies, feeling oh-so-cool. We looked like a cross between prostitute and alternachick. Alternatutes perhaps?

After the moccasin craze simmered, we noticed something new in their place: tan sheepskin boots. The same week, Kate Hudson was pictured wearing them in the pages of *US Weekly*. So were Pamela Anderson and Drew Barrymore.

"*Uggs!*" Karen cried. "I started wearing them when I was a freshman in college! A surfer chick from California introduced me to them and I lived in them all through school. And I swear, I was just thinking of getting a new pair the other day!"

She quickly put on a pair. They felt like the most delicious slippers in the world. Especially because they're meant to be worn barefoot. "I'm taking them! I've missed them so much! You don't understand how they cradle your feet like a warm blanket. They're the best. Mel, you have to have them!" she cried.

Karen explained that Uggs, first born in 1978, came from Australia, where beach bunnies and surfers wore them with bikinis when it got cold after dips in the ocean. "They're soooo sexy with bathing suits," Karen chanted. At first Mel resisted the Ugg-explosion. They were flat-heeled,

ELIZABETH LIPPMAN

Uggs and chunky fur hats spell snow-bunny sophistication.

after all. She was wary. But she was soon envious of Karen's ultra-comfort . . . and how cute the boots looked over Juicy Couture sweatpants, accessorized by a yoga bag and a fur hat. Within months Uggs were everywhere. You couldn't walk a block without spotting at least two pairs. Karen kept urging Mel to get them. "You must own these. They will change your life. I even wear them around my house as slippers," Karen persuaded.

Mel finally caved. (Karen thinks it's because they passed model Helena Christensen on the street, walking hand in hand with her adorable blond straggly-haired son, Mingus . . . and they were both wearing Uggs.) "All right, you win! I'll get them! Take me to your leader," Mel said. "Besides, they would look kind of cute with the sweatshirt housedress I wear when I'm writing."

Once Mel put them on her feet, they never came off! She couldn't believe it had taken her so long to finally get them. Now they are the only shoes we wear other than our four-inch stilettos. Our must-haves are Manolos, Jimmy, and Ugg. And we'll never take them off, even if the trend is long over.

The Hosiery Question

For several years, hosiery was simply out of the question for fash-ionistas. Bare legs in winter was a hard-and-fast rule. Fashion be-fore comfort, dahling. This was very trying, especially for fashionistas who lived in colder climates and did not want to die of pneumonia. But for daytime, the rules have bent a bit, and fash-ionistas are now filling their hosiery drawers with the following:

• Fishnets—Now a fashionista classic. Their versatility is the key. They can be worn during many fashion movements: punk, slutty secretary, neo-cancan girl. In addition to classic black, keep a host of fishnets in a riot of colors. We love magenta, nude, and glittery silver. Classic black is a must-have. Quirky fashionistas get creative and wear colored fishnets over black opaque tights or black fishnets over brightly hued tights. Sophisticated fashionistas pair them with pencil skirts, cashmere, fur coats, and heels.

• Patterned tights—Plaid, lace, and crocheted tights are a great way to spice up something basic. Steer clear of black-and-white horizontal-striped numbers. (They'll make your legs look fat, dear. Just ask Mel, who had a bad fashion moment in 1987 while wearing zebra-striped tights with an all-black ensemble.)

• Socks—Like tights, socks go in and out of acceptance. Striped, colored, fishnet, patterned, and fun socks have become a perennial mate for all stilettos (especially open-toed versions). Buy rainbow stripes, polka dots, cartoon character–covered, or graffiti socks. You can never be too crazy when achieving this aesthetic. Very cheeky. Warning: Best worn between the ages of thirteen and twenty-seven.

We have to add, however, that if you are going to a fancy evening ball—a black-tie wedding, a museum benefit, a swishy cocktail party—and are planning to pull on that exquisite swanlike, floor-length gown, or a knee-length strapless black dress and a fur shrug—you must *not* wear hose. *Never.* If you need some control-top action, get super-body-hugging stockings and cut off the legs.

DIANA VREELAND ONCE SAID, "BREVITY IS THE SOUL OF LINGERIE"

While some extreme fashionistas avoid underwear altogether ("But I'm allergic!"—Karen), most of us like a little support down there. The rules for wearing fashionista underwear differ according to garment. While underpants must *never* rise up above one's trousers or skirts (sorry, but the thong-flashing look is just so *not* fashionista, unless, of course, Tom Ford is advocating it in an ad campaign, then by all means), baring bra straps is totally acceptable.

Under Where?
✻ MELISSA ✻

I used to be a white-cotton-underwear girl. As a good Catholic schoolgirl, I wore underwear my mother purchased for me at Sears, Mervyn's, or some other reasonably bland retail emporium. My underwear was either white, cream, baby blue, or candy pink. Then one day during my senior year in high school in 1988, my best friend and I walked several blocks to the Victoria's Secret downtown. Ling-yi was as demure as a Chinese girl could be; she laughed with her hand cupped in front of her mouth. She was a National Merit Scholar and in the running for valedictorian, and like me, she wore our school's uniform shirt chastely buttoned up to the neck and her skirts right on the knee. She was the last person you would think would own a black push-up bra.

"Have you been here?" she asked as we tiptoed into the frilly, superfeminine store, oozing with estrogen. I shook my head. I was too embarrassed. The sight of all those teddies on display made my head spin. Why on earth would anyone want to wear anything like . . . that? Some of it looked uncomfortable, even downright tawdry. Nothing like Catholicism to make me feel guilty for being in a lingerie store!

"They've got great stuff," she insisted. She pulled out drawer after drawer of silky camisoles, boy shorts, tap pants, and thong teddies. I was mortified, yet I couldn't look away! I fingered a pair of black cotton underwear (I can't even write the word *panties*, I'm so shy!). I fell in love with an ivory-colored camisole set with embroidered pearl and lace insets. At $14.99, marked down from $39, as I recall, it seemed a real bargain. At Ling's urging, I bought the set, as well as two pairs of sexy black lace underwear.

They sat in my dresser drawer for months. I couldn't imagine what I would tell my mother if she ever saw them. "They feel *dirty*," I explained to my girlfriend later. And I got all neurotic over it for nothing. When my mother saw my new lingerie, she said nothing but "Oh, how pretty!"

Still, I was always skeptical of paying premium for good lingerie. Good bargain shopper that I am, I liked buying my bras 90 percent off at the outlet mall rather than paying full price for scraps of nylon and lace. And even as much as I want to be the La Petite Coquette girl, the Agent Provocateur chick, I'm still the fourteen-dollar-half-price–Calvin Klein lady.

Revelation came when I was shopping with Karen, the girl who doesn't even wear undies. She was wearing a beautiful nude strapless bra as she zipped in and out of Dior dresses. I was so impressed with what it did for her bust that I was driven to finally invest in my own fab bra. I was thirty-one years old and I was overdue. I treated myself to a gorgeous push-up bra for fifty dollars from the French lingerie line Chantelle. Unlike my other bras, the straps didn't bunch or fall, and it gave me a nice clean silhouette under even the thinnest T-shirts. I was hooked. While I've learned to appreciate designer underwear, I still can't go the next step and embrace the full-on-vixen thing. Lately, fashionistas like Karen are advocating going commando as an alternative to the annoying thong-in-the-bum-crack problem or visible panty lines. I'm still skeptical. Maybe I'll break down later, as I always seem to at some point. But for now, it just seems way too naughty for my taste. And I don't want to suffer the fate of Paris Hilton and *Basic Instinct* my way out of a car anytime soon!

Boob Job
✳ KAREN ✳

I hate underwear. I find it restricting, constraining, and uncomfortable. I like to be free, to breathe without fabric, underwires, and elastic in my way. I do wear it for show, however, and when I do, I go all-out. But that's beside the point. I resisted wearing bras for as long as I could growing up. I finally caved when my tennis coach suggested my mother get me something because all that running on the court led to distracting breast floppage during matches (one of the most mortifying hours of my life). To this day I try to get away with avoiding them as much as possible. The problem is, I do not have the perky 34Bs I once did. Gravity, sadly, has taken its toll.

After seeing a photo of myself—where I wasn't wearing a bra—I was sick. My "girls" were practically sagging to my belly button. At that moment I decided to suck it up and buy some boob gear. I headed to La Petite Coquette, the swanky lingerie store near my home, where a woman measured me properly, tightened the straps just so, and showed me how to get the most support out of a bra. My breasts looked so round and good that it didn't bother me to spend $70, even $80 on a piece of lace and well-constructed underwire. It felt racy, dangerous, and indulgent. Soon enough, however, I stopped wearing the bras. They became a hassle. Yes, I liked what they did for my chest, but I always felt the presence of the bra against my skin. It didn't seem natural. So I gave up.

Until I visited Alice Cadolle in Paris, one of the most luxurious lingerie shops in the world, first started by Herminie Cadolle, who invented the bra in the late 1800s. Couture lingerie! Custom-made pieces for the rich and international jet set. Now, I am neither rich nor international. But I was twenty-eight years old and in desperate need of help. If I didn't find a bra I liked, my breasts would sag more and more as the years went by. I saved a good amount of money and had a fitting. A blonde Frenchwoman, wearing a pink pincushion on her wrist as if it were a watch, took my measurements and handled my breasts with gentle care. "They fall flat," I was told, as if I needed to hear that! I needed a bra shape to promote them to point upward from the bottom. She asked me what I wanted out of a bra. I thought for a minute and came up with this: something so natural and perfect, I wouldn't even know it was on me. I was not interested in the ways of seduction—I have my Agent Provocateur for that. Instead, I requested form, fit, and shape. I wanted my girls to look like they did when I was fifteen.

Sketches were made. She talked about where the elastic should be (apparently more in the back, less in the straps is ideal). And we discussed fabric. Silk is not good. It's not supportive or long-lasting. Lace is better. But nylon netting, somewhat transparent, is best. Obviously, I want the best. We also contemplated color. I went with a plush pinkish nude to match my skin tone. After the visit, hours (actually weeks) of fine craftsmanship went into cutting, fitting, constructing the perfect bra for *moi*. When I finally got it and put it on, it was like a giant white light shone over me, the heavens opened, and the angels sang. My breasts never looked so immaculate, so plump, so fine. With clothes I appeared a good few pounds thinner, at that! I was in awe, so enamored that I didn't even mind the $700 price tag . . . until I lost the bra on a trip to Florida three months later!

I have been devastated—and braless—ever since.

Let's Take a Peek into the Fashionista Lingerie Drawer

- Thongs—Make sure they're nice and low for those hip-hugger jeans. We love Cosabella. But then, who doesn't?

- Boy-style briefs—No ordinary panties for the true fashion-ista. We adore ones that have funny sayings all over them, like "Welcome," "Spoil Me," and "Ring My Bell." Or fifties-style ones with the ruffled bottom or a peekaboo bum to reveal tushie cleav-age. They are especially cute when worn with a button-down for nights when you're entertaining your man at home. Target has a great selection at very reasonable prices.

- Everyday fashionista bras—They're utilitarian, and fashion-istas know where to find nude bras in all subtle hues in order to find the right one for their skin tone. Lingerie designer Jean Yu is known for that. Though fashionistas appreciate the go-with-anything nude tone, they may make an exception for the leopard print.

- Tank tops with built-in bras—All the support, none of the nui-sance.

- Hanro camisoles—Supercomfy to wear in lieu of a bra.

- Nipple tape—To wear underneath all those plunging gowns and backless halters. (Just make sure you pluck stray nipple hairs before sticking it on!)

- Sexpot possessions—When fashionistas go vixen, they do it right. Agent Provocateur's playful pieces are a must when you're feeling saucy (fringe panties, sequined pasties, lace bras with nipple cutouts), and La Perla's sexy sophistication is always classic for exotic honeymoons.

- Silk nightgowns—Diana Vreeland insisted on getting fitted for her nightgowns. While custom-made couture nightwear is a thing of the past, true fashionistas insist on sleeping in style.

JEAN-IUS
My Dad's 501s
✳ MELISSA ✳

My dad is only twenty-two years older than I. We share the same birthday. When I was eighteen years old and left for college, he gave me several pairs of his Levi's. My father was the kind of guy who wore suits from Hong Kong by tailors who'd been trained in Saville Row. He was just as discriminating in his taste of jeans. He always swore by Levi's 501s, straight-leg. He was fitted for them the same way as for his suits. He would buy several to last him for a year, and my earliest memories of childhood are of my father taking cuticle scissors to remove the leather label. He allowed the red Levi's tag, but he despised wearing such a large patch. It distracted from the simplicity of his belt.

Papa gave me three pairs of his treasured Levi's, waist size thirty-one (his waist had ballooned to thirty-three). One of the pairs was so worn there were holes in the knees. It was a lightly colored jean that was as smooth and comfortable as pajamas. The other pair was regular wash, and the third a dark wash. They were the coolest things I owned. I arrived at college with fourteen over-size cardboard boxes filled with Outback red camp shirts and jungle-print shift dresses from "Jean Nicole" (don't ask!) but the jeans immediately gave me instant boho cachet. I could never stop my friends from borrowing my dad's jeans. They loved the vintage feel, the flattering leg, and the stories behind them. I could never keep them in my closet. For four years, as many as six girls wore those pants.

I finally had to retire the jeans when the holes got too big to patch, but I still consider them part of my first true inheritance.

My Introduction to Cool
✳ KAREN ✳

From fourth grade through twelfth, I went to a school where there was a dress code. No jeans, no sneakers, blazers mandatory. Because I wasn't exposed to urban cool, I wasn't aware of the perfection of broken-in Levi's. Instead, the jeans I wore were supertrendy. Remember the Guess? jeans with fold-over acid-wash snap pockets? And the Et Vous pair with baby-pink patches of planets and aliens? And the stretch Farlows that may as well have been tights? That is what I wore.

During the summer of 1989, I went to London to intern for a neurosurgeon (that's when I thought I'd grow up to be a doctor—to give you an idea of how clueless I was) through an organized program that set up high school students with jobs across the pond. We stayed in some form of a Y on Tottenham Court Road. While we had evenings free to roam the city at will, there were weekend activities and trips we had to take as a group, a small circle of fifteen kids. I became insta–best friends with a girl named Laura, who was probably the coolest, grooviest chick I had ever met.

She was the type of girl who would go out all night, flirt with guys, lie about her age by ten years, roll out of bed first thing in the A.M., and look immaculate at breakfast, hangover or not. I was immediately taken by her energy. She had a carefree, fun attitude, and long, wavy, unkempt hair that somehow looked chic even when she didn't shower. Everything about her was appealing, right down to her internship at Hilditch & Key, an exclusive men's fashion brand. To go out at night she wore nothing but Levi's, cowboy boots, and tank tops. It was so simple and undone, yet so sharp and done at once. I would throw on full-on matching outfits. I felt so daddy's-girl, prep-school geek next to her.

And then one night she came into my room as I was getting ready for our outing on King Street. (Luckily, in London we didn't need an ID to get into a bar.) As I began to put on my ruffle-bottomed skirt and blazer, she said, "Hold it right there, Robinovitz." I stopped. "A gift. Something you never knew you always needed," she said, handing me a bag. Inside, a beat-up, worn-in pair of vintage Levi's 501s. "You wear the worst jeans and pants," she said. "If we're gonna keep hanging out like this, you need something that's good. Now put these on with a white Hanes T-shirt and your boots and let's go."

I was in heaven. Vintage Levi's! Mine! From the first time I saw Laura in the airport, sitting there with Armani sunglasses, Levi's, black shoe boots, a tank top, and a motorcycle jacket, I was obsessed with her lax, hip, "I don't look like I care, but I really do" sense of style. It was much more effortless than the look I had—big, blown-out hair, the occasional blazer with shoulder pads (I was a Jersey girl, don't forget). With my new jeans, I was suddenly city girl with an edge. They fit me perfectly. They hugged my butt just right. They flattered my thighs and made my legs look lean. They were slightly too long, so just the tip of my shoe peered out from the hemline, which was tattered and fraying. She walked into my room minutes later and victoriously sighed. "Finally! You have no idea how long I've wanted to do that to you.

"You were cute before, but now you're hot," she said.

With that, we ceremoniously threw away my Farlows and my Et Vous and said good-bye to my suburban image. Forever.

P.S. I still have and wear those jeans all the time, and they get better with age.

Blue-jean Baby

Fashionistas love jeans. They live in them. They wear them underneath vintage nightgowns. They roll them up to show off their pointy boots. They throw on stilettos and a wife-beater and they're good to go. And they call the look "studied casual," even when it comes with a suit jacket or sheared chinchilla.

Here's what you'll need:

• Superlong jeans—You're wearing four-inch heels, and there's nothing that looks worse with stilettos than high-waters. Jeans must be long enough to cover every part of the shoe except for the very tip of the toe.

• Superdark jeans—Dark indigo is the preferred color. Black jeans are over. Don't even go there.

• Superlight jeans—Because every few seasons they come back in fashion. For variety, try superbleached jeans as well.

• Supercute skirts—Every self-respecting fashionista must own a denim micromini for hot nights on the town (or to the beach with a hoodie sweatshirt over your bikini top) and one knee-length number to pair with high boots for conservative (corporate-casual) moments.

The ultimate designer jean from Alexander McQueen

• Designer jeans—For dressier nights, designer jeans can take you from a film premiere to dinner at the trendiest restaurant in town.

• Staple jeans—The everyday jean that fashionistas depend upon, on thin

The Levi's Super Low Stretch Bootleg: such a fashionista staple

days and fat days, bad-hair days and dirty-laundry mornings. This is where Levi's come in. The original American jean, they have the most diverse styles on the market and something that is right for everyone in every size.

- Trendy jeans—Because fashionistas must always be on the cutting edge. The trendiest jeans on the market at time of publication: Seven (notice little tag with "7" and embellished stitching on the back pocket) and Paper Denim and Cloth (their signature is light worn in denim with whiskers in the front and knees and one curved yellow stitch from one side of the pocket to the other).

- Utilitarian back-pocket—A favorite for those who want to show off a sculpted behind.

- Indie jean—The secret, cultish lines with interesting, hard-to-find details, like 5 percent spandex. Everyone asks where you got them! (We love Rock & Republic.)

- Fun denim—Jeans with a noticeable appliqué. A true fashionista would go subtle. Think jeans with one patch on the back pocket. Warning: Avoid denim covered with embellishments and embroidery all over the place. It's tacky.

As a hard-and-fast rule, fashionista jeans are never:

- High on the waist. That's so Gramps!

- Acid-washed. They're to be avoided at all costs.

- Regular length. No fashionista would do anything that's "regular." Dressing fashionista is about indulging in the left-of-center and the over-the-top.

- Relaxed fit. Comfortable clothes are anathema to the fashionista. You must suffer for fashion! No pain, no gain!

- Baggy. Best left to old MC Hammer videos. And we all know what happened to him!

- Stirruped. Giddyap, little fashionista, is not a look to go for.

How to Buy Jeans

• Decide whether you will wear them with sneakers or with high heels and get them tailored to the correct length. If you want to wear the same pair with both, hem or cut them so they work with the heels rather than with the sneakers. There should be a break in the front of the foot, and from the side the jeans should appear to skim the floor. It's okay if they drag when you wear them with sneakers. In fact, that's a good thing.

• Check the rear view. Does it ride up? Or worse, divide your behind? Extra-small or extra-large pockets are not flattering. Regular square pockets are the best bet.

• Check the crotch. By all means, avoid the camel-toe look. But on the other hand, you don't want the crotch to be too long either.

• Bootleg cut with the extra flare at the ankle is a safe basic, but we also recommend trying the boy-leg, fully straight jean and stretch Lycra jeans (sooo comfortable). Low-waisted jeans are more flattering; just don't go too low—the stripper look is very nonfashionista.

• Remember, while there are some clothes fashionistas would never wear, what makes you a fashionista is your desire to wear *anything* as long as it's in fashion. Therefore, the fashionista "rules" are not rules at all. Feel free to break them when the trend points toward high-waisted, relaxed-fit, regular-length jeans (although we won't hold our breath). But you'll learn. You'll go back to your dark-indigo, superlong denims in no time.

BOTTOMS UP

Fashionistas cannot live on jeans alone. While most of us do anyway, we happen to have a very large collection of pants and skirts of all shapes, sizes, and styles. Below, you'll find the other ingredients for your dream closet.

Show Them Who Wears the Pants! These Are the Basic Requirements

• At least one pair of slammin' black pants with a flat front and a crease down the front. Wear with high heels and any kind of top, sweater, halter. Will take you to hot dinner dates, parties, and day-time meetings.

• Evening pants, be it tuxedo, velvet, beaded, Harlows (a.k.a. very wide legged, named after Jean Harlow, who wore them in the thirties), or shiny and satiny numbers, will get you through any benefit gala, black-tie affair when you don't feel like donning a dress, or even daytime with a tank top and boots.

• Cigarette pants. Skinny-legged friends—that ski-pant look—great for sixties resurrection moments.

• Slouchy men's-style trousers—Menswear tailoring is a fashionista's best friend. The flattering fit, the straight leg, the longish hem—heaven. Masculine is always the new feminine, folks.

• Gauchos (or culottes)—Is it a skirt or a pair of long shorts? It's a skort! Wear in winter with knee-high boots and a Victorian blouse.

• Leathers—You'll need one pair of leather pants at some point in your fashionista life. They can be red rocker style motorcycle pants that get yer motor running when you head out on the runway, custom-made bad boys that tie up the front, or any style that suits you. Just make sure the leather is supple and the fit is slightly too small at first. Leather stretches—and bags at the knees—over time. Also, they require special dry-cleaning services.

• Cords—Basic boy-style, flare-legged, or low-slung hip-huggers are the way to go.

• Cargo—Pants with large pockets in the back and extra-large pockets in front. Dress them up with heels and halters, but be warned: They go in and out of style. Keep a pair on deck. You never know when you'll need them.

Skirting the Issue

Fashionista skirts are always in interesting fabrics or shapes, trumpet flares, ruffled tiers, or deconstructed denim being some favorites. While every other style guidebook will tell you never to buy calf-length or pleated skirts for fear of adding poundage to your waistline, we're here to say "Indulge away." Fashionistas are allowed to make fashion faux pas and laugh about them later.

A Few Basic Shapes and Styles

- A-line—Slightly flared that looks like the letter A.
- Asymmetric—Any skirt that falls diagonally at the hemline. Often it's ruffled and full of flounce.
- Fishtail—Skirt with an extra panel in the front or back that is reminiscent of a fish's tail.
- Handkerchief—Skirt with a hemline cut so it falls in points as if it were made from a series of hankies.
- Inverted pleat—Its marked characteristic is the two folds of fabric that meet at the center line in front and/or in back.
- Kick pleat—Straight skirt with just one pleat.
- Midi—A hemline that falls between the ankle and the knee. Recommended for tall women only.
- Mini—An extremely short skirt, first popularized by British designer Mary Quant in the sixties.
- Peasant—Full skirt with gathers. Likely to have bands of embroidery, eyelet details, even fringes.
- Pencil—Sophisticated, slinky, always a crowd-pleaser, it's fitted from waist to hem.
- Prairie—Flared skirt that gathers at the waist and has ruffles at the hemline.

- Sheath—Straight skirt. No flare.
- Trumpet—Straight skirt with one circular flounce at the hemline that resembles the instrument that bears its name.

WHAT'S ON TOP
Choke on This
❊ MELISSA ❊

It was my first reading. I had been asked to read an essay about my fashion and financial foibles as part of the bill at a downtown theater space. As I recall, the piece was titled "Money to Burn" and documented how I had wasted my money on my affinity for outrageous clothes and boozy champagne blowouts. I chose my outfit carefully: an asymmetrical black top—one shoulder had no sleeve, the other had an extra-long sleeve that dragged on the floor.

I had shown the shirt to several skeptical nonfashionista friends, who joked, "When you catch a cab, make sure your sleeve doesn't get caught on the door. You could choke!"

Ha. Ha. Ha. *Not.*

As I walked up to the stage in my four-inch stilettos (with only the toe peeking out from my pant hem), I tripped on my extra-long sleeve. There was an appalled silence. But I quickly managed to pull myself together and shrug it off. The essay was a hit. Especially when I told everyone how after being in credit counseling for four years, I had just been approved for a brand-new credit card—with a limit of $200!

Later, my flaming fashionista friend told me that the sight of my extra-long sleeve as it floated hither and yon beside me as I read was one of the most beautiful things he had ever seen. "You looked like such a fashionista. So unapologetic. I felt so proud."

SHIRT THING

What fashionistas wear on top of all those superlong jeans differs wildly from fashionista to fashionista. Some fashionistas prefer colorful, flirty, feminine jewel-tone ruffled blouses, while others stick to a uniform of torn T-shirts, slim-fitted designer sweatshirts or black sweaters, and tops in every variation of style and fabric: cowl neck, turtleneck, V-neck, cardigan, three-quarter sleeve (guilty as charged—Mel). This is the part of the fashionista closet where anything goes (ruched, extra-long sleeved, fringed, tattered, sequined, backless), especially since what's in one year (tie-neck blouses, nautical stripes, puffed sleeves) might be out the next. That said, there are some classic wardrobe builders to be aware of, as follows:

- Zip-up hoodies for errands or with heels. Cashmere is ideal.

- A crisp button-down oxford-style blouse. You never know when you'll need it.

- Oversize shirt, cut extra large and extra long and great with a belt to cinch the waist on the beach or on the town.

- Safari, an African-inspired look with lapels, large front pockets, and buttons down the front. First made chic by Dior in the mid-sixties, it makes a vital resurgence every now and then.

- Tunic, a straight, loose-fitting knee-length number. Work it for a big night out and the next morning over a bikini on the beach.

- One shouldered. Nothing beats that Studio 54 feeling.

- Blouson, a full-fitting blouse that tends to gather at the waist and evoke a rich hippie-chic vibe.

- Camisole, often called "cami." A lingerie-inspired look that is short, fitted to the bodice, and equipped with spaghetti straps for the shoulders.

- Tank tops, plain and racer back, and halters are also great staples.

JACKETS REQUIRED
Death by Fendi
✳ MELISSA ✳

It's nearly impossible for me to resist a good bargain, and during the winter of 1996 I fell prey to a Fendi sample sale when a fashionista friend e-mailed me the following news: "Fendi sample sale! Run, don't walk!" This was during the baguette years, when everyone from suburban soccer moms to downtown gallerinas were obsessed with the tiny Fendi pocketbooks, reminiscent of baguette rolls from chic Pareeeee.

I arrived at the sale breathless, and after securing my first baguette (opting for the larger "Mama" version), I inspected the clearance bins. The Fendi store on Fifth Avenue is an immaculate temple to Italian design. It looks more like a museum than a store, and without the sale I would never have had the nerve to step inside. It was an absolute pleasure to see all the merchandise haphazardly stacked and the store packed to the rafters with voracious fashionistas.

Then I saw it: a $3,000 leather jacket with beaded and embroidered appliqués on the shoulder and spread collar. It had a tight silhouette and was the color of hot buttered caramel. Better yet, it was reduced to $189! Can I repeat, $189! I grabbed it from the hanger and put it on immediately. The jacket nipped at the waist and had a one-of-a-kind raffish edge. It was the perfect thing to wear to Fashion Week (conveniently scheduled for the following week!).

I went home with my new purchase, giddy over my exquisite loot. The next Monday I put on the jacket, zipped it up, and wore it to the first fashion show. I was soon surrounded by cooing, awed fashionistas.

"Your jacket!"
"Where did you get it?"
"It's handmade!"
I basked in their admiration, and told them about the Fendi

sample sale, and how much I paid for it. (Did I mention $189?) The consequent charge out the door trampled the art students in the standing-room lines. I took my front-row seat and felt very self-congratulatory. Then it happened. I noticed that when I bent my head down, the little beaded plastic sequins on the collar of my jacket cut into my neck. It was painful! My jacket was attacking me! I had several little nicks all over my neck, as if I were suffering from a bad rash.

The worst was yet to come. When I got home that afternoon, I pulled down the zipper. But it wouldn't budge. I was trapped in the jacket like meat in sausage casing. I pushed, I pulled, I sweated, I panted, I cursed the designer. I got it halfway up my head but then I found I couldn't breathe! Finally I had to ask my super to help me out of the jacket. He had to use a pair of pliers to release me from my Fendi stranglehold.

Unfortunately, the jacket was final sale. No wonder it had been reduced to that price. I kept it in my closet for three months, and then one day decided to risk it again. This time my super was not amused when I knocked on his door for fashion 911. I still own the jacket. I can't seem to part with it. I guess this is what they mean when they say "Fashion hurts!"

Rabbit Stew
✳ KAREN ✳

During the spring of 2003 I fell in love. And I do mean really in love. The kind of love that makes you smile when you walk down the street in the pouring rain. The kind of love that keeps you up at night just because you can't stop thinking about it. The kind of love that makes your heart skip a beat. The kind of love that inspires you to be more than what you already are. I was sure I had met the one: a white rabbit-fur jacket with ruched leather elastic bands at the wrist and around the waist and a fantastic collar. It was sporty, yet elegant. Sophisticated yet fun. And a fortune at $3,600.

Totally impractical, this jacket was. Probably the precise reason I had to have it. I first saw it at an Alexander McQueen trunk show. I practically knocked the model over as I pounced her way to pet it. "I have to have it," I told the store's manager. "You don't understand; I have to!" At trunk shows, it's easy to lust after everything and get so caught up in the moment of it that you think you can actually have it all. Just saying you want it doesn't mean anything. Unless it's the kind of trunk show where you have to put down a deposit, no money is exchanged and nothing is set in stone. But Moselle, the tall, exotic-looking saleswoman whom I work with at McQueen, took down my name for the white jacket. The store was getting in only two, and only one of them would be my size.

"It's the best," she assured me, congratulating my choice.

I thought about the white jacket for months, eagerly waiting and fearing its arrival. I knew that when it showed up, I would not really be able to afford it. But I had to find a way. What girl doesn't need a sporty white rabbit jacket with leather cuffs and waistband? In June it arrived with the store's first delivery of fall merchandise. Pressure was on. I had to decide right then and there if I'd take it. I came in and tried it on. It was perfection. An angelic slice of heaven against my pale skin. It made me feel like a rock star. But that lofty price tag! Ouch!

I put it on hold so I could think about it and I prayed that money owed to me would trickle in soon. A week went by and I got no checks. "I can't do it," I explained to Moselle. "I wish I could, but I won't have money for a month or two." She did me right and put it aside for me. "Just take it when you can afford it," she said. Three months passed. And then one day, something beautiful happened. A very large check that I had worked extremely hard for appeared in my mailbox.

I called Moselle, exclaiming, "I have it! I have it! I have money!" I ran over to the store and wrote a check. I sent the jacket to New Jersey in order to save the tax. Upon receiving the jacket days later, I admired my new pet, but I also felt sick. Nauseatingly sick. I could not believe I spent so much on rabbit fur, the lowest of all fur on the totem pole of luxury (after squirrel). I couldn't return it. Not after it was put aside for three months. While it's the hottest thing I ever had in my hands, it was also the thing that made me feel terrible about myself and my bad shopping habits.

What to do, what to do, I stressed. My therapist urged me to take it back. So did my accountant. And after another month of deliberating, I finally did, so proud (though mortified and embarrassed, I must confess) of my obvious psychological growth (not so long before that, I never would have brought it back—or even considered it). Sadly, it wasn't in the cards. The store would no longer allow me to return it. Not even for credit. I was stuck with the thing, which serves as a constant reminder that I have got to get a grip!

JUDGE A GAL BY HER COVER

It's the first thing people will see you in, so your coat just may be the most important statement a fashionista makes. Here's what you should consider (mind you, you don't need to buy them all, but of course, it wouldn't hurt if you did):

• Fur. It doesn't matter if it's vintage, new, faux, or your mom's, but some form of warm fuzzy jacket, chubby, or floor-length coat is in order.

• Vests. It could be an ironic sporty down or fleece vest, something in fur, or a doctored-up denim with grommets. They're great for fall.

• Denim. A little cropped denim jacket is an easy solution to slight breezes.

• Military. A fitted, often double-breasted jacket or floor-length coat that borrows military details (gold buttons, epaulets, high collars) will make everyone stand at attention.

• Long sweater coats, ponchos, capes, stoles, and wraps are always a good thing to collect and bust out for variety. Wraps, capes, and stoles are especially chic for evening.

- Puffy down jackets, whether from the Gap, a ski or snow-board company, Nike, or Gaultier, keep you warm and sporty cool. A winter basic. Just don't get one that makes you look too puffy.

- Maxi coat, a floor-length drama piece for high-powered meetings, black tie galas, and whenever you want to make a lasting impression of classiness and grace.

- Midi, a mid-calf-length coat. The same function as a maxi, but not as serious.

- Bathrobe style. Much like a bathrobe, it's midthigh length, with a sash to tie it closed.

- Smoking jacket, a manly style with a shawl collar and a sash tie. Much like the bathrobe. Called "le smoking" by the French, as it was first made chic by YSL in the mid-sixties.

- Fleece. You'll need something laid-back for when you do your errands. Note: You can also use your vest or puffy jacket for this purpose.

EXCESS-ORY: AN OUTFIT JUST ISN'T AN OUTFIT WITHOUT THE RIGHT ACCESSORIES

The Bag Ate My Hair!
✳ KAREN ✳

My red Chloe handbag with the chunky silver chain shoulder strap, outside zipper pockets, and luggage tag is one of my most cherished possessions. Wherever I go, people compliment it, from the hostess at the diner and my mother and her friends to bitchy drag queens I pass in the Meatpacking District on afternoon walks and even bitchier fashion editors. I wear it with everything and every color. It is my bag soul mate, the one I've been searching for my whole life. Like the right man, it's the addition to my world that makes it just that much more complete.

Yes, the right bag can do all of that.

I have spent time polishing the silver chains, treating the leather, and organizing all of its contents in order to maintain the bag so that it never looks worn and beaten down. I have given it 100 percent of my love and attention. I bring it all over town. I show it the world. I treat it with the utmost respect, adoration, and care. I hold it on my lap at movies and on airplanes. I would never banish it to the floor! I never take it for granted, especially considering that I'm one of the few who snatched it from the shelves before it sold out (a karmic blessing).

No different from some of the guys I've dated and treated well only to be stomped on, my red leather friend has an aggressive way of showing me the feeling is not mutual. More often than not, the chain gets tangled in my locks and bites down so tightly on them that no amount of sweet manipulation will set me free. I am forced to tug and pull, often removing large chunks of hair along the way. It happens at the most inopportune moments—in the elevator on my way up to meetings with important editors (I actually walked into one fashion director's office with the bag attached to my head. She got out the scissors and said, "This will hurt you more than it will me"), while trying to hail a taxi, and shopping in the Chloe store, where the bag, I think, should be on its best behavior. It is, after all, where it came from!

It's a sad, sad thing when good fashion goes bad. But it happens to the best of us. And you know what? It's worth the fight. I am confident that we'll be able to get through this try-

ELIZABETH LIPPMAN

Exhibit A. Mel, carrying the hair-eating chain-link handle. It's safer that way.

ing point of our relationship in time, which, luckily, heals all wounds. Thank gosh. I have a bald spot just above my right ear!

Speak Softly and Carry a Great Handbag

Most fashionistas are either shoe people or bag people. (Okay, most are both, but we don't like to sound so greedy.) Like shoes, you can never own enough handbags. These are the styles that will set you apart as a member of the tribe (MOT).

ELIZABETH LIPPMAN

- Clutch—A strapless bag, fabulous for the P.M. A mini clutch is a very small clutch.

- Envelope clutch—A longer clutch shaped much like an envelope. (Easy to hail taxis with, bad for also holding shopping bags!)

- Evening bags—They tend to be small, often are bejeweled, and may even have a bracelet handle.

The clutch! Look, ma! No straps!

- Messenger bags—Bags with a long strap that crosses the chest diagonally so that the roomy pouch sits at the hips. Named after bike messengers who carry this style to transport packages.

- Oversize—Whether it's a tote, a doctor bag, a bowling bag, or just a large hobo, you need one extra-large bag to trundle all your stuff in.

- Doctor—The classic doctor bag is a great sturdy shape for everyday use.

- Tote—A utilitarian bag with an open top, two handles, and a square pouch usually large enough to hold a few magazines, running shoes, a sweater, a small umbrella, a notebook, and all of your necessities. Similar to the shape of a shopping bag.

• The man purse—Any kind of bag a man holds. Typically, older, graying Euro-trash carry clutches (yeesh!) and urban hipsters go with messenger styles. Note: Straight men should never have a Prada bag.

• Designer—You can have as many knockoffs and fakes as you please, but all fashionistas own at least *one* real, bought-at-the-flagship-store, spent-all-my-money-on-it, superdesigner handbag, even if it meant saving up for years. Gucci, Louis Vuitton, Prada, Fendi, Bottega Veneta, Hermès, logoed or unlogoed, it doesn't matter. Barrel shape, lunchbox style, satchel, or any shape will do. Just make sure to buy one if you haven't already.

The beloved Balenciaga motorcycle bag.

• A bag for Jean-Claude—Fashionistas like to carry their little pooches everywhere; hence, it's very important to find a roomy bag for your pet.

Arf, darling. Arf.

The Contents of the Fashionista Handbag

• Cell phone—The smaller the better.

• MAC Blot tissue-paper wipes—Cure-all for shiny face.

• Kiehl's lip balm—Chapped lips are the devil's handiwork!

• Credit cards—Keep cash to a minimum.

• Orly nail file and nail polish—Carry your own color (and maybe a clear one to stop stocking runs).

• Chanel lip gloss and lipstick.

- Chanel blush/compact—Important to have a mirror.

- Flip-flops—Comfortable shoes to change into.

- Designer wallet with many credit cards, ID.

- Fabulous sunglasses.

- Change purse that doubles as a business-card holder. Karen's reads "get rich quick" on the front.

- Red kabbalah string—You never know when you'll have to ward off the evil eye.

- List of things to do—"Meet Todd at 6:00, Oyster Bar"—the fashionista Palm Pilot.

- Croc notebook—For taking down notes at the fashion shows.

- Tiffany pen.

- Kiehl's Crème de Corps hand cream.

- Ouchless hair bands—Without the icky metal thing.

- Crest White Strips—Whiter teeth for the fashionista.

- MAC Studio Lights cover-up—great for under-eye concealer.

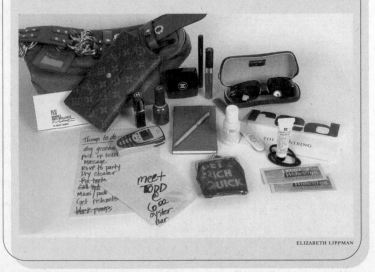

ELIZABETH LIPPMAN

IT'S ALL IN YOUR HEAD

The opportunity to add *more* clothing to any outfit is always welcome in the fashionista mind-set; therefore, fashionistas are staunch proponents of headgear. Especially since hats are a difficult accessory to pull off; fashionistas can't resist a challenge. Some people should never wear hats. They look silly and pretentious. Fashionistas don't mind looking pretentious (sometimes you can't help it if you're a fashionista), but looking silly is fashionista death. Therefore, hats are for varsity-level fashionistas only. If you must indulge, which of course, you must, here are some of the hats that will keep your head warm and your style impeccable.

The Mad Hatter
✳ MELISSA ✳

I saw it in the shop window of Barneys: an oversize black top hat made of velvety mink fur. I fell in love, and walked into the shop in a daze. Sometimes things just come out of the ether and you realize what you've been missing all along. For me, it was like that—when I saw it, I knew: *big hat!* My life was missing a big hat! How did I ever get dressed and walk out the door before this?

Once I put that big furry hat on my head, I never wanted to take it off. It was just the thing to wear with a slim, vintage leather coat that I was working all season. (You can never wear fur headgear with fur or chubby jackets—keep the line slim at all times, and make the large hat the exclamation part of the outfit.)

"Do you want this wrapped up?" the salesclerk asked.

"Nah! I'll just walk out with it," I told her. I went home, hugging the huge hatbox and feeling extremely giddy. New Yorkers don't normally smile at other New Yorkers; we are a breed that likes to keep to ourselves. But somehow, my joy and the sight of the fur hat were infectious. I got comments like "Cute hat!" and "Cool hat!" and "Awesome hat!" all the way from Madison Avenue to Carmine Street in the West Village, where I lived at the time.

My hat even got the highest regard that I could think of. I wore it to Flamingo East's Wednesday-night "salon," a nightclub frequented by my coterie of gay friends and several high-profile gays. The designer Marc Jacobs was lounging in the center sofa (the "it" table where you could see everyone), and as I walked by, I felt the weight of his stare as he looked straight at me.

"That is a fucking amazing hat!" he said.

I was too thrilled even to squeak a thank-you.

Fashionista Headgear

• Fuzzy wool cap—Preferably knitted and in a shocking color. Ear flaps are cute. But caps with actual "ears" sewn in are a little too cute. You're a fashionista, not a fourteen-year-old. If you are fourteen and a fashionista, go right ahead!

On Mel (left), corded suede newsboy by Eugenia Kim; on Karen (right), leather driving cap by Marc Jacobs

• Newsboy—Similar to a driving cap, but a bit fuller on top with a larger brim. Wear with a long ponytail or slightly tilted to the side with wild, sexy hair.

• Fedora—A classic topper. Never wear with a trench coat (too Humphrey Bogart and not the look you're going after). Pair with slinky black jumpsuits or your too-dark superlong jeans.

On Karen (left), red pinstripe Philip Treacy bucket-fedora combo; on Mel (right), cowhide cowboy hat by Amy Chan

• Beret—Monica Lewinsky gave these a bad name, but berets, brimless wonders worn tilted to the side of the head, are very charming . . . and Parisian.

• Walk on the wild side with something bold that makes everyone stop and stare. Warning: Requires confidence.

• Fur—Fashionistas never pass up the chance to wear fur-trimmed or fur anything. The larger and furrier the hat, the more fashionista. Wear with slim leather jackets. Never with your fur chubby. Otherwise you'll look like a muppet. Beware of tofu-tossing activists.

Extra Touches

Other things to add to your accessory collection:

• Gloves, be it driving or opera.

• Scarves for braving the cold front and giving a French flair to whatever you wear.

• Strands of pearls of varying lengths.

• Lots of earrings, including chandelier and hoop.

• Cocktail rings.

• Cameo from Grandma.

• Brooches, to add to hats, to close jackets, to doll up the hip-bone area of jeans. Get one that doubles as a pendant.

• Classic belt. Hermès is ideal.

• Hip-hugging belt, worn not to hold up your pants, but to give oomph to low-slung pants, jumpsuits, shirt dresses, oversize shirts, and slinky dresses.

THRIFTY WOMEN: SOME THINGS ARE BETTER THE SECOND TIME AROUND
What's Old Is What's New
✳ KAREN ✳

I believe in reincarnation. Our souls live one life in one body and another and another and another, each time around learning new lessons, projecting new identities. The same goes for clothes. I look at vintage clothes with a vision. I don't see it for what it is (or was). I see it for what it can be. When my mother gave me a hanging bag of her honeymoon trousseau (the new threads you get for the first romantic vacation a couple takes as husband and wife), all of which evoke the spirit of the late sixties; blouses from the seventies and eighties; and her luscious mink coat from the early eighties, I was in awe. Such a gift! If those threads could talk! They were full of a youthful energy of the younger version of my mother, who was a lot like I am now. Having her pass on her most special pieces—then splurges from a store called Mademoiselle in Bayonne, New Jersey, and Westfield, New Jersey—was a way of sharing memories, a piece of her life from an earlier day, a part of herself.

The fabric! The stitching! The details! While nothing was from a noteworthy designer, it was all so flawlessly unique, meticulously crafted, and very Jackie O. There was a pink-gold-and-silver-patterned cropped sleeve, A-line mock-turtleneck brocade dress with thick Lurex threading and heavily jeweled embellishment that was $300, a fortune at the time; a cream ornate floral lace sleeveless A-line mock-turtleneck dress with a pink bow behind the neck, which stood perfectly straight up due to intense boning; a white A-line (she was obviously very into A-line silhouettes) tank dress with silver Lurex zigzag horizontal stripes and a matching three-quarter-sleeve knee-length swing coat with a crystal-studded ball attached to the zipper; and a simple white shantung silk A-line knee-length dress with lace sleeves. Extraordinary. But not very wearable.

The dresses hung in my closet for years. My friend Sally wore one once to a sixties theme party. But other than that, they got no play. Until I heard of Guillermo Couture, an alterations wizard, who has his own collection and can apparently knock off anything from any designer to a T (all you have to do is show him a picture from a magazine). Well, I brought the pink and lace dresses to him to see what we could come up with. We chatted about what we could transform them into. The pink could be a short bolero jacket and matching skirt (kind of Prada-y from spring/summer 2003). After a few sketches, we decided to turn the pink into a mod evening coat, the kind of thing I could wear with sexy dresses at night or jeans and a tank top. As for the lace frock, I wanted something sexy. Maybe even backless. He turned it into a feminine scoop-neck, open-backed tank dress. The original bow from behind the neck is now above the bum. It reminded me of something you'd see on the Valentino runway.

So taken was I with my new creations, I went through my closet to find more things I could make over. I brought him old A-line skirts, which he tapered into pencil skirts. Next, he's getting a green Gucci beaded top that I never wore (you'll read about that in the shopping chapter next, entitled "Really, I shouldn't have!"). I'm pretty sure he can shorten it from the top so there would be more width over my chest and then rescoop out the neckline. His sister is said to be a master beader.

Mom's giant mink coat went to Anne Dee Goldin, a furrier who has designed for Karl Lagerfeld. The mink, she thought, was in mint condition. But to modernize it, she suggested shearing it. The shape of the coat, however, was a different story. It was very oversized—huge shoulders, a wide, full bodice. Totally overpowering for my frame. I had a number of choices, as there was a lot of material to work with. A short chubby—and make the remainder a hat, scarf, and pillow; a peacoat; a straight long jacket; a poncho. After trying on dozens of styles from her vault, we came up with a sharp design: a mid-thigh-length bathrobe style with a dramatic pseudo-hood collar and a sash. With that, she took my measurements, and two weeks later I came in for a fitting in muslin, a canvaslike fabric, in order to make sure the pattern was right. It was.

A week later my coat was ready. Sheared, the fur had a fresh, sumptuous feel—like smooth liquid butter. The color, once chocolate, was lighter and richer. And the fit—like a glove. It is the most perfect custom jacket I could imagine. I get compliments on it wherever I go. And then came Mom's old shirts. I brought them to Guillermo, who cinched one at the waist, trimmed another, shortened a third. And just like that I had a new wardrobe of reinvented vintage, better than anything I could buy new or find on a thrift store rack. The best part: When I wear them, it's like my mom is with me. She's proud of what her old clothes have become. And we both wonder what my (future) daughter (if I have one) will do to give them a whole new life—again.

ELIZABETH LIPPMAN

I'm sure they were great in the '60s, but they're not now.

ELIZABETH LIPPMAN

ELIZABETH LIPPMAN

Now it's fitted, backless, and that constraining turtleneck is gone.

Guillermo puts the finishing touches on my fabulous new evening coat.

Scavenger Hunt: What to Look for When It Comes to Secondhand Clothes

• White and ivory ruffled blouses with puffed sleeves from the Victorian (1890s) era. Wear with distressed jeans you already own. So Chloë Sevigny.

• Black flapper dresses from the twenties. Wear to parties with a denim jacket à la Kate Moss.

• Fur. Psychologically, it's easier on the conscience to get an old fur rather than a new one. Besides, it's a fraction of the price.

• Belted dresses from the 1930s in voile prints, just like the ones Prada offered several years ago.

• Mink stoles from the 1940s. How Greta Garbo!

• Frothy 1950s prom dresses in pastel shades. Think Gwen Stefani and Marc Jacobs—the frothier and more many-tiered, the better. You can also have a tailor cut it to turn the bottom half into a fab skirt. Skip the embroidered sheath prom dresses from the same era; they are very matronly.

• Vintage lingerie, such as slips, bustiers, camisoles, peignoirs, and bias-cut nightgowns from the 1930s, makes great evening wear. Who needs to buy a new dress when you can wear an old nightgown? Stella McCartney used to ravage thrift stores for antique lace lingerie to use for her collections. Be choosy and pick fabrics in great condition, in the most flattering colors. The look is reminiscent of Madonna in her "Express Yourself" heyday.

• When buying vintage denim, beware of jeans that are too fussy—way too many buttons, rivets, and fancy stitching. These details are more frumpy than fashionista. Look for straight-leg Levi's with the red label. So Sheryl Crow.

• Vintage leather should be soft, thin, and well constructed. Fashionistas love leather in unusual colors rather than the typical black or brown.

• Keep an eye out for Emilio Pucci's psychedelic creations. The Italian designer turned out collections for swimwear, evening gowns, minidresses, halters, purses, skirts, pants, and lingerie. Jacqueline Susann was a Pucci fanatic, as was Marilyn Monroe, who was buried in her favorite Pucci. Make sure it's authentic by looking for the Pucci signature repeated in the print. There's a lot of pseudo-Pucci out there!

Quality Control!
Make Sure What You Buy Is in Good Condition

• Check the lining. If the lining on a jacket is torn, it will be expensive to replace and not worth your while. Unless, of course, you love, love, love it.

• Hold the garment up to the light. Is the fabric so threadbare it's almost see-through? If so, leave it on the rack.

- Check for stains. If you have a fabulous dry cleaner who can get red wine out of ivory lace dresses (can we have his number?), then you might be able to salvage it. However, if it's a very dark grease stain, it might not come out, and you're left with a fashion don't.

- Take a good, long whiff. If decades of body odor waft from the garment, no amount of dry cleaning will help it. Leave that stink at the store, where it belongs!

- Never buy underwear at the thrift store. Slip dresses, fine. Underpants, no. But did we really have to tell you that?

Warning: Some designers licensed their name to everything, and while these items might carry brand names, they are actually very cheaply made and not fashionable at all. For instance, Pierre Cardin allowed his name to go on everything from sunglasses to umbrellas and ugly men's ties. It's very hard to find a real sixties piece. If it's polyester and Pierre Cardin, don't buy it. Halston is another one whose name was heavily licensed. Get a Halston original only if it's a gorgeous dress.

CLOSET MAKEOVERS WITH SUPERSTYLIST MICHAEL PALLADINO

We had heard about legendary stylist Michael Palladino for years. Michael's clients call him from hospital rooms after plastic surgery saying, "Michael, I'm thinking plunging necklines! I've got breasts now and they're gorgeous!" Michael tells them to hang up and call back when they're off the Demerol. "I'm not taking advantage of their weakened state to sell them fashion," he says. As director of client and studio services of Henri Bendel, one of the city's most cherished department stores, one of his services is to weed out the good from the bad and the unnecessary from the racks—and his clients' closets—and help them fill the gaps in their wardrobes. We invited him to do ours.

Michael arrives at Mel's apartment and immediately sifts through her closet like a madman. Mel wants to know which items to keep and which to discard, as she is moving all the way to Los Angeles, the land where the height of fashion is a Juicy sweatsuit and a pair of Uggs. Mel is a bit of a pack rat, and has kept every trend she has worn. He roots through and throws away all of her old, faded J.Crew dresses ("I didn't peg you as a preppy!") as well as several itchy and unflattering sweaters. Gone are the white vinyl miniskirts and the bulky wool tops. "Too many dark colors, too much black; for Los Angeles we need to get you into a color palette, something vibrant," he decides.

At Karen's, Michael takes one look at her walk-in closet and begins to toss beloved items in the "go" pile: an Imitation of Christ eighties prom dress that he describes as "part of the Cyndi Lauper therapy fund," a Morticia Adams–style lace cardigan, and a Balenciaga dress with too many trends in it (topstitching, denim, leather, flounce). He tells Karen, "You have such a fun, whimsical style. What you really need are connectors, things to carry you through life and daytime. You have all of these wild event clothes that most women would never have the guts to wear. So let's find you some basics. I'd like to see you in things that will last a lifetime, not just through a great party."

We all pile into a cab and head to Henri Bendel to do some shopping. It's the first time we have made use of a stylist, and we realize how helpful it can be to have an objective eye take a look at your wardrobe and run around the store to pull things for you. Fashionistas sometimes live in too much fantasy, and it's good to have an outside voice ground you in reality. (We decide we must make use of this service more often, especially since every department store from Macy's to Bergdorf has a personal shopper department to provide styling advice.)

At Bendel, the three of us dash from floor to floor. Michael grabs things while an assistant hangs them on rolling racks and carts them off to our respective dressing rooms. After MP's closet analyses, we are focused with specific tasks at hand in order to meet each of our needs. Mel holds up a Plein Sud shearling. "Lightweight, Mel, lightweight!" Michael barks. Karen ogles more event clothes. "This white marabou jacket, is it a connector?" she asks. Michael shakes his head, staring at his shoes like a disapproving parent who always knows best.

We fall in love with all things Missoni, but the price tags ($2,500 for a coat Mel lives for) don't allow us to consummate, and Mel, again, reaches for fur! This time, a rabbit-lined Juicy sweatshirt. ("What, it's Juicy," she rationalizes. "You said I need Juicy.") She'll never learn! Every time MP shows Karen practical connectors like a cargo skirt or a decent raincoat, she protests, *"Boring!"* and points to a crazy pair of black sequined cigarette pants and pleads, "Can't this connect?"

"Sure," he says sarcastically, "it's perfect for running out to get the paper." He is determined to help us break bad habits and make our lives whole. He finds several cool mod shift dresses and light chiffon skirts for Mel that she can wear tripping along in flip-flops in Cali. But for Karen, he gives up. "You want flash. That's who you are. Stick to it." He brings her a micromini satin black corset Luella Bartley dress and tosses her a knit hat that says "*Slut.*"

"Oh, Michael. You know me so well," she says approvingly. Le pièce de résistance: a Swarovski-encrusted Agent Provocateur riding crop, which Karen uses to spank him (and Mel). Inspired, he brings her a long Rick Owens oxblood-colored part-chiffon skirt, which she turns into a strapless

We came. We saw. We shopped.

Saying good-bye to Michael, double-air kisses

dress by lifting it above her breasts (elastic waist) and twisting the extra fabric around her body to cinch it, closing it with a brooch. He adds in the fleece jacket Mel wanted and—voilà!—screams, "Yes! A connector!"

With that, we are royally escorted out the glass double doors on Fifth Avenue. We hop in our chariot—a yellow taxi—with dozens of delicious Henri Bendel signature brown-and-white-striped bags. Ah, life is sweet.

How to Organize Your Closet

The secret to a well-dressed fashionista is a well-organized closet.

• Fold jeans, don't hang them, and pile them on a shelf. This way they occupy less space.

• Never hang leather pants; always fold. Hanging stretches the leather.

• Organize clothing by group: pants, sexy tops, button-downs, skirts, dresses, coats and jackets, each should have its own section. Within sections and subsections, organize by color, so things are easy to find.

• Don't hang the pieces of your suits together. Keeping them separate may inspire new outfits.

• Don't fret about seasonality. If you don't have storage space to keep winter clothes when it's summer and summer clothes when it's winter, it's fine to keep it all together (the seasonless closet). Just stick to the groups per above.

• Fold sweaters and keep on a shelf. Arrange in piles according to color and thickness.

• Keep dry-cleaning bags to a minimum. They tend to "suffocate" the clothes. Clothes must breathe, just like people.

• Consider fur storage. Fur should be kept in optimum temperature conditions.

• Nail hooks on the wall for your hats, bags, and belts.

CLEANING OUT THE CLUTTER

Some of your clothes will never come back in style. It's a hard fact of life you will, at some point or another, have to face. There is no better way to make room for the new than to clean out the old. Getting rid of the things you don't wear and will probably never wear again is not always easy, but it's an occupational hazard that is par for the course. If you're not sure what to keep and what to trash, follow our guidelines. But don't feel like you have to follow things too closely. There are a bunch of dresses lurking on hangers in our closets that we refuse to give up, no matter what.

What to Give Away

• Trendy one-season wonders.
• Whatever you haven't worn in over two years.

- The stuff that's way too small on you. It's too much pressure to squeeze back into it. You'll feel better about yourself if you don't have a constant reminder of your weight gain.

- The frump that's too big on you.

- Whatever you never really, really wholeheartedly loved in the first place.

- Whatever looks a bit too worn and is too costly to repair. An $800 dress with patches of missing sequins deserves fixing, but a trendy dress from H&M with aging fabric does not.

- Reminders of old flames. You don't need the karma of an ex in your future. Exorcise your demons and make room for new fashion memories.

Tip: If you are afraid to let go of something, take it out of your closet, fold it, and put it in a box someplace else. Let time go by. If you don't miss it, it's your sign to take the next step . . . to Goodwill.

CHAPTER 3

The Shopping Commandments: One False Move and You're in the Back of a Magazine with a Black Bar Over Your Face

Now that you understand the essential building blocks of the fashionista closet, it's time to shop, darling, shop. For fashionistas, shopping is a full-contact, hard-core sport that leads to joyous feelings of triumph and victory ("Oh, my God! I finally got that red leather jacket, the one I've been saving up for, the one in all the magazines! And there was only one left in my size. And it's only because someone returned it just as I walked in the store. It was meant to be! Such a coup!") as well as the agony of defeat ("I shouldn't have bought this. I can't afford it. I feel sick. I'm out of control. I'm a bad person.").

We are a nation of consumers. No doubt shopping is one of the most pleasant ways to spend an afternoon, bonding with your mom, your friends, your new boyfriend's sister. It can be the ultimate escape, a mind-altering, deliciously dizzying buzz. The excitement typically begins in the mind the second that we fashionistas decide to take a shopping excursion. As we near our desired location, the spring in our step gets bouncier. Our pace gets faster. Our heart rates increase as if we were in an aerobic boxing class. Our breath deepens. If you were to monitor our cardiovascular signs, the graph would be as wild as the stripes of a Missoni dress.

Shopping can also be a vehicle to fill a void (Warning: It doesn't really fill that void, even when you think it does in the moment). Stanford University Medical Center published studies that claim that compulsive shopping disorder (CSD) is an actual illness, likened to alcohol and drug addictions, which can be so destructive that it disrupts daily life. Sufferers actually feel like the only thing that will make them okay is the pièce de résistance of le moment—a new cashmere blanket, leather pants, a white moleskin coat, even Puma sneakers. (They're limited-edition, Ma! I had to have them!)

Telltale Signs of CSD

- You believe that whatever you buy will make things all right.

- You're unable to think about anything other than shopping.

- After the high of the buy, you're overcome with guilt, remorse, regret.

- Every time you buy, you swear you won't do it again for X amount of time, knowing full well you will.

- You forgo important bills (or responsibilities) in order to get something new.

- You lie about what you spend.

- You're powerless over shopping desires.

Shopping is, let's be honest, a frivolously fun way to relive the girlish innocence of playing dress-up (with one trip to the dressing room and a few hangers in our mitts, we can be Madonna circa 1984, the prom queen, Kate Moss). No wonder it's often better than therapy and more therapeutic than sex (retail orgasm!). It can be a quick fix to cure a bad day. And while it may give you an instant high—the smell of new clothes, racks of fine threads, a community of like-minded people who understand your fashion fantasies—it can also be a dastardly way to come face-to-face with your mental demons, especially body image (ugh, don't get us started on the mental wars we've fought over our thighs).

Let's forget the negative shopping side effects and focus on the good ones! As a fashionista, you must appreciate every type of shopping destination, bitchy, prodding salespeople aside. We're talking all: flea markets (where else can you boast, "I got this for two dollars!"?), discount designer outlets like Loehmann's (last year's designer must-haves are always on a rack or two), department stores (and their amazing seasonal sales), mass-market retailers like Kmart, Wal-Mart, and Target (the best place for your basic ribbed tanks), small posh boutiques (personalized service!), army-navy stores (authentic camouflage pants and peacoats are very important), and anyplace where you can exchange monetary denominations for material goods. Call us a sentimental breed, but we hate leaving without taking a little token of our experience with us, be it a sweater, a denim skirt, another white button-down shirt, or some supercute socks.

Fashionistas also have all sorts of shopping philosophies, specific rituals they follow, knowingly or not, and particular getups they like to wear while shopping. Every shopper has his or her own belief system. A religion, if you will. The two of us certainly have ours. They're often different, but we have each learned from the other and expanded our horizons—and closets—throughout the journey of our friendship. Just remember, no matter what your manifesto, nothing is set in stone. Changing your mind—and MO—is as simple as returning a dress to Saks if you have your receipt. In your shopping career as a fashionista, it will be important to figure out what works for you and what doesn't.

Think of this chapter as your guide to shopping well. We coach you through various shopping creeds, bargain hunting and thrifting tactics, the beauty of putting things on hold, and the extravagance of big-ticket items (everyone needs at least one!). We provide tips for surviving and succeeding at sample sales and spotting knockoffs, and show you the difference between being a fashion victim and a fashion maven. In addition, we introduce you to the benefits of consignment shops, eBay, and the occasional faux (a.k.a. fake). We walk you through shopping destinations anyone can reach, whether you live one mile from Madison Avenue in New York City or in the kind of small town where most civilians think Nordstrom is a side effect of SARS. Time to get your credit cards ready! Or at least Celexa, the drug now prescribed for CSD.

CONFESSIONS OF THE SHOPPING OBSESSED
Kirna Zabete, Number Three on My Speed Dial
✳ KAREN ✳

Shopping, for me, is as much about the camaraderie I have with the people who work in the store as it is about the items I covet. I can't hit the shoe department of any of my favorite establishments—Alexander McQueen, Henri Bendel, Jeffrey, and Kirna Zabete—without kissing (or air-kissing) every store employee (or employer) along the way. Mel once called me the shopping mayor. "You know everyone," she yelped in amazement the first time we shopped together. Having this kind of rapport is my equivalent to going to Cheers, a place where everyone knows your name. It's like having built-in friends who can be my voice of reason ("I understand why you want that satin motorcycle jumpsuit, but it's for tall girls") when I get sensory overload and hallucinate, thinking the most ridiculous things are timeless classics (though I cannot say that I haven't, at one time or another, been steered in the wrong direction and purchased an item or two I've never worn, like—ahem—a ruffled belly-revealing coral top that makes me look like a Dallas stripper).

The point, however, is this: Knowing everyone in a store turns shopping into a party. And I'm always up for a good party. In my world, there is no such thing as making a five-minute quick trip to the boutique. I have an uncontrollable urge to chat with everyone who works in a store. Full-on, in-depth conversations is more like it. We know about one another's doctor appointments, hot dates, fights with our significant others, and breakups. I have plopped down on seating cushions, ordered lunch, and talked to the storekeepers for hours while thinking about whether I should get something or not.

Like real friendships, I have nurtured these relationships over time. They come with holiday cards and gifts, social phone calls for no reason at all, dinners, yoga classes, and morning trips to flea markets in search of vintage accessories while talking about everything from hemlines to what's going on in the Middle East. If I come into the store in a bad mood, they know how to cheer me up—and when to leave me alone—just by observing my facial expressions. And unlike money-hungry mongers out for only commission, I can trust them all to tell me when something looks bad—or when I don't need something, which has happened on many occasions. (One salesperson actually ripped a white feather bolero jacket out of my hand and said, "No! I will not allow you to do this, and believe me, taking it away hurts me more than it does you!")

My favorite salespeople have all, at one time, met my family (though they have often been instructed to act as if I never really buy anything when my mom and dad are in the house because my parents lecture me about my foolish spending habits to the point of nausea—though I don't deny I am in need of a good lecture or two on the topic!), my boyfriends, my friends. It is because of these warm and genuine connections that I love shopping so much. I feel comfortable stripping in front of them (they've seen my areolae—and comforted me through bathing-suit traumas). They've all been in dressing rooms with me, helping me squeeze into narrow sheath dresses I could barely get over my hips and struggling to get me out of tops with all sorts of ties that are impossible to figure out.

Because these people have become so aware of my lifestyle, social calendar, and schedule and have such an intimate knowledge of my body—what fits, what flatters, what doesn't—and my issues (can't wear strapless because it does bad things for the armpit fat; no high-waisted anythings because it shortens my already too-short torso), they have keen insight into what I really need. And it leads to a much more personal, successful, strategic, and fun shopping experience.

It's also nice to be treated well. Who doesn't want to shop in a place where people offer you water, show you their baby pictures, gossip about what celebrities are wearing, and make you feel like you matter? I can't forget about the fact that these kinds of relationships afford me VIP treatment galore, such as extra-long "can I put this on hold" periods (sometimes up to three months!), scoring the occasional dress on sale before it actually goes on sale, and after-hours shopping when the store is closed to the public.

Over the years, my sales-pals have become so familiar with my taste that they go on buying trips with me in mind. Kirna and Zabete, the charming Southern-born style impresarios of Kirna Zabete, a brightly colored, sophisticated mecca of the best designers, located in Soho, have returned from Paris on many occasions, chanting things like "We finally found you a winter coat!" and "We bought you a gunmetal hip-hugging belted miniskirt from AF Vandervorst and the most amazing red beaded matador pants from Gaultier. Oh, and tons of inexpensive play clothes you can work into everything you already own. This will be your best season yet!" I've spent so much time in the store that other customers have actually called to ask if I'm working! I tend to get so into the moment that I will start helping other people, too. Joyfully scurrying around to style someone I don't even know or fetching a random girl a sweater in her size is not unusual.

It has always been this way for me. In sixth grade, I remember my mother taking me shopping for school clothes. We spent an entire day chatting it up with the owner of the store and her daughter, who was my age. The woman actually closed her shop early so we could all go to dinner. In college I became best friends with Anthony, a large gay black man with a gleaming bald head, perfect white teeth, and the sweetest voice and disposition. He was the salesman at the Joan & David store, and this was the time in my life when I was obsessed with clopping around in clunky, men's-style shoes, which were called, in Joan & David factory terms, "08." During weekend days, when my roommates would take to the pool and I wanted to avoid skin cancer, I hoofed it to the mall, where I sat on a banquette, schmoozed with Anthony, tried on all of the shoes, and discussed the cute boys who worked at the Gap across the way. When I didn't show up, he would leave me giddy messages

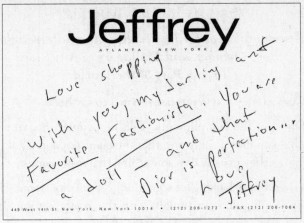

Jeffrey

ATLANTA   NEW YORK

Love shopping and with you, my darling and Favorite Fashionista. You are a doll — and that Dior is perfection... Love, Jeffrey

449 West 14th St. New York, New York 10014 • (212) 206-1272 • FAX (212) 206-7064

This is the love you get when you befriend store owners!

on my machine: "Girl, get down to the store! We have new 08s that you'll love. Besides, I miss you!"

Years later, I was browsing at Jeffrey in New York, a hip and über-chic department store in the Meatpacking District, and all of a sudden I hear "My 08 girl! My, have you grown up!" It was Anthony! He wound up in New York, and thus our love affair over shoes (now, however, it's all about four-inch skinny stilettos and pointy toes) has continued and blossomed. To this day I make friends with salespeople wherever I go. Mel laughed at me when we went to a random shop in upstate New York once. I put something on hold so I could think about it, and when I returned to make the commitment, the woman greeted me with open arms, singing, "I knew you'd be back!"

"Maryanne, you know me so well," I gushed. She gave me her card in case I needed anything in the future. I gave her mine, in case something came in that reminded her of me, as if she actually had any inkling as to what I'd really like or who I am. Mel watched in confused amazement. "I don't get how you do this," she said. I just shrugged my shoulders. I can't explain it. It just happens. For some reason, making friends while shopping and leaving the store with a hug (and bag in tow) makes the experience complete for me. Or maybe it just allows me to respect myself in the morning.

WHERE'S THE PARTY?

Behavioral Tips for Befriending the Salespeople,
Store Owners, and Managers in Any Store
in Any Part of the World

- Consistency. Go in often, even just to say hello.

- Dole out the compliments. Tell the people who work at the store that you love it there and that they look good in what they're wearing, as they usually don something that is also on the racks.

- When you're looking for something, be specific about why you need it. "I am going out tonight with this really hot guy. It's our third date. I'm not sure how he feels about me yet. But I want to knock his socks off, so I need something amazing and super, super sexy. Oh, my God, this guy is the best. He's . . ." Then you should go into his vital stats and perhaps consider opening up your dating history—and asking an innocent question about the personal life of the one who's helping you. Salespeople are often treated with disrespect by obnoxious shoppers who suffer from an extreme sense of entitlement. Showing the staff that you want to hear a bit about who they are is a way to create a bond.

- Treat them as if they're you're best friends. Call a day or so later to give a full report on how the outfit felt—and what the guy had to say about it. Go one step above and beyond and send a thank-you note. Trust us, it will make you stand out, and the next time you're in the store, these people will seek you out and pay a lot of positive attention to you.

- When you refer a friend to the store, have that person ask for your favorite salesperson and say that you recommended he or she. Instruct your friend to flatter, too, by saying something like "Karen swears that no one is better than you!"

- Always be polite. Say "please," "thank you," and "you're welcome" when need be. Don't turn your nose up at anyone. And never pull attitude.

• Show your appreciation and acknowledge others for being helpful and supportive. "You're good" you can say when a salesperson gives you something to try on that you love.

• Don't leave the dressing room a mess. Show some respect.

• Return things as infrequently as possible.

• Try things on and show the salespeople how they look. Even if they're outfits you couldn't imagine walking out of the house in. Be their guinea pig. They need to know how things fit in order to get to know the product they're pushing better. Besides, it may lead to a new style you never knew you always needed.

• Call before you come in and inform your contact of your impending arrival. This way, the store is prepared to receive you and may even have a dressing room full of things for you to try. Bring your point person (or people) something. We recommend candy. They could probably use a sugar fix.

The Stealth Shopper
❈ MELISSA ❈

Shopping is an extremely personal matter to me. It's not just about buying; it's about reimagining who I am, fantasizing about what I want my life to be, and forgetting about all the problems of my day. Whenever I'm in distress, I never run for a therapist or for a prescription. I work it out on the sales rack. It's called "brand-aid."

When I shop, I get into "the zone"—I don't see anything but the clothes and shoes and bags in front of me. The stress of the daily grind wears away. I don't hear the ring of my cell phone. And all I'm left with are extremely interesting, critical questions, like: Can I pull off shiny vinyl pants? Do I need another white fringed handbag? What would go with this fishnet-sleeved shirt?

Because I have a constant running dialog in my head, I have never really enjoyed shopping with other people. I see them as unnecessary distractions who take away from the pure, unadulterated joy of shopping. For one thing, I don't trust other people's opinions.

I am a tenacious bargain hunter, one who has learned to find the diamond in the rough. I pull clothes from the pile that no one would look at twice. And I know that if I put it on, whoever I'm with won't see the possibilities I see.

For example, I have several brightly colored polyester floor-length gowns that I bought at a Cleveland thrift store for a dollar each. They looked odd and garish on the rack, but I knew that once I got them taken in and hemmed to the right length, they would make amazing evening dresses for spring benefits. Don't get me wrong; I still enjoy shopping as a social occasion. Karen and I have made Kirna Zabete a frequent stomping ground and a fun "break" from working on our books. My friend Jennie and I have a standing date to shop every Sunday, and when I visit my parents, there's nothing my sister, mother, and I like to do more than hit the mall. But they are not real shopping trips for me, merely a pleasant way to spend time. I never find my greatest treasures on a group outing.

I am also very skeptical of the ministrations of overly familiar salespeople. I like to survey the store, disappear into the dressing room, and decide what to buy all by myself without someone plying me with empty flattery just for a sales commission. I also feel guilty about hurting someone's feelings if I don't buy something. Most of the time I prefer to slink away if things don't "work out." I hate disappointing people. But sometimes I just can't escape.

For instance, my favorite store in the whole world is Century 21. A world-famous discount emporium, Century 21 has last season's must-haves at bargain-basement prices. I thrill to see $300 Balenciaga coats (from $1,800!), or Vera Wang wedding dresses for $99. When I worked down on Wall Street, Century 21 was across the street from my building. I hated my job, and I spent many happy hours at Century, fantasizing that I was a fashion editor instead of a computer consultant. For almost a decade I was at Century 21 every day for two hours at a time. I guess I should have been resigned to being recognized.

One day, one of the green-jacketed salesgirls asked me for my name. The next time I went, she had put things aside for me that she thought I might like. She told me about the store's personal-shopper service, and while I had mixed feelings about it, I soon reveled in all the attention. She put aside a cream-white Helmut Lang funnel-neck coat that every fashionista was dying to own (and I bought it for $399 from $1,200!), and she also dug up a leather Alexander McQueen dress I had been lusting over at Barneys. But because I had a personal shopper, I felt exposed every time I visited. I could no longer just rummage through the racks, lost in thought. In the back of my mind I knew she was there, waiting for me to make a purchase.

I couldn't handle the pressure (or the expense to my wallet—she kept unearthing such great things that I felt I had no choice but to buy them), and I missed having the triumph of the discovery. She did all the work. All I needed to do was pony up my credit cards. Where was the fun in that? After a few weeks I kept away from Century 21 (I was hiding from my personal shopper!), and I didn't go back for a season or more. A month later I returned, and found out they had discontinued the service.

I was back in the racks, alone with my thoughts and fantasies once again. It was heaven.

THE LONE SHOPPER
How to Keep Your Distance and Maintain Your Personal Space While Shopping

• Enter the store while talking (or faux talking) on your cell phone. No one wants to bother a person who's in the middle of a conversation.

• Don't bring a dog or a baby. Everyone always wants to ooh and aah over that sort of thing.

• Don't dress to impress. Keep a low profile. If "they" suspect you could be a high roller, they're likely to be all over you.

• Don't make eye contact with anyone. Not even for a second.

• If someone asks to help you, give the obligatory "No, thanks, just browsing."

- If you find yourself being hounded by a salesperson who can't take a hint, plead laryngitis to put an end to the conversation. Just be careful that you don't blow your cover if your phone rings, you bump into a friend, or you yell in excitement when you successfully close size-four pants.

- Brashly give them the ol' "talk to the hand" gesture. What's wrong with that? Isn't the customer always right?

WHERE TO WEAR
The Shopping Uniform
✳ KAREN ✳

What you wear to go shopping says a lot about you. There are women who dress to the nines because they want to impress and project the "I'm a good customer" image of "big spender." There are those who dress in a way that's conducive to slipping in and out of what they're wearing. There are those who dress for comfort. And then there's me. I'm very strategic. As far as tops, anything goes. From a zip-up Juicy hoodie or a tank top to a basic sweater or a white button-down shirt, I don't concern myself with shirts. My only rule is that they're comfortable and not constricting. I focus on other necessities.

First and foremost, I'm all about jeans, especially when I try on tops, which I find I often need more than anything else because I can wear jeans twenty-four/seven and change the entire look with whatever goes on above the waist. So I always wear jeans (unless I'm actually shopping for jeans, in which case I tend to wear Juicy sweats or a denim mini because they're both easy to get into and out of). Trying on things when I'm already wearing my favorite jeans gives me a clear indication of how the piece will really work into my wardrobe and life.

Step two in shopping uniform: heels. Heels are a must. Even if I'll be spending the entire day on my feet, I wear four-inchers (okay, maybe three if I want to be practical—or wedgie slides if weather permits). Being equipped with heels gives me the illusion of longer legs, which makes me feel more svelte, which promotes more of a buying attitude. When I feel short, squat, and thighish, I'm not apt to buy. Now, the heels have to be neutral, the kind that go with anything and everything. A basic pointy-toed black-patent pump, perhaps. Or a nude-colored knee-high boot. That way it doesn't matter if I'm trying on pants, skirts, dresses, jumpsuits, or what have you—because I have shoes that do whatever I'm donning justice.

I have learned the importance of wearing good heels the hard way. When I'm in sneakers or cozy Uggs, I have to stand on my tippy-toes to get a feel for how the items would translate from store to real world. And being that that's an uncomfortable way to walk around, I wind up trying on shoes from the store. And therein lies the problem. They, of course, bring out the most spectacular footwear, something that goes magically with what I'm wearing, serving to tempt me to spend more money. As a woman with very little sense of self-control—and an insatiable fetish for new shoes—it's hard for me to just say no. Being armed with my own heels saves me money.

As for another trick I've picked up: I keep a strapless bra in my bag at all times. That way, when I try on a sheer top, a bustier, a cute cami, or some kind of strapless situation, I never have to wonder what it might look like with the proper lingerie. Bra straps can be so obtrusive. That's it. It's very simple. And it leaves my mind free to contemplate more important things—like how I'll pay for what I want.

DRESS TO BUY!
What to Put on (or Tote Around)
for Any Purchasing Jaunt

• Something that makes your life easier. Think about your needs, not what a salesperson might think of what you're wearing. One of the most affluent women we know wears a cheesy one-piece zip-up terry-cloth jumpsuit, so she can dress and undress without a fuss.

• If you're in a time crunch, consider a trench coat, heels, and nothing else. It will save you the hassle of buttons and buckles and zippers when you're in the dressing room.

• A thong. It prevents panty lines. Nothing says dowdy like panty lines.

• A catsuit for shy types when venturing out to places like Loehmann's, where there are community dressing rooms. It saves you embarrassing naked moments. Besides, your stretch marks and cellulite are no one's business.

• A great-fitting T-shirt. It works with everything down south.

• Juicy sweats. They're easy, relaxed, and cute as hell.

• One fabulous accessory—great hoop earrings, a cool scarf, a chic clutch, a hot fedora—to enhance your potential new threads.

• Lipstick. A girl's got to feel good about how she looks when she's shopping. Our favorite: MAC's Diva Matte.

RETAIL THERAPY
Glamour Girl: Where to Splurge
Your Heart Out Around the World
✳ NEW YORK CITY ✳

• Kirna Zabete, a haute haven, filled with Chloe, Gaultier, Balenciaga, Ungaro, Hussein Chalayan, AF Vandervorst, Rick Owens, Andrew Gn, Adam Jones, Valentino handbags, Pierre Hardy heels, and special accessories, like glamorous Indian pieces by one of Nicole Kidman's favorite designers. Also, they have candy and a more affordable section of play clothes downstairs! 96 Greene Street (212) 941-9656.

• Henri Bendel, a happy department store where you'll score Philip Treacy hats, Rick Owens, Catherine Malandrino, Diane von Furstenberg, Plein Sud, Anna Molinari, wacky frocks from Bernard Wilhelm, and the hottest emerging British designers, like Alex Gore Brown and Emma Cooke. Plus, a great beauty department: Bobbi Brown, MAC, Trish McEvoy, DVF Beauty, Mary

Quant. Fragrances: Jean LaPorte and Santa Maria Novella. 712 Fifth Avenue (212) 247-1100.

• Other high-end department stores, such as Barneys, Bergdorf Goodman, and Saks Fifth Avenue.

• All important flagship boutiques, such as Alexander Mc-Queen, Prada, YSL, Gucci, Louis Vuitton, Chloe, Gaultier, Hermès, Balenciaga, Ungaro, Valentino, Dolce & Gabbana, Helmut Lang, Marc Jacobs, Chanel, Burberry, Stella McCartney, Versace, Bottega Veneta, Harry Winston, Cartier, Van Cleef & Arpels, and more.

• Jeffrey, New York, a highbrow shopfest, complete with DJ and a crazy selection of Marni, Alaia, Zac Posen, Gucci, YSL, Jil Sander, Galliano, Dries Van Noten, Anne Demeulemeester, Pucci, Narciso Rodriguez, Henry Duarte jeans, and the sickest shoe selection in town (Brian Atwood, Manolo, Jimmy, Prada, Gucci, YSL, Christian Louboutin, and, oh, we can go on!). Known for great sales staff and huge dressing rooms, to boot. 449 West Fourteenth Street (212) 206-1272.

• Seven, an avant-garde refuge of often hard-to-wear, but the most interesting collections from As Four, Bernard Wilhelm, and Raf Simons, and it's the only store in the city that carries Imitation of Christ's menswear line. 180 Orchard Street (646) 654-0156.

✳ LOS ANGELES ✳

• Tracey Ross, a jewel box of a boutique where all the celebs get their doses of Stella McCartney, Juicy, Chloe, and Marc Jacobs. Also carries unusual knickknacks: $300 to $800 smoking pipes from Vietnam, cotton pajamas from China, and beaded jewelry pieces from Tanzania and Kenya. 8595 Sunset Boulevard (310) 854-1996.

• Maxfield, a center for the eighties resurgence with brand masters Comme des Garçons, Yohji Yamamoto, Dolce & Gabbana, and Gucci. 8825 Melrose Avenue (310) 274-8800.

- Mademoiselle Pearl. Owned by Jennifer Nicholson (yes, daughter of Jack) who reconstructs vintage clothes with a modern twist for celebs who like to play, like Lara Flynn Boyle and Shannon Doherty. She also carries her favorite designers: Stella McCartney, Galliano, and Ernesto Esposito. 1311-B Montana Avenue, Santa Monica (310) 576-7116.

- Fred Segal. There are two stores—one on Melrose and one in Santa Monica. Both have everything you'd ever want, from posh to retro hip: Armani, Colette Dinnigan, Chloe, Helmut Lang, Marc Jacobs, Earl Jean, Katayone Adeli. 8100 Melrose Avenue, West Hollywood (323) 655-3734; 500 Broadway, Santa Monica (310) 458-8100.

- Lily et Cie. A highly curated, hand-picked vintage museum gallery where all the celebrities get their glorious vintage gowns, often worn to award ceremonies and black-tie events. Haute couture collections include Yves Saint Laurent, Balenciaga, Givenchy, American designers Pauline Trigere and futurist Rudi Gernreich along with handbags from Hermès and Chanel, and Miriam Haskell and William De Lillo jewelry lines. 9044 Burton Way, Beverly Hills (310) 724-5757.

- Important flagship stores (Celine, Gucci, Chanel, you name it) are located on and near Rodeo Drive.

✳ MIAMI ✳

- Bal Harbor, a shopping center with the crème de la crème: Dolce & Gabbana, Gucci, Armani, Prada, Bvlgari, Cartier, Chanel, Gianni Versace, Escada, Hermès, Christian Dior, Salvatore Ferragamo, Ungaro, Tiffany & Co., along with Neiman Marcus and Saks Fifth Avenue specialty stores. 9700 Collins Avenue (305) 866-0311.

- Merrick Park, another shopping center. Located in Coral Gables, it has 115 stores: Diane von Furstenberg, Hogan, Jimmy Choo, Gucci, Tiffany & Co., Vespa, Carolina Herrera, Roberto Cavalli, and more. 358 Avenue San Lorenzo (305) 529-0200.

❊ DALLAS ❊

• Stanley Korshak is the mother ship for the rich and famous for European and American collections, including Oscar de la Renta, Carolina Herrera, Donna Karan, Armani, Paul Smith, and many things that glitter. 500 Crescent Court #100 (214) 871-3600.

• The Dallas Galleria is the home of department store biggies Nordstrom, Macy's, Saks Fifth Avenue, and essential designers such as Louis Vuitton, Gucci, Cartier, Tiffany & Co., Gianni Versace, Max Mara, and Hugo Boss. 13355 Noel Road (972) 702-7100.

• Neiman Marcus. The Dallas store is where this superstar megastore began. 400 Northpark Center (214) 891-1280; 1618 Main Street.

• Highland Park Village, the Rodeo Drive of Dallas, where Jerry Jones, owner of the Dallas Cowboys, and Ross Perot live. Calvin Klein, Prada, Hermès, Christian Dior, Bottega Veneta, Chanel, Escada, and Harold's all live here. Mockingbird Lane at Preston Road (214) 559-2740.

❊ CHICAGO ❊

• Oak Street is where superposh shopaholics lurk, as this part of town—on the north side—has it all, from Prada, Jil Sander, and Kate Spade to Luca Luca, Hermès, Giorgio Armani, Versace, and more.

• Chicago Underground, a minimalist space for tapered hipsters seeking Gianni Versace, Roberto Cavalli, Zanella, Jean Paul Gaultier, Gianfranco Ferré, shoes by Lorenzo Banfi and Cesare Paciotti. 72 East Oak Street (312) 787-9557.

• Department stores like Barneys New York, a New York favorite in Chicago for high-end classics like Donna Karan, the entire Vera Wang bridal selection, and a fine selection of Balenciaga.

• George Greene, a men's-only haven of Kiton, Luciano Barbera, Oxxford, Zegna, Yohji Yamamoto, and Christian Dior. 49 East Oak Street (312) 654-2490.

• Ultimo, a breeding ground for upscale hipster stuff from Katayone Adeli, Jil Stuart, Randolph Duke, and Armani to Issey Miyake, Miu Miu, John Galliano, Michael Kors, and Chloe. 114 E. Oak Street (312) 787-1171.

✻ PHILADELPHIA ✻

• King of Prussia Mall is world-renowned. With Louis Vuitton, Gianni Versace, Donna Karan, and Neiman Marcus, it's no wonder. Route 202 at Mall Boulevard (610) 265-5727.

• Aptly named Jeweler's Row, one of the oldest diamond districts in America, this area offers little fingers big, fat stones of diamonds and pearls and colorful gems: Check out Sansom Street between Seventh & Eighth.

• Rittenhouse Row houses a cluster of specialty stores like Nicole Miller, Polo/Ralph Lauren, Francis Jerome, and Sophy Curson.

• Joan Shepp. A wonderful mix that includes Dries Van Noten, Prada shoes, Wolford hosiery, Chloe, and Yohji Yamamoto, to name a few. 1616 Walnut Street (215) 735-2666.

✻ BOSTON ✻

• Louis Boston, considered the city's answer to Barneys or Harvey Nichols in London. Two floors of women's, three floors of men's, and everything you'd ever want from Balenciaga, Prada, the groovy Aussie line Sass & Bide, Zac Posen, Dries Van Noten, and Foley + Corinna. 234 Berkeley Street (617) 262-6100. www.louisboston.com.

• Saks Fifth Avenue, Armani, Donna Karan, Calvin Klein, and Michael Kors are all at Prudential Plaza, Back Bay (617) 262-8500.

• Neiman Marcus. Needs no explanation! 5 Copley Place, Back Bay (617) 536-3660.

• Alan Bilzerian, posh and high-tech refuge with Yohji Ya-mamoto, Ann Demeulemeester, and John Galliano on the racks. 34 Newbury Street (617) 536-1001.

• Hermès. Another one that needs no intro! 22 Arlington Street, at Boylston Street, Back Bay (617) 482-8707.

• Ríccardi has all the bold chic there is: Vivienne Westwood, Thierry Mugler, Comme des Garçons, D & G, and Chrome Hearts. 116 Newbury Street (617) 266-3158.

• Serenella, the only Boston shopping pocket good enough for Narciso Rodriguez, along with Pucci, Balenciaga, Dolce & Gab-bana, Moschino, Ann Demeulemeester, Miu Miu, and Alaia. 134 Newbury Street (617) 266-5568.

✳ LAS VEGAS ✳

• Tallulah G.: Strike it rich on the craps table and blow your wad on sexy Chloe, Marc Jacobs, Daryl K, Foley + Corinna, and other hard-to-find labels. And don't worry about what time it is—they're often open for high-rolling winners till midnight. Fashion Show Mall, 3200 Las Vegas Boulevard South (702) 737-6000, or Boca Park Fashion Village, 750 South Rampart Boulevard (702) 932-7000.

• Fashion Show Mall. This place is conveniently located in the heart of the strip. Neiman Marcus, Saks Fifth Avenue, and Bloomingdale's may be a better bet for your money than the craps table. At Spring Mountain Road, across from Treasure Island (702) 933-7777.

• Caesar's. Ooh-la-la. We're talking Louis Vuitton, Gucci, Cartier, Emporio Armani, Dolce & Gabbana, Christian Dior. 3570 Las Vegas Boulevard (702) 896-5599.

• Bellagio Casino Mall. With Giorgio Armani, Chanel, Gucci, Hermès, Fred Leighton, Moschino, Prada, and Tiffany, you will definitely get lucky. 3600 Las Vegas Boulevard (702) 693-7111.

❋ PARIS ❋

- Colette. Every time fashion editors are in Paris, their first stop (even before the hotel) is Colette, a flashy multilevel, lofty emporium of the best designers (from the bigwigs like Gucci, Chanel, YSL, to the darlings of tomorrow), rockin' accessories, chic books, home accessories, rare CDs, and a restaurant downstairs with a pretentious water bar, where bottled numbers are imported from all over the world. 213 rue Saint-Honoré (33 1) 55-353-390.

- Maria Luisa, a small boutique with a meticulously edited collection of Dior, Gaultier, Tomas Maier, Veronique Branquinho, Anne Demeulemeester, and more. Very high society. 4 rue Cambon (33 1) 42-60-95-48.

- L'eclaireur, a ritzy boutique with hippie-chic designers like Dries Van Noten and Comme des Garçons. 12 rue Malher (33 1) 44-542-211.

- Onward, a groovy outpost, catty-corner from Louis Vuitton, and the apartment of Marc Jacobs, with an eclectic mix of avant-garde finds, including Veronique Branquinho, Martin Margiela, Viktor & Rolf, hard-to-find innovative designers you read about in *Vogue,* and the occasional art exhibition. Our personal favorite. 147 Boulevard Saint-Germain (33 1) 55-427-755.

- Aside from Rue St. Honore and the Champs-Élysées, where you'll find all the classic flagships—Christian Dior, Hermès, Yves Saint Laurent, Rive Gauche, Balenciaga, Chloe, and then some— we recommend wandering the Sixth and Seventh districts, where you'll find Martine Sitbon, Sonia Rykiel, Christian Louboutin, Yohji Yamamoto, a small YSL store, and petite boutiques that are *très jolies.* Also, it's where Marc Jacobs keeps an apartment (see onward).

❋ MILAN ❋

- 10 Corso Como is the first non–department store to introduce the combo of big-name designers with unknowns, as well as art, books, and miscellaneous cool things you probably couldn't find anywhere else. The owner, a style icon called Carla Soazzani, scours the globe to find the right mix of merchandise, which ranges from Prada and Moschino to Yohji Yamamoto and Comme des Garçons. Top, top, top of the line. Check out the boutique chic hotel (three rooms only) above the store, also owned by Soazzani. (39 02) 654-831.

• Clan International, a cute and kitschy boutique that offers cool, hip young new designers like Alessandro Dell 'Acqua and Lawrence Steel, who used to design for Prada. Via Pontaccio, 15–20/21 Milano.

• In the hip artsy area, check out Via Solferino, which is more like Soho in New York, and full of lots of unknown names but great shops nonetheless.

• Salvagente, which means "lifesaver" in Italian, offers Prada, Armani, Alberta Ferretti, and other top names. 16 Via Bronzetti (39 02) 76-110-328.

✳ LONDON ✳

• Bond Street, Sloane Street, and Regent Street have all the big names, like Prada, Alberta Ferretti, Louis Vuitton, Etro, Kenzo, Gucci, Versace, Burberry, and such.

• Covent Garden is where you'll find your hipster chic: Paul Frank, Diesel, Mooks, Tiger, Boxfresh, Paul Smith, Frop, Duffer of St George.

• Selfridges & Co.: Ranks alongside Harrods with all the top-top designers, including hot English designers Emma Cook, Jo Casely-Hayford, Nicole Farhi, and Fake London. 400 Oxford Street (44 0870) 837-7377. www.selfridges.co.uk.

• Harvey Nichols or "Harvey Nicks," as it's known. Along with high-end brands, Stella McCartney, Marc Jacobs, Balenciaga, Alexander McQueen, John Galliano, Dries Van Noten, Dolce & Gabbana, Dior, Yves Saint Laurent Rive Gauche, Comme des

Garçons, Nina Campbell, Mulberry, Ralph Lauren, Designer's Guild, Barbara Bui, Burberry, Diane von Furstenberg, DKNY, Eley Kishimoto . . . there's also an Aveda Spa. 109–125 Knightsbridge (44 207) 235-5000.

• Harrods: Sonia Rykiel, Chloe, Cartier, Celine, Jean Paul Gaultier, Hermès, Kenzo, Christian Lacroix, Christian Dior. 87–135 Knightsbridge (44 207) 730-1234.

• Liberty, a groovy stop for Balenciaga, Carpucci, Dries Van Noten, Eley Kishimoto, Yohji Yamamoto, and others. 214 Regent Street (44 207) 734-1234.

• Browns, also known as heaven! Sonia Rykiel, John Galliano, Dior Home, Emanuel Ungaro, Azzedine Alaia, and so much more, it's madness. 23–27 South Molton Street (44 207) 491-7833; 6 Sloane Street (44 207) 514-0040.

DISCOUNT DARLING
Where to Find the Über-chic on the Über-cheap
❋ OUTLET MALLS ACROSS ❋
THE COUNTRY

• Woodbury Commons in Central Valley, New York: Barneys! Saks! Chanel! YSL! Prada! Celine! Puma! Gucci! Dolce! Bottega Veneta! Dior! Frette sheets, even!

• Manchester, Vermont: Burberry! Coach! Ralph Lauren! Armani! Calvin Klein! Tse Cashmere! Versace! (J.Crew, Levi's, and Gap, too!)

• Desert Hills Premium Outlets in Palm Springs, California: YSL! Gucci! Sergio Rossi! Giorgio Armani! Tod's! Judith Leiber! Samsonite! Bottega Veneta! Max Mara! Calvin, Donna, Ralph! John Varvatos and Zegna (men's designers we love)! Versace! And Levi's, Vans, Izod, Earl Jean, and Lucky Brand blue jeans!

• Secaucus, New Jersey: Calvin! Donna! Gucci! And more, more, more!

- SawGrass Mill in Fort Lauderdale, Florida: Off 5th Saks Fifth Avenue Outlet, Last Call! The Clearance Center from Neiman Marcus, Disney's Character Premiere, Kenneth Cole, Tommy Hilfiger Company Store, Mikasa Factory Store, Banana Republic Factory Store, Calvin Klein Outlet Store, Gap Outlet, Polo Ralph Lauren Factory Store, and more.

- Franklin Mills in Philadelphia is one of the world's largest outlet stores with outposts for all the essential designer stores, including Neiman Marcus, Saks Fifth Avenue, Polo/Ralph Lauren, Escada, Donna Karan, and Kenneth Cole. 1455 Franklin Mills Circle (800) 336-MALL.

✳ OTHER CHEAP AND CHIC ✳ ALTERNATIVES

- Consignment shops, which sell amazing designer clothing that other fashionistas have previously owned. In New York City, Naomi Campbell and Gisele Bundchen have been known to unload bags upon bags of samples and free clothes they've gotten from designers as gifts at I.N.A.

- www.ebay.com and other Web sites, like www.yoox.com, which is known for selling discount end-of-season designer clothing and iconic vintage pieces.

- Sample sales (they are often listed in local or regional magazines like *TimeOut,* and Web sites like www.dailycandy.com). If you're ever in New York City, loiter in the lobbies of the Hachette Filipacchi, Condé Nast, and Hearst buildings, where you may come across flyers for sample sales geared for insiders.

- End-of-season sales. Just as stores start getting in the next season's clothes (about three to four months before the season begins), current season's merch goes on sale. If you become very friendly with the salespeople, they just may put something aside for you and bring it back out when it's 60 percent off.

• Discount stores like Loehmann's, Marshalls, TJMaxx, Filene's Basement (fabulous fur salon!), and Century 21, which is in New York City, have designer wares, but success is hit or miss.

QUIZ
What Is Your Shopping M.O.?
Answer These Three Questions and Find Out

1. You need a dress for a fabulous soirée and you want to look hot. You:

a) Blow off whatever you have to do during the day so you can devote yourself to hitting every major store you love in search of the perfect look. You find it immediately. In fact, you find two . . . three . . . four! Such decisions! You rationalize: They're all different and you could really use each of them. While you're at it, you pick up another pair of black strappy shoes (of course you need a new pair for the dress—God forbid you wear any of the three other pairs you have just like it!), a couple of sexy tops, a handbag, and earrings, all the while putting a few other things on hold. In your frenzy, you forget about lunch—and the conference call you scheduled a week in advance. By the time you get home, you call one of the stores, frantic! You really need a jacket or some kind of wrap to go with these new things. They must have something they can messenger over!

b) Happily get something new—if it's at least 40 percent off of retail . . . or more.

c) You get one thing you're into. But you're not quite satisfied. So you run out and find more. And more. And more. You bring everything home, try them on again, and pick your favorite, which you keep. Ridden with guilt of overbuying, you return everything else in the morning.

d) Make do with what you already have and, if you must, you get something new. A classic piece that lasts a lifetime. You want an investment, not a fad you'll get sick of or won't want to be caught dead in next season.

e) Raid your mom's closet for something she wore on her honeymoon or find a way to make an old frock feel new.

2. You have extra money to burn. You:

a) Spend every last dime (even if it's only for one thing)—and then dip into your funds for bills, rent, or whatever else you're obligated to. If you have to bounce a check while you're at it . . . well . . . who cares. You'll deal with it later.

b) Get giddy with excitement and get as much as you possibly can within your budget, which is a lot, considering you got it all at a good price. Heh, heh, heh!

c) Binge! You can't get enough. But you crash after the high and bring everything back as soon as possible.

d) Put it aside for a rainy day. You're sure you'll need something chic at some point, and when you really do, you'll be prepared.

e) Hit the thrift store with a vengeance. There's a Pucci velvet jacket you've been dying for.

3. Your mom/husband/very practical best friend asks you about your day after you go shopping. You:

a) Hide the bags, throw away the receipts, rip the tags off everything you bought, and discard all evidence. It's called "lie and deny."

b) Brag about the deal you just got. They were practically giving the stuff away!

c) Try to sell them some of the things you bought and don't need, but are interrupted when your therapist finally calls you back.

d) Show them the timeless, trans-seasonal item(s) and explain all the many uses you'll get out of them.

e) Bust out the new threads and a book with an old picture of Jackie O, who had the exact same thing!

The Profiles

If you answered a) to the above, we have one thing to say: Danger, Will Robinson! Houston, you have a problem! In your world, more is more! You'd better make a lot of money—or marry well, my friend. Otherwise, it's time to consider the Priory, the Betty Ford Clinic of London. It may cost about $4,000 a week, but it will save you from financial ruin (and buying many unnecessary things, like, ahem, a white Alexander McQueen rabbit-fur jacket) in the long run.

If you answered b), you're a discount diva—a bargainista—who revels in the thrill of a good deal and navigates sale season with precise, scientific skill. If there's a pair of YSL shoes for $99 within a twenty-mile radius of you, you'll find it. Your closet may be worth thousands—hundreds of thousands, even—but nothing cost you more than $100!

If you answered c) to all of the above, you're what's known as the "bulimic buyer." You fill voids by buying, buying, buying, and buying way more than you really want and need. Overcome with painful feelings of guilt and regret afterward, you have to purge, purge, and purge by taking almost everything back to the store. Warning: Avoid all shops that have a "store credit only" return policy. And consider herbal remedies like kava kava. It's very good for curbing obsessive compulsive behavior.

If you answered d) to all of the above, you're Miss Practicality. You appreciate sales, yet you don't have a problem plunking down a grand or two if the item(s) in question are true assets. You avoid big trends and anything that's "of the moment." You hate to be "dated" and recognized for wearing something that can easily be identified to a specific season. No one will ever say, "Love that Calvin, fall/winter '02" to you! You're a smart, elegant shopper, the type who really thinks about what you buy and doesn't do anything rashly. You buy only what you'll get a lot of wear and use out of. (Mel and Karen hate you for being so controlled and balanced. You're what they call "n.f."—no fun!)

If you answered e) to all of the above, you're the thrifty lady. You abhor anything designer-y, flashy, and new. You spend hours sifting through racks at vintage stores, flea markets, army-navy shops, and Mom's and Grandma's hand-me-downs. You can tell what year something was made and which designer did it just by glancing. With a collection of old belts, handbags, shoes, and lingerie from the twenties to the seventies, you have a natural boho style and an uncanny way of turning dusty old frocks into modern masterpieces. You think that most contemporary high design is all hype, glorified by the media—and no one crafts clothing, creates textiles, and manages details the way they used to. All of today's collections are just knockoffs from yesteryear anyway. And you mock the high price tags of modern-day fashion.

*If you had a mix of answers, God bless. You're a true fashion darling. There's a little bit of each of these personalities in your soul.

SCENES FROM A MALL (OR, OUR CRAZIEST SHOPPING ESCAPADES . . . OY!)
A Day at the Outlets
✳ KAREN AND MELISSA ✳
(GUEST-STARRING SALLY, OUR FASHIONISTA FRIEND)

A day of outlet shopping at Woodbury Commons in Central Valley, New York, is serious business. We woke up at the crack of dawn so we would arrive before the crowds poured in. At seven-thirty A.M., we piled into the bright, shiny, chic red Volvo convertible (borrowed for the day—when you're shopping, you have to look good, even driving in l'auto . . .).

"Welcome to my world," Mel said, leading us to the entrance. A seasoned pro, she studied the map and marked off a path for us to follow in a manner so meticulous, you'd think we were Frodo, trying to bring the "precious" back to its rightful place.

At Dolce & Gabbana, we pounced on diaphanous dresses, white corduroy suits, eel-skin heels, all things we coveted seasons ago and could not afford. The prices? Amazing. $200 for patchwork leather pants that were originally at least two grand, and a rack of goods for $100. Sadly, everything was too tight, too revealing, too sexy, even for Karen, whose style tends toward the tight, revealing side. Sally, whom we brought solely as a voice of reason, to keep us in check when we begin sale-goggling and start buying too many things we don't need, made the first purchase—a pair of pointy-toed pony-hair pumps.

Next stop: Chanel. Several totes were examined. Everything is in the $500 range instead of the $1,500 range. It's heaven. Karen put a $400 black-patent clutch on hold, afraid to make her first buy so soon into the game, without seeing what else was out there. Mel contemplated a clutch, emblazoned with Lichenstein-esque graphics, and decided to pass. "Not for my first Chanel," she said. "A girl's first Chanel has to be classic."

We left empty-handed. A miracle. We were starving. Time for food court action. But—oh!—there's Prada. Like magnets we were drawn into the store. We had our priorities. Inside, it was like the pages of *In Style* had come to life. There was the dress Cate Blanchett wore to a premiere. And—look!—Nicole Kidman looked unbelievable in that! We flipped for the ruched $5,000 goddess dresses from Mt. Olympus (a.k.a. Hollywood), but sadly, we mere mortals could not pull them off (a relief—they were still $1,500 a pop). We contemplated a $75 transparent plastic raincoat and wondered if it was too *victim*. It was.

Before making our exit, Sally scored another purchase: a jewel-tone orange blouse that looks gorge against her creamy skin. Karen convinced the salesperson, her new best friend, to put a lavender chiffon poofy-sleeved blouse on hold—even though the store had a no-hold policy. Sally walked out with two bags. "I can't believe I'm the one shopping! I was supposed to tell you guys to stop shopping!" she yelled. Outlets can do that to a person!

After a quick lunch (cheese steaks sans bun, and wilted greens), we hit the mother ship. The Gucci outlet was pandemonium. It was as crowded as the Gap with Japanese tourists elbowing one another for $50 logo wallets. We ripped through the racks. Karen decided on a satin skirt, a top she had loved last season (which was still classic enough to wear now—a real find!), but was torn over a lavender dress—it was one of those "it would look bet-ter if I lost five pounds" kind of things. Mel picked up her first pur-chase—a $140 tank top (bargain?), down from $500—and we took off, leaving $1,400 of Karen's merchandise on hold so she could think about the purple dress.

At Dior, Sally and Mel got matching skirts—crazy, embellished, Mexican fiesta–inspired works of art, bedecked with elaborate beadwork. Mel also bucked up for a leather dominatrix skirt—a size too small (leather expands!), and Karen finally took the plunge—smokin' tapestry-print midcalf boots, the same pair that Sally bought (she was getting out of control, our so-called voice of reason).

At the Barneys outlet, Mel was drawn to enormous corduroy-and-suede Balenciaga bags for $260 (from $1,260)! Should she or shouldn't she? The pressure! Sally thought it looked like a diaper bag. Karen screamed, "I think it's fantastic! It makes a statement: 'Here I am with my humongous Balenciaga bag!' " It was a state-ment Mel was prepared to make. She put down the AmEx. But the guilt started to kick in. Although it didn't stop her from making a pit stop to pick up $149 Bottega Veneta snakeskin shoes (they were originally $600!), and Sally got one last thing at Fendi—a wal-let—while Karen picked up her load at Gucci, making her total $1,800—$800 more than her "allowed" amount.

Lugging our bags, we perused Tod's—and the doorman actu-ally said, "That's enough! You girls should go home." (Signs you know you've gone and done it!) After a quick lap and a final perusal of Chanel (which Karen finally decided against), it was time to go home.

We couldn't fit all the bags in the trunk, and Mel, who sat in back, was almost suffocated by our purchases. There was no talking on the way home. Silence. We were so depressed. It was a day of reckless, fun shopping, and we spent money we did not have. Ugh, fashion. Such a disease. Would Mel fess up to her husband about what she'd done? In the car, she talked about getting home quickly so she could hide the bags. She freaked out even more when she checked her messages—and there was one from the bank, making

You know you've overshopped when you can't even close the trunk!

sure someone didn't swipe her credit card (you know you're in trouble when . . .).

Did we really need this stuff, we wondered. Why couldn't we just be happy with Banana Republic and J.Crew? Actually, we are, but we get that extra thrill from high design, making runway clothes a reality. Anxiety and all. By the time we got home—and unwrapped our loot—the guilt subsided. The stuff wasn't returnable anyway. So we might as well enjoy it. And we made a plan to return the following week!

OUTLET PREPARATION
Things to Keep in Mind for a Day in Manic Paradise

• Get a map, so you're aware of all the goods and the key areas you'd like to visit. Otherwise you'll spend half the day walking aimlessly, wasting your precious energy.

• Be patient. Sometimes you'll hit an outlet and find your dreams. Sometimes you'll find *nada*.

• Don't bring credit cards, only enough cash to pay for what you can really afford.

- Keep a Balance bar in your bag. If you forget to eat—or can't find sustenance in the food court—you'll need something to keep your blood sugar from crashing.

- Do a sweep of the entire mall first. Get an idea of what's available. Put things on hold if possible. And then take time to think about your decision in order to make a smart one.

- If you're the type who has trouble saying "when," take your most antishopping friend (or boyfriend), who will put a time limit on your day.

- Examine things carefully. Sometimes outlet pieces have been tried on so many times that the fabric is pulled, ripped, or discolored. Also, there are sometimes stained designer rejects.

- Bring a car with a large trunk!

YOU WON'T BELIEVE WHERE WE GOT THIS!
The Wonderful World of Target and Paying Less
✳ MELISSA AND KAREN ✳

There are a few things we appreciate more than anything else in life: family, genuine friendships, and the thrill of a cheap purchase that everyone admires and asks us about. And there's nothing we like more than stretching our dollar at one of the most fabulous places in town. We're talking, of course, about Target. (Or Tar-zjay, in the French pronunciation.)

Target is so much cooler than Kmart or Wal-Mart. For one, the store actually hires real designers, like Todd Oldham and Stephen Sprouse (who, unfortunately, is no longer with us, making his graffiti bikinis we own collector's items), to create their wares. We are in love with all the Michael Graves kitchen gadgets, and can't think of a better place to buy a plastic doggie bowl ($10 from design guru Karim Rashid!). We start by pawing through the latest stuff from Isaac Mizrahi. The ebullient designer has a collection of American classics at the store: $29 clogs, $50 cotton trench coats, and $20 cashmere-cotton sweaters. It's fantastic, but we're more excited by the Juicy knockoffs.

"I love these sweatpants!" Karen exclaims, pouncing on several pairs. At $18 each, she could buy ten for the price of one designer sweatsuit. A Mossimo rack holds a white oxford shirt sewn into a V-neck sweater. We had lusted over a similar one from AF Vandervorst at Kirna Zabete for $495. At $19, what could we lose? We take three. Target is a great place to find basics, and we stock up on tank tops with the bra already sewn inside, as well as a bunch of vintage-ish T-shirts with funny seventies ski logos. (They're only $8 each. We buy ten!) Our shopping cart loaded

Parting is such sweet sorrow.

with all our treasures, we head back to the city, where Mel takes Karen to the local Payless. Yes, Payless.

"This is, like, my favorite store from high school," Mel explains, pulling out purple booties with the "fold," which are so retro eighties and just the thing for right now. We find Mary Janes that look just like Prada for $7, and gem-encrusted strappy sandals that could have walked off the Manolo boutique (almost). Sheepskin-lined boots are $13 and kick-ass combat boots are a mere $17. While we still love our high-priced heels, there's certainly nothing wrong with making room for a little pleather in our lives.

BARGAIN HUNTING 101!

The best advice we've ever received was from our moms: Don't wear expensive designers from head to toe. In fact, when you mix the high with the low, no one will be able to tell what's what. Here's everything you ever wanted to know about affordable destinations and (shhh!) knockoffs.

• Basic white T-shirts and wife-beaters? Try Hanes, the boys' underwear section of department stores, and prepackaged sets of three that are sold at Wal-Mart and Kmart. Just note: Avoid the Kathy Ireland section of Kmart at all costs.

• Target. We've seen some darn good Manolo Blahnik knock-offs here (remember the Timberland stiletto boots J.Lo wore in one of her videos?), not to mention great T-shirts, workout clothes, teeny tanks, cotton thongs, socks, and inexpensive collections from noteworthy designers like Liz Lange (maternity) and Isaac Mizrahi.

• Club Monaco. The perfect place to pick up Marc Jacobs and Prada imitations that your friends will swear are the real thing if you mix them with one designer piece.

• Old Navy. Choose wisely and you'll find a $10 facsimile of whatever is the "it" bag, top, and silhouette of the season. Just tell everyone it's Miu Miu. We swear, they won't doubt you.

• H&M. In fashion circles, it's become known as the hip European retailer of "disposable" chic. Big in Sweden, H&M is the ultimate purveyor of cheap, trendy looks that will update your wardrobe instantly without bankrupting your wallet. But a caveat: It's not made very well.

• Victoria's Secret. Consider it the home of the sexy, feminine lace-trimmed camisole, the perfect thing to pair with leather pants, straight jeans, and velvet evening trousers.

• Any army-navy store. Go for old-school peacoats, army fatigue jackets, and little sweatshirts that say "Army" or "Navy" and wear them with something more refined and pricey. Very Kate Moss.

• Vintage fur retailers. Fur, when vintage, is not as "rich bitch" or guilt-inducing as new pelts. Consider raiding your mom's or grandma's closet and bringing an old coat to a furrier for a modern makeover.

• Flea markets. Whether you're in Paris, Notting Hill, or a local street fair, you can always find chandelier earrings, luxurious fabrics for sarongs or scarves, a leather jacket, or something to enhance your wardrobe without dipping into your savings account.

- Top Shop, the Target of London, where top designers like Matthew Williamson and Clements Ribeiro have cheapie, but supercute collections. 214 Oxford Street (44 207) 636-7700.

COPY CATS: SOME THINGS ARE MEANT TO BE KNOCKED OFF
Mom Won't Lend Me Her Birkin
✳ KAREN ✳

If there's one mark of a fashionista, it's her handbag, a veritable symbol of who she is and the image she wants to project. The mother of all handbags: the Hermès Birkin, a $4,000 (and up) emblem of sophisticated, classic luxury. The Bentley of accessories. Named after sixties British starlet Jane Birkin, the leather satchel has a four-year waiting list, and comes in a rainbow of colors, hides, and skins (can you say $30,000 for croc?) and either gold or silver hardware (diamonds for $80,000). Whether you're wearing Gap or Gucci, a Birkin is the kind of statement piece that complements, enhances, and completes your style. Unlike all other bags, it will truly last a lifetime. My mother has been nagging my dad for one forever. So much so that even my younger brother, Jason, has said, "Dad, just get it for her already," and actually searched for one on eBay. My dad has always been reticent, unable to understand how his wife could spend that kind of money on something that he deems so frivolous.

One fateful afternoon, Jason and I were meeting my parents for lunch at Taboo on Worth Avenue in Palm Beach, Florida—a few steps away from the Hermès store, where my mother often drools on the wait list. My parents were late. And J. and I were starving and annoyed—they knew how hungry we were . . . how could they keep us waiting for so long! "I bet Mom walks in with an Hermès," Jason said.

"No way. Dad is so not going there," I snapped.

"He's caving. Trust me," Jason said assuredly.

Minutes later, my mom walked in with a black leather Birkin on her arm and a beaming smile longer than the train of a Vera

Wang wedding gown. She held it up as if it were a new baby. "Isn't she gorgeous?" my mom purred. My dad shrugged his shoulders and sighed. "I'm a sucker." Apparently the bag had come in just as my parents entered the store, and when the salesgirl called the people on the wait list, they weren't home . . . and she broke all the rules and sold it to my mom on the spot. I don't want to know what my mom promised my dad in return for the gift. But I do know that Birkin is now a family member. My mom loves it so much, I'm surprised she hasn't marked off its height on the wall the way you do with children as they get older. We joke that Birkin is lonely and in need of siblings—a sister named Kelly (Kelly being the Hermès bag named after Grace Kelly) and a girlfriend named Constance (yet another Hermès style).

Birkin almost never leaves my mother's side. It's like she's nursing. I have asked repeatedly if I can borrow the bag. To that she says no. "I don't understand," I have begged time and time again. "It's just a bag. I won't do anything to hurt it." And she responds, "You don't need to walk around with a notable $4,000 bag at this age. It's inappropriate, even pretentious." I have explained that many, many girls my age (and younger) have Birkin sidekicks, but that argument has gotten me nowhere. And she said, "You can have one when you can afford one. I want you to have something to look forward to." I took the approach of "carrying it for even a day will certainly give me something to look forward to." But she just won't part with it. No matter what.

Her attachment to the bag, while I understand it in a way, is a bit much. If, God forbid, something happened to it, I swear she'd have a funeral and sit shivah (Jewish for mourning) like a full-on Orthodox (covering mirrors, wearing black, the whole megillah). Soon after Birkin was adopted, my parents traveled to Florence, Italy, where they met a fellow Birkin owner from New Jersey who informed my mom about a man I'll call Paolo (for legal reasons, I cannot divulge his real name), who runs a normal, innocent-looking newsstand near the Pontevecchio, often called the "Jewelry Bridge," and peddles all kinds of faux designer bags that look *exactly* like the real thing (for $100 to $300) on the side.

It's a process to make the connection and secure the loot. Upon arriving, my mom was instructed to say "Adrienne sent me." The man at the newsstand told her to return later. Paolo wasn't there. She did. Three times. Finally Paolo emerged and told her to return at four P.M. sharp. They were to meet at a corner, at which time he would lead them to his storage warehouse. "Trail me at thirty paces and don't look like you're following me," demanded Paolo, burly, swarthy, and unshaven, as if he were explaining a CIA op. At four o'clock, my parents arrived with two other New York couples, who had heard of Paolo. They stealthily walked around the corner, as Paolo cautiously looked over his shoulder, ensuring that no one pulled any funny stuff or called the cops.

Paolo opened a door to some kind of trucking garage space, made sure the coast was clear, and waved everyone in. He closed the door. The room was pitch-black. Mom prayed she wouldn't be mugged, and suddenly the lights went on. Floor-to-ceiling shelves revealed thousands of faux bags—Diors, Guccis, Fendis—on every wall. The women gasped over the sight, as if it were the crown jewels.

They sat on plastic bags filled with more fake bags and inspected the merchandise. My mother refused to believe that a respectable faux (isn't that an oxymoron?) existed. She brought the real Birkin to compare the feel of the leather, the weight of the lock and key that hangs off the top, the interior. It was perfect, even stamped and engraved with the Hermès insignia in all the right places (above the strap and clasp, on the hardware of the clasp, at the bottom of the lock, and on the inside of the strap). These fakes even had a stamp with the year it was made and a code, real or fake, to signify which craftsman made it. My dad was sure Paolo had a friend on the inside. It was a little too perfect.

She bought the bag on the spot! Upon her return, she delightfully showed it to her most meticulous friend—a woman who has no less than six Hermès bags. She could not tell it was fake. Not even for a second. She even brought it into the Hermès shop, just to see if they'd notice (they didn't!). I examined it, too, and was unable to decipher the difference between the real and the fake. I figured my mom would surely lend me the fake one. But no! She didn't want her daughter projecting the image of "I have a $4,000 handbag," even if it was only $300. She compared it to kids who get BMWs for their first cars and thus have no respect for the dollar, or wind up living a life where they have a grotesque sense of material entitlement. Um, I'm a thirty-one-year-old woman! But she promised she'd leave me her Birkin (and two Kellys) in her will (they are heirlooms, after all). I hope I don't inherit them for a long, long, long time. In the meantime, if you know anyone going to Florence, do let me know!

By Any Other Name
✳ MELISSA ✳

My family immigrated to San Francisco in 1985, the year I turned thirteen. My parents became proprietors of the employees' cafeteria in the back room of the Sears department store. We went from having servants to working in the service industry. Worse yet, my mother, who was never without her three-inch mules in Manila, now ran around in sneakers. I had never seen her in sneakers before. It disturbed me immensely.

For my thirteenth birthday, my mom had always planned on taking me on a mother-daughter shopping trip to Hong Kong, like the kind she and my grandmother and her three sisters used to take every month. Of course, Hong Kong was out of the question now. We could afford only Kmart. The first designer label I owned was from the Jaclyn Smith Collection. I still remember the outfit: pink velour sweater, pink flannel calf-length skirt.

A few years later, when I was off to college in New York City, I asked my mother to sew labels from my dad's old Ralph Lauren button-downs on my Mervyn's-bought clothes to "make them designer." In college, a friend rummaged through my closet and remarked on my homemade Lauren. "That's funny. It kind of looks like someone sewed the label on this to pretend it was Ralph Lauren," she said.

I turned beet red. I became an expert at thrift-store shopping after that.

HOW TO SMELL A BAD KNOCKOFF A MILE AWAY

- Misspellings. There's no such thing as a Kate Spude bag, but come on, we didn't need to tell you that.

- Discolorations of any kind. Be aware of the exact hues of the authentic version, whether you study it in person or in a magazine, so you can compare and contrast.

- Examine the zippers. A real bag will have a sturdy zipper of a certain kind, so before making an investment in what might be a fake, check out the real thing and take note of the color of the zipper, the thickness, the weight, and any engravings on the metal. If the Louis Vuitton zipper is gold, don't buy a bag that has one in silver.

- Glue remnants. Fakes often have labels that are glued, not sewn, on.

- Crooked stitching.

- You found it in Chinatown.

- The feel of the fabric. Fakes are notoriously stiff and rigid.

- Look at the lining. The color and textile of the inside of a handbag—if it's bad—is a dead giveaway.

- Open the bag and search for a stamp or label inside. Make sure it doesn't peel off and that it's centered.

SPLURGE! OUR BIGGEST-TICKET ITEMS, GOD BLESS THEM!
The Girl's Gotta Have It!
✳ KAREN ✳

Here is the thing about splurging. It's like having the most decadent, delicious, sumptuous, silken cupcake that tickles your taste buds into sugar-induced ecstasy. If you've never had one, you're fine. You don't need one. You don't know what you're missing. The second you do, you're hooked, transformed, full of urging—and you wind up craving more and more and more, thinking, *It was so good the first time, it doesn't matter if I do it again . . . and again . . . and again.* Over time you're getting two, three, four, five at a time . . . and possibly gaining fifteen pounds. Shopping big is no different. Once you buck up to higher and higher price levels for fashion, it has a tendency to become a habit as de rigueur as getting the morning paper.

My splurging infatuation began innocently, as all bad habits do. 'Twas the summer of 1998. My aforementioned friend Sally was getting married. And as a part of the wedding party, I was allowed to wear whatever I wanted, as long as it was a soft candy shade of pastel pink. The ceremony was an urban-hip affair at an all-white loft in Chelsea. I searched high and low for something that was sexy and cool and that I could wear again. Trips to Barneys, the boho hippie store Calypso, a little fashionista boutique called Jane Mayle on Elizabeth Street, and Bergdorf Goodman got me nowhere. I came close at Cynthia Rowley with a strapless, tight, short satin dress, but not close enough (it didn't do great things to my armpit area). I found an amazing hot-pink skirt and camisole, but Sally put the kibosh on it. Too bright, she said. Saks and Bloomingdale's had nothing. And this was before my days of thinking it was acceptable to pop into Gucci, Dior, YSL, or some kind of major designer store where things start at $1,000 (however, it was this very search that wound up leading me to such future behavior).

I was frustrated. And my $500 budget kept getting higher and higher. I went to Los Angeles to visit a guy I was dating at the time and I figured I'd surely find something there. That city is all about color. But the groovy stores like Curve and all the shops on Robertson were barren in the pink department. Finally I went to Fred Segal Santa Monica. I fell for a slip dress by Patty Shelabarger, but it was too small. Out of curiosity I stepped into the "couture" department. And there it was. The first thing I saw—a lovely baby pink V-neck, superfitted Blumarine short-sleeved sweater with a rabbit-fur (detachable) collar and pink pearlized flower-shaped buttons down the front. Stunning. I tried it on with a pink Pucci shantung silk skirt of the exact same shade. And the guy I was with popped out of his seat and yelped, "This is the one. I'm in love with you."

It was $1,800 in total. And I couldn't get one piece without the other. Finding matching pinks like this almost never happens. I couldn't imagine dropping such a load on one outfit. But I could wear the skirt with anything, and that sweater was a classic—with white pants, jeans, little miniskirts. I put it on hold for a day so I could think about it. I agonized over doing it or not. The next day I called back and asked to keep it on hold for another day. This went on for four days until—after a fight with the guy that caused me to leave his house and stay with a friend—I said, "Screw it! I'll doll myself up in something extraordinary and find a new boyfriend." And that was that. Don't think I wasn't breaking out in a cold sweat, clutching my friend Jennifer's hand as I gave the saleswoman my ATM card, which sucked the money right out of the bank! In fact, I felt sick about what I had done until the day of the wedding. When I put it on—along with baby-pink roses in my hair and silver high heels—it made me feel glamorous and adult. I got over the $1,100 sweater and $700 skirt after the bride and groom had their first dance and some cute guy I had my eye on told me I was a knockout. After that, $400, $500, $600, even $800 sweaters didn't seem so outrageously priced. Not compared to the Blumarine.

The same thing happened soon after with boots. I was dying for a knee-high pair, but had no luck due to my very muscular calves (a result of gymnastics and genes). In the beginning of the trying-on-boots marathon, I thought maybe I'd splurge by dropping $400 or so. After nothing zipped—or allowed my blood to circulate to my feet—I decided to go into the Manolo Blahnik store. It was my first time behind the doors (before that, I had always salivated in front of the window, dreaming of the day I could afford them). Among the pressed, nipped, tucked, manicured, blown-out, made-up shoppers in the "shoe salon," I felt like a bit of a misfit (maybe it was the Rollerblades and Adidas sweats).

Then Ben, an angelic Asian man with satin butt-length black hair and a perfect size-two body, came to my rescue. "Cutie, how can I help you?" he said sweetly. I explained my plight. Before I could finish, he had the solution—stretch suede chocolate four-inch-heel pointy-toed boots. They were divine. I slipped them on, and just like that I was in heaven. I handed over my credit card without asking about the price (I heard that money is not to be discussed at Manolo!) and almost puked when

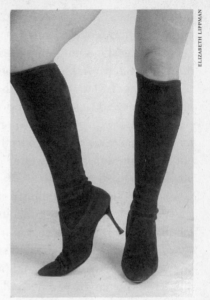

The $1,200 Manolos in all their glory

I got the receipt back—$1,200. I thought, *I'd better wear these to death*. And I did—and still do. They remain my favorite boots. They're incredibly comfortable. They hug the curve of the legs just so. They look smashing with pants, denim, and skirts of all hemlines. And just like that, spending $400, $500, $600, $700, $800, $900, $1,000 on footwear stopped feeling painful.

It became—scarily—normal. Just don't ask me how I allowed myself to get $2,000 pants! I still haven't quite recovered from that one.

It Happens to the Best of Us
✳ MELISSA ✳

I don't have a "biggest splurge" story. Most of my clothes are in the $50 range, marked down from $500. I've never paid more than $500 for a handbag (usually they are down from $1,200 to $2,000). When I was working as a computer consultant, I spent my Christmas bonus on "real" things, like throwing my parents their twenty-fifth anniversary party at the Yale Club, or buying a new computer, or paying off my college loans.

My biggest clothing splurges at the time consisted of a fitted military greatcoat in black cashmere with brass buttons that was reminiscent of Madonna's, which I found in a cute West Village boutique for $300. (I paid full price, which is a "splurge" for me.) At the time, I wasn't the label whore I am now, and I don't even re-member who made the coat, only that it was an extremely flattering cut and kept me warm all winter. (Oh, for the days when I could be satisfied by such things!)

So, no, I don't have a splurge story.

What I do have is a story about the time I fainted at the Marc Jacobs outlet. It was the year of my wedding. Also known as the year I left my corporate job and started to freelance. Otherwise known as the year I didn't buy any shoes. Or the year without fash-ion. Even though my parents and Mike's parents each kicked in the price of a fancy new car to help foot the bill for our wedding, Mike and I were still several thousand dollars short. Money was very, very tight, and there was no room in our budget for my frivo-lous shopping habits.

But my husband, being a kind man, had agreed we could visit the outlet mall that summer. I left him at the food court and walked around, eagle-eyed, as I tried to make the most of my visit. I knew I wouldn't get another chance to spend on myself for the next six months. I walked into the Marc Jacobs outlet.

90 PERCENT OFF CLEARANCE SALE! the signs read.

My heart started to beat wildly. At the time, Marc Jacobs was my absolute favorite designer. I died for his puff-sleeved jackets, his satin prom dresses, his "San Francisco"–seamed jeans. I gin-gerly stepped toward a rack and began to feverishly riffle through it. I looked at the price tags . . . $10 for a chiffon tank top, $17 for a cashmere sweater, $29 for a silk printed dress . . . I swooned. It was like a dream I wasn't sure had come true. I felt dizzy. I started to have double vision. The world became pixelated, little colored dots like a computer or a Seurat painting.

The next thing I knew, I was looking up at Mike's face.

"Are you all right?" he asked.

I was on the floor. Everyone was staring at me. What had happened?

I had fainted! Oh, my God. I was so embarrassed. My skirt was in a bunch and my sandals had fallen off my feet. "They had to go through your wallet, and found my number on your cell phone." He said, "Are you feeling okay?"

"Let's get out of here," I mumbled. I couldn't face the other shoppers, or the concerned salesclerks. I told Mike it was probably because I hadn't eaten breakfast that morning, but I knew the truth. I couldn't believe the prices. It just didn't seem possible that I was lucky enough to have the opportunity to buy such expensive things for so little money. The whole premise seemed insane.

I walked around for an hour to clear my head. Finally, when I deemed myself calm enough to shop, I reentered the store. I needed a cool head, after all, to be able to work through the sale carefully instead of helter-skelter grabbing at the loot like a starving vulture. I spent close to $250 and came home with my whole summer wardrobe. The store even had shoes for $10, but alas, they were all size ten! It was one of the best days of my life. So no, I don't have a crazy biggest-splurge story. Oh, wait. I just remembered that a year later I purchased a beautiful sky-blue Marc Jacobs coat for $1,500. But it was marked down from $7,000, so really, it doesn't count.

WHEN IT'S OKAY TO GO ALL THE WAY

There are some days when it's acceptable—even necessary, to shell out the big bucks for just the right outfit.

- For a special occasion. Don't scrimp on your wedding dress, a black-tie gown, or an outfit for your graduation portrait. Those pictures will last forever.

- A good winter coat. It is an investment that will pay off over the years.

- Good shoes and bags. The right bags and shoes pull together any outfit. Also, you will always feel better knowing you are wearing leather, not plastic, unless the shoes are by Stella, who uses plastic and charges $500.

• Cashmere. It's worth it to spend the amount to buy four-ply winter warmth from an Italian designer. The knockoffs at the mall are not even close to the real thing.

JUSTIFY YOUR LOVE

Shopping—or overshopping, rather—can lead to grief, anxiety, and stress. But don't feel bad about yourself. True or false, here are some foolproof mantras that will ease your pain.

• I'm not selfish. It's for my daughter . . . someday.

• I deserve it. (This is a good time to find something positive about yourself, whether you got a good grade in school, did a great job at work, or lost those three pesky pounds. A girl's got to reward herself, you know.)

• I only live once.

• I don't have a child to support. I'm not married. I have no mortgage. I don't have to be responsible just yet.

• I won't buy anything for the rest of the season. (This one can be used over and over again. As long as you believe it at the time, it'll do the trick.)

• I won't go out to dinner for the rest of the month. I'll make my own coffee instead of spending $5 at Starbucks. And I'll give up luxuries like taxicabs and Charmin TP to make up for the expense.

• It makes me look really thin. (There is no price tag on skinniness.)

• It's a size smaller than I normally am! (See above. Feeling svelte is invaluable.)

• It's for a very special occasion and I will treat it with the utmost respect and care.

• It's a classic. I'll have it forever. (Who cares if it's a hot-pink velvet capelet with an Edwardian-inspired ruffled neck that you'll wear only once?)

BUY IT OR LEAVE IT?

Can't figure out if you should get it or not? This is your guide to making strategic shopping decisions:

- Has it been editorialized (meaning: shown in all the magazines) to death? If so, it's a no-go. It will be right for only that particular season. However, if it's smashing on, it may be worth the splurge . . . but herein lies the rub: After it's had its moment of glory, you can't wear it for at least five to eight years. When you do, you can call it vintage.

- Can you buy something exactly like it at J.Crew, Club Monaco, the Gap, or Banana Republic? If so, get it there and save the splurge for something special no one else sees every day.

- How do you feel in it? Fierce, slammingly hot, and amazingly thin? If so, run, don't walk, to the cash register.

- If you don't love, love, love it, leave, leave, leave it. Don't lay out a large sum of cash on something that doesn't rock your world.

- If you say "It would look better if . . . (I lost ten pounds, I were four inches taller)," don't get it. It's not worth the pressure (sometimes!).

- If you're afraid you won't wear it, you probably won't. Enough said.

- If you are dying for it but don't think it has a purpose in your life or closet, get it and create a purpose for it. It will make you feel decadently lavish and fabulous.

- Remember that comfort and moving are overrated. It's okay if you can't walk in a pair of shoes or sit in a tight skirt. If it looks good, that's all that matters.

REGRET ME NOTS?

For every fashionista, there are always a couple of things you didn't buy and wish you had. We call those the "ones that got away."

Farewell, My Concubine!
✳ KAREN ✳

Minutes before Mel's engagement party is about to start, I am running around my bedroom, freaking out over the fact that I have nothing to wear. I hate my clothes! I have tried on a dozen things, from hot and sexy to modern to uptown lady. And all of it is sitting on my bed, piling up, as I rummage through my racks. Can't wear the army-green backless halter and newsboy cap—wore it last week and I'm sick of it. Refuse to put on the black slip dress with rose details and a lace hemline—I always thought it was a bit cheesy. The way my favorite Balenciaga ruffled skirt ruches in the midriff makes me look fat—that's not gonna do.

If only I had that white backless Chloe jumpsuit with the draping neckline and the Studio 54 edge. It would be so fantastic with my white open-toed Prada patent-leather forties-style shoes, circa 1995—and the straw fedora with gold trim. When I tried it on, it was love at first sight. I stepped out of the dressing room as if I were Bianca Jagger, one of my style icons. It was fun, yet sophisticated, feminine yet strong, hard yet soft, and sexy without being too revealing or showy. The ultimate party wear. At the time I needed something for a swank dinner party, and it was between the jumpsuit and a black dress with a plunging neckline and giant cockatiels at the base of the spaghetti straps.

I went with the dress. I thought it was the smart choice at the time. Who doesn't need a black dress with giant cockatiels? I wore it once . . . and discovered that that plunging neckline was a *lit*-tle too plunging. And those birds? They were patches that got kind of itchy. While the dress is fierce, it just isn't the jumpsuit. And I can't tell you how many times, other than Mel's engagement party, I have wanted to wear the jumpsuit.

The store had only one. It was sold (to Celine Dion, of all people). I called a dozen stores that carry Chloe. No one had it. I called Paris. I have looked many times on eBay. I have searched consignment shops. And I have come up empty-handed. If I could trade something in my wardrobe for it, I would in a hot second. It pains me every time I think about it. I look for something like it each new season. I have tried vintage stores, all to no avail. Almost two years later, I still haven't let it go. I miss it. Maybe in my next life I'll meet up with it again. Until then, I hope Celine appreciates it as much as I would have.

Haunted, While the Minutes Drag
✳ MELISSA ✳

There's a closet somewhere that's stuffed with all the clothes I wish I had had the good sense to buy. The Balenciaga lion vest that launched Nicolas Ghesquière into the forefront (and was marked down to $199 from $800), the Eley Kishimoto red calf-length jacket with oversize buttons ($399 from $700). It happens when you're an inveterate shopper. Once in a while, you let your guilt or your good sense get in the way—the voice that says, hey, maybe I should pay my rent this year instead of buying that Chanel skirt. So you stand there, coveted item in hand, put it down, and walk away.

Then it haunts you forever.

There's a certain fur-trimmed black Byblos coat that never leaves my mind. It had a shawl collar with the fluffiest, fattest fox fur, tinted just this side of violet-black. It shone lavender in the light, and it was divine. The coat was a slim-fitted black cashmere, Italian, and lined with silk. It was only $250 from $900. My memory for prices—and their markdowns—is uncanny. Once a friend told me, when someone complimented me on my clothes, that I don't have to tell them all the details—designer, original price, and what I paid for it. A simple thank-you would suffice. But old habits die hard!

Unfortunately, I put the coat down. I had already spent my limit for the season, even though I really "needed" a fur-trimmed coat. *Next time,* I promised myself. I couldn't sleep that night. I kept thinking of that coat. I woke up early and went to the store the minute it opened. But it was already gone. I still think of that coat, and I've never found anything close to it. It was irreplaceable. It's more real to me than the dozen winter coats that hang in my closet. One day I know I'll get over it. I hope.

LETTING GO—IT'S NEVER EASY

There are no tips here. If you didn't get it, that ship has sailed. It wasn't meant to be. Like a boyfriend you break up with, move on. We sympathize. So here are some emotional tools that will get you through this difficult time.

• Burn sage and smudge, a Native American spiritual tradition that cleanses the aura and energy. This will help detoxify your spirit.

• Light candles and take a moment of silence to recognize and pay homage to whatever it is you're mourning so you can have some closure. That should help you get over it.

• Make a list of all the things that you would wind up finding wrong with the item(s) in question (i.e., it has to go to a special dry cleaner, which is really expensive; this kind of fabric gets pilly; the color fades after being dry cleaned so many times; I can't wear it on my fat days; I'm sure those fringes would wind up getting caught in the car door and ripping off, etc.).

• Click your heels three times and say, "This too shall pass, this too shall pass, this too shall pass."

• Put on your absolute favorite things to wear and dance around your apartment. You have such chic style, you didn't really need it anyway.

• If the above suggestion doesn't work, just drink lots of chamomile tea and cry if you must. It's a very soothing coping technique.

• Find solace in the fact that if you had that outfit, sweater, pair of jeans, or whatever it was you regret not buying, you'd still be standing in your closet, half-naked, thinking, *I have nothing to wear.* The fact is, you only want it because you don't have it. Just like relationships and boys, there will be a new (and cuter) one around the corner when you're not looking for it or expecting it.

BUYER'S REMORSE

Definition: The feeling of shame and sorrow that often comes with having wasted hard-earned money on something that you never, ever wear.

Really, I Shouldn't Have!
✳ KAREN ✳

Shopping tends to cloud the mind. I very easily get caught up in the excitement of it all, unable to see straight. It's sort of like drinking too much and spending the night flirting and making out with a guy you think is really cute, only to find out the next day, when you're sober and bump into him, that he is the ugliest guy you've ever seen. Such is the case during many shopping sessions. Buzzed from the scent of new clothes and the fantasy the garments represent, I have made many terrible decisions that have left me, a.) broke, b.) depressed, c.) in the awful predicament of having nothing to wear.

Let me bring you to a moment I had during an end-of-season sale at Gucci's. The store was packed with pushy women getting their fix of things that were up to 70 percent off. You could hear the screeches of joy emerging from dressing rooms. "It's only a hundred dollars! Get two!" "It's too big! But for this price, it pays to have it fully reconstructed by my tailor." "I don't care if the shoes are too big. I'll put pads in them." Sandwiched in an overcrowded rack of evening gowns, where I was browsing "just for fun," I came across a kelly-green backless halter top made of nothing but dangling beads, some of which dripped down to the middle of the thigh—the very same piece that Jennifer Lopez and Elizabeth Berkeley were photographed wearing with jeans earlier that season. It was divine. Originally $2,000, it was down to a mere $300, and I was not letting it go.

"If you don't get that, will you please let me know so I can?" pleaded a woman who went to reach for it at the same time as I did. "Of course," I said, knowing full well that there was no way in hell I was giving this masterpiece up. I brought her to the dressing room so we could get to know each other (the top, I'm talking about) more intimately. I needed to know how she (again, the top . . . it's definitely a she) felt against my skin. I tied the green satin string around my neck and hooked the metallic green puckered strap around my lower back. I took a step back to admire

ELIZABETH LIPPMAN

Yikes! The only way I can wear this is if I hold my chest all night!

her. And the only thing I saw were both of my breasts, which were fully popping out of the sides of the top, which didn't come close to covering my chest because the silhouette was too narrow.

Noooooo! I thought. *It can't be. God cannot be this cruel!* There had to be a way to make it work. I squeezed my breasts together to make them fit. They didn't. But I had the brilliant idea of taping them together. Yes, that would be perfect. When I went to pay for it, the saleswoman gasped, "Lucky girl! This top is soooo good." My sense of accomplishment soared, like I had won a Pulitzer. I beamed and excitedly rushed home to tend to the masking tape.

Once my breasts (a.k.a. "the girls") were pulled close together in the center of my chest, I put on the top. It was a match. Sort of. While there was no side cleavage, you could see the indentations the tape left on my boobs through the fabric, which did not lie properly across me. I pulled the tape off briskly (it didn't tickle) to try again, this time only a little more loosely. Still, you could see where the tape was through the fabric. *Well,* I thought, *it's not like*

I need to wear this anytime soon. I'll just put it aside and deal with it later.

Although it has never been worn outside of the confines of my own home (actually, not true—I loaned it to a small-breasted friend for a fabulous wedding she attended in Capri, Italy), I admire it on the hanger every now and then and think, *One day, my sweet . . . one day.* It's been four years. And it's still hanging in my closet!

What Was I Thinking?
❋ MELISSA ❋

Viktor & Rolf are a pair of avant-garde German designers who made their name by creating outlandish, superfabulous outfits that are worn by the likes of Cecilia Dean, the editrix-in-chief of *Visionaire* magazine, and my fashion heroine. Cecilia is part Filipina, which accounts for my hero worship. She can always be counted on to wear the most exciting things from the runway, and she was an early supporter of the duo.

One of their signature pieces was a white seventies "disco suit" edged with black satin ruffles, so that the white suit "popped" out of the background. Another was their "Babushka" collection, when they sent models down the runway wearing all of the clothes designed for the season at once. They looked like stuffed kewpie dolls. The spring of 2001, they designed their "Americana" collection, wherein they splashed the Stars and Stripes all over ruffled silk shirts and white bootleg jeans. (Later that year, when patriotic chic was in, fashionistas showed their colors by wearing their V&R outfits!)

I had been following their career and work for years, but their pieces were priced way above my comfort level. So you can imagine my delight—my intense joy—when I found them at Century 21. There it was—a ruffled leather shirt, puffed and slim-fitting. It was a classic Viktor & Rolf statement, and at $299 from $1,500, it had my name all over it. I immediately took it home with me, and showed it to Karen the next day.

"Oh . . . my . . . God. This is *major!*" she said, oohing and ahhing over the shirt. She caressed the leather tenderly. "It's *beyond!*" That week we were getting our pictures taken for our author photos. I wore the shirt with a pair of pink wool trousers. I felt pretty fine.

Then the photos came back.

Instead of supreme fabulosity, I looked like I was wearing a shirt made of rubber tires. It was a disaster. The

The failed photo shoot with the disappointing leather top!

shirt bunched up and reflected light in the oddest places. I almost cried from disappointment and grief. But I couldn't return it. It was a little piece of fashion history that was all mine. Someday I know it's going to hang in a glass case with the note "Viktor & Rolf, 2002, on loan from the collection of Melissa de la Cruz."

HOW TO HANDLE BUYER'S REMORSE IN STYLE

• Give the object of your nonaffection to a friend who will love it—and wear it.

• Turn it into art. Frame it in Lucite with a plaque that marks the date it was purchased or something tongue-in-cheek like "Momentary lapse of reason, November 2001."

• Have a theme party where everyone has to come dressed in something they bought and never wore.

• Use the fabric and turn it into a pillow (calling in a professional will probably be necessary).

- Bring it to a wonderful tailor, capable of reincarnating it into something exciting and new (pants can become miniskirts or shorts; blouses, halters; sweaters, shrugs or leg warmers; A-line, pencil-shaped skirts; coats, vests or bolero jackets; a long dress, a top or a cowl neck to accessorize a simple top).

SAMPLE SALES! SAMPLE THE FUN, SAMPLE THE FRENZY
That's My Handbag, Bitch!
✳ KAREN AND MEL ✳

It's six A.M. We're sitting in a dark hallway in front of a door, watching the time tick by. Only three more hours until we're allowed inside the discount den of heaven—the Chanel sample sale! It is an invitation-only event. Forget about museum balls, film premieres, fancy restaurant openings, this is the one happening that no one in the fashion industry misses. Inside these very doors lie Karl Lagerfeld's fanciful creations, from shrunken tweed jackets and chiffon tops to outrageous gowns, Coco-style suits, and—oh, my God!—handbags, handbags, handbags for practically nothing. Shoes for $50, dresses that were $3,000 for $200, and $99 accessories. It is insane.

We're not even first in line. Armed with coffee, carb-free breakfast, gossip columns, *WWD,* and cell phones, these people have been here since five A.M. Maybe earlier. "I hope they have that black rocker chain-mail bag. I've been dying for it," we overhear one woman say. Judging by the look of the crowd—austere fashion girls, stylists, editors, and socialites with perfectly ironed straight hair, sky-high heels, oversize sunglasses hiding the bags that we're sure lurk under their Creme de la Mer–moisturized eyes, and long, lean (yoga-toned) arms—we've got quite a battle ahead of us.

The line piles up (wraps around the corner, rather) as the clock gets closer to nine. We can feel the sense of urgency and anxiety building. Once inside, it's a no-holds-barred, take-no-prisoners grabfest. It's like the first time Charlie, Viola, Veruca, and TV Mike were let loose inside the Chocolate Factory and allowed to freely drink from the milk-chocolate stream, pick over-size Gummi Bears off trees, and feast on all the confectionary delights at their fingertips. At a sample sale, everything is so temptingly deliciously enticing, you just want, want, want, even if it doesn't fit.

The click of a door unlocking is heard. The gates open. A woman with a snappy attitude (and fabulous eyelashes) checks names off the list. The space is a giant dream closet. Racks full of immaculate twinsets, puckered leather skirts, and sheer tops bedecked with sequins are arranged by size. Tables are covered with quilted bags in every color, shape, and size imaginable, floral pins, pearl necklaces, chain belts. And armies of women are running loose, snagging things right and left. Prices are so low, you'd think the mighty Karl himself was giving everything away.

"Are you taking those? If not, do you mind if I try them on?" one woman asks Mel, who's holding satin ballet stilettos that lace up the calf. "Yes," Mel snaps, "they're mine," knowing full well she won't even be able to walk in them, they're so high. We don't even really look at what we're taking. And it doesn't really matter—it's all Chanel! Besides, we hardly have any room to fully examine the specimens before us. It's so damn crowded, we can't walk a straight line without knocking someone over. Women are pawing the hand-bag buffet as if they were at one of those all-night $5 food spreads in Vegas. And others are leaving the checkout counter with six, seven, eight large brown paper shopping bags, each overflowing with grade-A, prime designer filet mignon.

Karen's phone rings. It's Mel from across the room. She's standing near the dresses and commands, "Come to this section . . . you will die." Karen scoops up some ribbed sweaters, a pair of hot pants (?), some graphic-print blousy silk tops, and something with feathers on it, and makes a mad dash for the dress section, where Mel is triumphantly holding a crazy, sexy black ruched dress. "It's so you," Mel shrieks.

"Oh, my God! Divine," Karen says. "It's so coming home with me!"

In the corner, two women look like they're arguing over a strapless lace dress ("I saw it first. . . ." "No, I did. . . ."). And the racks are getting thinner and thinner by the minute. It's not even ten A.M. and half the stock is gone.

In the end, we each wind up with five extraordinary pieces for ourselves, wallets and makeup bags for our moms, and a few ridiculous patent-leather flower pins we're pretty sure we'll never really wear. All for under the cost of what one tiny thing would have been if it were retail. Our shopping bags are not as full as we had hoped they'd be, but some things look better on the hanger (or on women who are much taller and thinner). It was sad leaving such beauty behind. But we relished our achievements, nonetheless. And the fact that neither of us suffered any bruises, battles, or black eyes.

SAMPLE SALE SURVIVAL SKILLS

• Arrive early. Very early. We're talking, plop down on the floor and camp out hours in advance. It's no different from sleeping in front of Ticketron overnight for U2 tickets. It's the only way to ensure the best selection, before it's all picked over.

• Don't stop to engage in idle chitchat. The rules: First come, first served; shop now, be friendly later.

• Embrace the "elbow shove," a shopping style that involves jutting out the elbows to the side while rummaging through racks, making it impossible for anyone to invade your personal space.

• Strength-train. You may wind up in a ferocious game of tug-of-war. Biceps will be your saving grace. Remember these wise words: All is fair in love and fashion.

• Grab whatever you think you might want. There is no time for hesitation and taking a moment to think about things in the midst of the frenzy. It's best to stake your claim right away, and after you have everything in your possession, you can make an educated choice.

• Wear something that will allow you to try things on without getting undressed: a skirt (you can put pants on under it) and tank top (nothing bulky so you can put something on over it).

CHAPTER 4

Embrace Your Inner Galliano: Girls, Get Your Fabric Scissors Ready!

Fashionistas are multitalented. They make social statements with the way they dress. Their ever-altering sense of style changes the way people think. And while they may not be able to sketch, sew, paint, or draw, they are wizards with the scissors. They are always looking for creative ways to reinvent their clothes, tweaking T-shirts and turning them into cutting-edge knockouts, transforming old jeans into miniskirts, and adding just the right touch to turn a white Hanes tee into something that looks a lot like what the best designers are sending down the runway.

They also have a genius way of looking at clothing and seeing it for more than what it was originally intended to be. For a fashionista, long skirts become strapless dresses, which can become ponchos, which can also turn into scarves. Tube tops double as skirts. And skirts, tube tops. The list goes on. The beauty of being a true fashionista is having the wherewithal to magically put a personal spin on whatever you wear by way of shredding, cutting, trimming, deconstructing, reconstructing, and simply getting more mileage from what you already own.

This is your do-it-yourself guide, a chapter revolving around unleashing the designer that lies within (trust us, there is one itching to break loose). It will not only teach you how to deconstruct, reconstruct, readjust, modify, doctor, alter, and trick out your threads, but give you the skinny on how to wear things in multiple ways, open up your "what to wear" options, and show you how to be a little playful. Because if you can't have fun, what's the point?

SNIP, TEAR, AND WEAR
Lessons from the Master
✳ KAREN AND MELISSA ✳

Try as we might, our technical scissoring is not up to fashionista par. We both envy the girls who have the perfect T-shirts that are slashed just right. Our homemade V-necks and tank tops have ended in disaster—and the garbage—more often than not. So we brought in the big guns, designer Elisa Jimenez, a New York icon who has made slinky goddess dresses for Marisa Tomei and Sarah Jessica Parker with nothing more than a pair of scissors and swaths of fabric. We have both been to parties in constricting T-shirts in the past and bumped into Elisa, who has promptly taken us to the bathroom, whipped out scissors from her bag, and with a few hand movements, manifested sexy tops that hang off the shoulder, droop down the back, and tie around the neck. It's something she's been doing her entire life. She was the cool girl in school who never had to buy anything new because she could always make something fresh out of nothing. We sat down with her in order to perfect our cutting skills. A few hours later, we successfully walked away with lattice lace-up-the-side crewnecks, T-shirt jackets, cowl-neck tops, baby shrugs, and a newfound confidence about Galliano-izing our lives. Here's what we did.

How to Do It Elisa-style
✳ T-SHIRT INTO HALTER TOP ✳

1. Lay T-shirt flat on the floor and fold it in half, vertically, so the armpits are on top of each other evenly. Pull the back out flat.

2. Remove sleeves by cutting a U-shape that begins a few inches under the neckline and travels closely under the armpit seams. The cut should be through both sides of the shirt.

3. Create an oval-like shape through the folded T-shirt three inches below the U-shape you just made. This will eventually be the sides of your halter top.

4. Unfold the shirt.

5. Cut a hole just under the neckline seam on the side that would normally hit the center of the right side of your neck.

6. Continue to cut the neckline off moving toward the back of the T-shirt and stop at the point that would hit the center of the left side of your neck.

7. When you have a full circle of the neckline (the front half of which remains intact and attached to the front of the T-shirt), snip the back so it can be used as ties for around your neck.

8. If you want to crop the top, cut it shorter above the bottom seam.

Note: If you want to draw on the T-shirt before you start cutting, put your feet through the bottom of the T-shirt and open your knees in order to stretch out the fabric as if it were a canvas.

✳ T-SHIRT TO SIDE LATTICE TOP ✳

1. Fold T-shirt in half on the vertical edge (the long way).

2. Make sassy cap sleeves by cutting diagonally from the bottom of the armpit seam to the top right corner of the short sleeve.

3. Make two parallel cuts along the long edge of the side of the T-shirt where the arm is. The first cut should be one to two inches from the side, and the second an inch or two next to it. And both cuts should start at the level of the armpit seam and go through the bottom of the tee. These long pieces—much like car-wash slits—will become the ties that will lace up the sides.

4. Make holes two inches apart from one another next to the

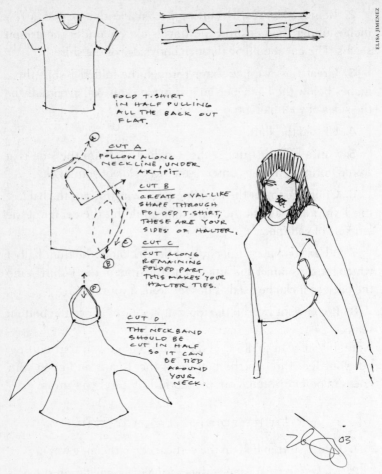

HALTER

ELISA JIMENEZ

FOLD T-SHIRT
IN HALF PULLING
ALL THE BACK OUT
FLAT.

CUT A
FOLLOW ALONG
NECKLINE, UNDER
ARMPIT.

CUT B
CREATE OVAL-LIKE
SHAPE THROUGH
FOLDED T-SHIRT;
THESE ARE YOUR
SIDES' OF HALTER.

CUT C
CUT ALONG
REMAINING
FOLDED PART,
THIS MAKES YOUR
HALTER TIES.

CUT D
THE NECKBAND
SHOULD BE
CUT IN HALF
SO IT CAN
BE TIED
AROUND
YOUR
NECK.

Follow Elisa's step-by-step instructions to halter heaven!

second vertical cut you just made. These will be the holes through which you will stitch the ties.

5. Take the first tie next to the holes and weave it through each hole in a wrapping direction. The second tie should wrap through the holes in the opposite direction to create a crisscross braidlike effect.

Note: Remove the neckline if you want a more open neck. Or cut

ELIZABETH LIPPMAN

With our boring T-shirts and Elisa Jiminez, our fab teacher!

ELIZABETH LIPPMAN

Karen's cool T-shirt with shrug, and Mel's sexy halter top!

a plunging V for a V-neck. Make a square shape if that's the look you're going for. Or just make one cut down from the center of the neckline.

❋ T-SHIRT TO JACKET ❋

1. Cut a T-shirt down the front from the center of the neckline through the bottom.

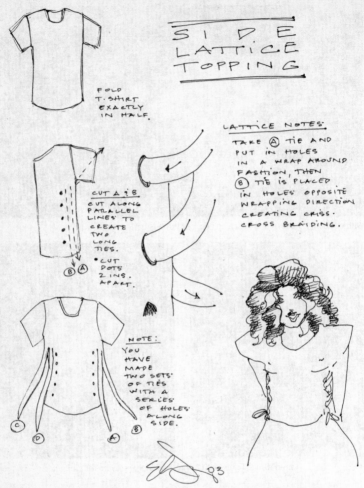

ELISA JIMENEZ

SIDE LATTICE TOPPING

FOLD T-SHIRT EXACTLY IN HALF.

CUT A & B
CUT ALONG PARALLEL LINES TO CREATE TWO LONG TIES.

• CUT DOTS 2 INS. APART.

LATTICE NOTES:
TAKE Ⓐ TIE AND PUT IN HOLES IN A WRAP AROUND FASHION, THEN Ⓑ TIE IS PLACED IN HOLES OPPOSITE WRAPPING DIRECTION CREATING CRISS-CROSS BRAIDING.

NOTE: YOU HAVE MADE TWO SETS OF TIES WITH A SERIES OF HOLES ALONG SIDE.

Follow the instructions to create a sexy side-lattice top for maximum peekaboo impact.

2. Shorten the T-shirt by lopping off a few inches from the bottom if you want it to be more cropped or raw-edged.

3. Two inches from the right and left of the center cut, which opens the T-shirt like a jacket, make slits from the bottom of the T-shirt three-quarters of the way up the top. These will become ties that hold the jacket closed like a button of a cardigan.

4. Tie a knot at the base of each tie so it doesn't accidentally rip.

5. Trick out the sleeves if desired.

❊ JEANS TO MINISKIRT ❊

1. Fold jeans in half, vertically.

2. For the longest possible hem, cut along the lowest crotch part, angling down, and moving sideways toward the outer thigh.

3. Then trim the crotch part so it's straight, as it will stick out into a point.

Note: Use jeans that are way too big on you. So do something with your ex's favorite jeans, the pair he left at your house and keeps asking you for!

❊ T-SHIRT TO COWL NECK ❊

Make a cropped T-shirt with a cowl neck—a great layering piece over a tight turtleneck or long-sleeved tee. A quick style trick that takes no talent, as scissors are not involved.

1. Turn T-shirt upside down and put it on so that neck is around the rib cage area.

2. Insert hands in sleeves and let the fabric that was originally the bottom half of the shirt flow forward like a cowl neck.

YOU CAN'T ALWAYS BUY WHAT YOU WANT . . . BUT IF YOU TRY SOMETIMES, YOU JUST MIGHT FIND, YOU CAN MAKE WHAT YOU NEED

Preppy to Punky

❊ KAREN ❊

I don't know why I bought it in the first place, but in the moment, it seemed like a must. Convinced the novacheck gray Burberry slip dress was sweet and sassy, I imagined myself wearing it and being charming at a lovely dinner to meet my boyfriend's parents. Never mind the fact that, at the time of purchase, I had no boyfriend to speak of. The stretchy frock remained in my closet. I put it on a few times, in the hopes of liking it on my body, but I could never seem to get out of the house in it. It made me feel so country club and so not me. It hung straight. It gave my body no curves. And the plaid! I appreciate Burberry, don't get me wrong. But it was just a bit too prim.

One night I was eating sushi and listening to lounge music at my apartment with my fashionisto friend Joseph Germonto, who at the time was the manager of Kirna Zabete and my favorite shopping consultant. Between conversations about the new spring collections and who would win *American Idol,* he suggested an activity—going through my closet to get rid of things I never wear. Out came Burberry. "Oh, my God! This is so not you," he exclaimed. "I can't even see you buying it!"

"Don't ask," I said.

We looked at it for a bit to assess the situation. "My vision is slashed-up punk," I told him. I went through my drawers to find old (original!) patches from hard-rock bands from the eighties (I had Whitesnake and Wham!, which is not hard rock, but still). I put the dress on and Joseph began to cut away at the length.

"Let's get asymmetrical," he suggested.

"Do it! Just lop it off," I told him. "Take no prisoners."

The new hemline began two palms' lengths below my left hip and ended one palm's length above my right knee. Then he slit the left side all the way up to the waistline, closing it back up with oversize safety pins. We were on our way. Next, the neckline. We made it much more cleavage-baring and we scooped out the back, as well. With the extra fabric, we took the two straps of the camisole and tied them together in the back to make them bunch up and create a circle of skin in the center of the back.

Once we had the shape, the fun really began! We attached the patches on the thigh, slightly askew, by using safety pins. To be cheeky, I cut out the Burberry label and pinned it in the center of the neckline to advertise what it once was. "Genius! I love it! It's sooo good," we both sang. "Kind of British schoolgirl gone bad! *J'adore!*" Designers like E2 and Imitation of Christ, who take vintage pieces and tweak them, had nothing on us! I threw on knee-high boots and a leather jacket, added big hoop earrings and red lipstick, and took Joseph out for cocktails to celebrate my Germonto-Robinovitz original, thinking to myself, *I doubt my future boyfriend's parents would find me charming in this naughty number . . . I'll just have to buy something else!*

More Tricks of the Trade

- Transform fishnets or old hosiery with runs up the legs into groovy sleeves.
   1. Remove crotch area with scissors.
   2. Snip a straight line across the feet.
   3. Put waistband, which should be upside down, over your head as if you're putting on a shirt; slide arms into the legs.
   4. Snip a small opening a few inches away from where the nylons hit your wrist—for a thumb hole, in case you want to do a Ziggy Stardust thing.
   5. Throw on a tank top over it and pair it with jeans or low-waisted pants.

- Morph oversize sweaters (the ones you haven't worn in a hundred years) into sexy little shrugs (good for throwing on over T-shirts when you need a cute getup to walk the dog or for nights out), which you can close with a brooch or thick belt.
   1. Remove neckline with scissors.
   2. Cut a straight line down the center of the sweater from the neck to the bottom.
   3. Lay the sweater flat on a table and cut a half-moon shape from the bottom corner of the left all the way to the bottom corner of the right side. This will crop the sweater's length and give it an angular, asymmetrical aesthetic that is very edgy, but make sure you measure this against your body first so you cut the right length for you.

4. Try it on, because you may want to make it narrower by making the opening in the front wider (just cut strips of fabric from each side).

• Make sleeves bell and flare by cutting them from the back of the cuff up a straight line. For slight flare, keep it four inches, but for dramatic bat wings go all the way to the middle of the triceps.

• Turn jeans into bell-bottoms by slicing them up from the hem to the knee on both sides. Let them flare freely or insert another kind of fabric or denim in the open slits by sewing or safety pinning or making holes up both sides and threading fabric through like we did with the lattice T-shirts.

• Use a leg of old sweatpants as a scarf. It's very cozy.

• Scoop out the back of a T-shirt or pullover top to give it a sexy twist.

• Create the perfect V-neck.

• Graffiti an oversize button-down shirt and wear it as a cover-up on the beach.

• Turn old cardigans upside down and put them on so the neck

Boring cardigan

Turn it upside down and slit the sleeves to make a chic shrug!

is down the back, toward the bum. This automatically turns them into shrugs with swooping cowl necks.

• Take a boring pair of old jeans and pump up their sex appeal with naughty lacing up the legs by cutting the entire side seam down the vertical and making holes two inches apart from one another up the entire cut on both sides (legs). Then lace through string, fabric, leather, or suede.

• Ruche anything by making small folds onto one another, as if you're making a fan with a piece of paper, and then from the inside of the garment, use a safety pin (or many) to hold it in place. A few inches of ruching between the breasts is always a nice touch on any V-neck.

Some Serious Supplies

• Vintage buttons. Add them to a T-shirt, from the center of the neckline, straight down to the bottom or just around the sleeves.

• Lace. Make cutouts on any T-shirt or top and insert lace in its place (you may need to visit a tailor to sew it well if sewing isn't your forte).

• Red tights are great as thread. Get rocker-chick crazy and slash tops (T-shirts and sweaters) down the center or the back, make holes up both sides of the slit, and thread strips of the tights through in a circular wrapping way to get a spiral stitch. You will need a sharp upholstery needle to thread it. Tie a knot at the end of the yarn and let the tail hang as part of the design.

• Spray paint. Apply strips of masking or duct tape at random or in shapes, letters, and patterns to a garment and spray-paint around it. Afterward, remove tape so there are clean chunks of fabric surrounded by color.

• Safety pins in all sizes. Slash something and close it with the pins. Use them to close V-necks that are a wee bit too low. Or pin them on something at random.

• Ribbon. Punch holes in fabric to make ties, or use it as thread.

- Patches. Vintage are best.

- Sequins from an old dress.

- Stain fabric with tea, beet juice, bleach, or red dye.

- Sharpie pens. Draw, doodle, write your boyfriend's name across your chest or a cute saying like, "Bad Girl."

Important note: Never throw away remnants from old garments you cut up. Karen has recycled strips of Burberry plaid and sewn them onto many T-shirts.

TWO, THREE, FOUR, FIVE IN ONE!
Maxiskirt to the Max
✳ KAREN ✳

Fall 2002, I bought a mesh-net elastic-waisted, fluid Jean Paul Gaultier floor-length skirt with swirls of earth-tone patterns and a fringed, uneven hemline. It's not typical of my style. First, I never wear maxiskirts. I always think I'm too short. It's also much more "hippie" than I am. But I lusted after it regardless and wore it all season with a black sweater, knee-high boots, a rust-colored corduroy military jacket, and a beret. In it, I always felt so French-schoolgirl chic. Like most things, however, I got sick of it. And one day, while I was standing in my closet, bitching over the fact that I had nothing to wear and how I hated my clothes, I pulled out the skirt and examined it.

It's very full, voluminous, with loads of floating fabric, which is slightly transparent. The first thing I did was pull the waist up over my chest. It hung like a tent, so I took the excess fabric from the side and wrapped it around my body to pull in the silhouette and make the fabric thicker, hence opaque. It still needed something. But what? I searched my closet and grabbed a thick black leather sash from one of my coats. I wrapped it around my waist as if it were an obi belt. The hemline, being that it was uneven in the first place, was jagged and asymmetrical. I added chunky gold earrings, a motorcycle jacket, and I was out the door in a hot new strapless dress. "What is that dress?" people said, ogling. "Ungaro?"

When I explained it was a skirt, they shook their heads and sighed. "Such a fashionista."

That was only the beginning. Inspired, I came home and played some more. I slipped the skirt over my head with the waist around my neck. I pulled it down a bit so that the waist went across my chest and off the shoulders. Again, I made use of the sash, wrapping it around my waist. The finished look: a belted poncho. Amazing! What else could I do? *There must be more,* I thought. I'm not sure what I did exactly, but with a little finagling, I turned it into a one-shouldered blousy dress. And then I put it back on as a skirt, wrapping the fabric around my legs and tucking the edge into the elastic waist to make it extremely asymmetrical and more of a pencil fit. I kept going. I used it as a headdress next and thought it very Moroccan sixties jet set. And I also wrapped it around my neck as a scarf.

That many looks for the price of $400! I haven't been sick of it since, and I know that if I ever dread wearing it one more time, I'm sure I'll come up with something new. Thanks, Jean Paul!

The hippie skirt as it was meant to be (left) and wrapped around my legs for a slightly more svelte silhouette (right)

ELIZABETH LIPPMAN
ELIZABETH LIPPMAN

The back of the strapless dress, and here it is as a one-shoulder show stopper

ELIZABETH LIPPMAN
ELIZABETH LIPPMAN
ELIZABETH LIPPMAN

As a poncho, a headdress, and a scarf

How to Expand Your Closet—and Horizons

- Wear tube tops as skirts and wear little baby skirts as tube tops.

- Starch the collars of your white button-down shirts so they don't wrinkle and so they have a sharp, stiff appearance. It's also a plus for times you want to wear your collar up.

- If your crisp oxford button-down shirt is wrinkled, dampen it, roll the whole thing up in a ball, wrap it with some rubber bands, and let it sit for a few minutes while you use a hair dryer to heat it up. Then unwrap and wear it as if it were supposed to be all crinkled in the first place. It's *très* Japanese.

- If your pants are too short, take a pair of scissors and cut about four inches up the seam from the ankle. This will give you a cute, flare-legged look that works with sandals, flip-flops, sneakers, and boots.

- Cut old jeans or pants into capris or pants that just skim the bottom of the knee. Wear with heels or knee-high boots.

- Use scarves as belts and headdresses.

- Wear lingerie slips over jeans for a groovy downtown-girl vibe.

- Befriend a very good tailor who will turn A-line skirts into pencil skirts and copy styles of designer clothes you love but cannot afford.

THE BITCH-AND-SWAP!

You know the drill. You're digging through your closet and finding a ton of things you haven't worn since Britney was a virgin. It's time to bundle up those clothes and—before trying to sell them on eBay or donating them to the Salvation Army or Goodwill—have a little fun with them! Throw a bitch-and-swap party with a few girlfriends!

ELIZABETH LIPPMAN

At a recent bitch-and-swap party we threw, we all came out winners! Here we are, holding our new scores!

The Rules

• Everyone brings stuff they don't like anymore and are okay swapping. No Indian givers. And no musty gross things either. Things should be laundered or dry cleaned. Basically, ready to wear, but for some reason, they just don't fit anymore, you're over them, or they never looked good on you in the first place.

• Each girl goes one by one, holding up said item and explaining why it doesn't work in her wardrobe anymore.

• Whoever wants the item in question speaks up to claim it. If more than one person wants the same thing, the group votes on who gets it. This happens very rarely—and when it does it helps to have invited close friends who aren't afraid to yell at one another or tell one another the truth, i.e., "You *know* Sheila has the smaller butt—let her have it!" without causing rancor or ill-feeling.

• Food is a must! Cocktails are good, too, if you're of drinking age. By the end, everyone will wind up leaving with something exciting and new—without having spent a penny.

Makeup, Not War:
Beauty, Skin-deep? Ha!

By now you've masterfully shopped for thrift-store treasures and knockoff finds. You've turned old stockings into sleeves. You've perfected the art of walking with grace in sky-high heels and jeans that drag on the floor. Your style is under control. It's time to consider polishing the pout, flattening the hair, and acquiring the fashionista beauty routine.

Fashionistas must be well-groomed, even if they're not blessed with the flawless genes of Carolyn Murphy. Need we remind you that Diana Vreeland, one of our most acclaimed icons, was no beauty queen? In fact, she was famously ugly. Some might even say an eyesore (God rest her *jolie-laide* soul). But DV worked her looks by exaggerating them to full effect—highly rouged cheeks, lacquered hair, prominent dark eyebrows—to create a fashionable impact.

There are variations on the beauty theme. Fashionistas from across the pond tend to stay on the rough side of polished with chipped nails, straggly haircuts, cigarette-stained teeth; fashionistas in New York like the slick, polished look that comes from weekly visits to the dermatologist and the beauty salon; West Coast fashionistas appreciate casual, well-tanned glamour. Regardless of where you live or what salon you frequent, be it a posh spot where you invest in a $200 haircut or pay the minimum for a quick blowout at Fantastic Sam's, your budget doesn't have to break the bank to make you feel like a million bucks. This chapter will help you keep a rigorous schedule of beauty maintenance.

Besides, what's a fashionista without her sea salt scrub and cleansing cream?

Eye Openers

"We are starting a new year. Faint, faint, if any eyebrows. Beautifully made up corners of the eyes, eyelids and above the eyelids. Rich-looking skin with a golden sheen."

—Diana Vreeland, September 11, 1966

Three years later, she was apparently done with faint, faint, if any brows.

"It is an appalling thing to see four hairs on the brow of a beautiful girl. What is this new kick . . . I am speaking of hair on the forehead of a good-looking girl."

—Diana Vreeland, June 12, 1969

Brow-beaten
✳ MELISSA ✳

When I was eleven, I was indoctrinated to the perils of eyebrow-line application. My grandmother, who was living with us at the time, was getting ready for a posh soiree and rooting around my mother's dressing room for an eyebrow pencil. Lola (*Grandma* in Tagalog) had overplucked her brows in her youth, so all that was left above her eyes were a few stray hairs. She looked like an alien without her eyebrows. She was also half blind.

"What are you doing?" I asked when I saw her applying her eyebrows.

"What do you mean?" she said.

"Lola, that's a *Pentel pen*!"

She had mistaken a brown Sharpie for an eyebrow pencil. We both collapsed in hysterics. Then she surveyed her reflection thoughtfully. The pen was a light brown, the same shade as her eyebrows. "No one will notice." She shrugged, and painted a half-moon over her other eye. That night, at the big fancy party, it was true. No one had a clue that my grandmother had literally painted on her eyebrows that evening.

Let your eyebrows do the talking.

It's always been my ambition to have perfectly arched brows, but it took a long, hard road to get there. I first started plucking my eyebrows at thirteen, when my mother took a good look at my face and decided it was time for "polishing." But I was a lazy plucker, and didn't pay much attention to it. Also, it took a while to get accustomed to the pain.

The worst eyebrow phase I endured was in college, when I applied such a dark eyebrow pencil that in photos of that time I look very, very angry. One night I tried the same trick as Lola. I was out of my espresso brow pencil, so I decided to use my black eyeliner instead. I started penciling it in, but it didn't look right. I kept filling in instead of washing my face and starting over. Big mistake! I looked like a cross between Frida Kahlo and Groucho Marx. None of my friends said anything, but I still cringe when I see the photos.

Maybe I should have used a brown Sharpie instead!

Tweezer (Wo)Man
✳ KAREN ✳

Growing up, I was fascinated by my mother's beauty routine, the way she kept her makeup immaculately stored in Lucite cases, cat-

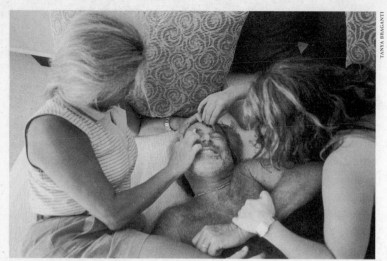

TANYA BRAGANTI

A family affair! Getting my father in on the brow action isn't easy. Mom holds him down while I go to work.

egorized by color. She had a kit of brushes and a magnifying mirror. She didn't spend that much time on her face, yet she always emerged from her bathroom with creamy, even skin, glamorously shaded eyes in earth-color combinations, enhanced by her perfect eyebrows, which she spent ample time shaping and trimming. She was obsessed with her Tweezerman tweezer, a professional quality stainless-steel tool with points so fine and sharp that they could pull up the tiniest and shortest of hairs, even the ingrowns.

She stored her Tweezerman with the same meticulousness—in felt bags in a box, as she did her Chanel bags. It was handled with the utmost care. Whenever I went out with my mother, at least one person commented on her flawless brows—they were curvaceously arched and thick without being too thick. And according to her manicurist, they "opened up her eyes."

I wanted my eyebrows to open up my eyes. And at the age of twelve, my mother gave me my first lesson. She told me to imagine the shape first and she held the side of the Tweezerman against my brow on a diagonal to show me a line to follow. The line began on the underside of the brow and sloped upward to the center of the brow. "Pluck below that line only," she instructed. And we be-gan . . . as I screamed in pain. Virgin skin is very sensitive. "You'll get used to it," she assured me.

And I did. Maybe too used to it. I started plucking religiously. Every time I saw even a trace of stubble, I went to work. But it was more than just grooming. Removing a hair, grabbing it from its root and ripping it from its follicle, gave me the same kind of sick thrill as popping a pimple. Then the inevitable happened: I overplucked. And I really do mean overplucked. By the time I was finished one Saturday afternoon, I had almost no hair left above my eyes. The line was so pencil-thin that when I took a step back to see the dam-age I had done in my attempts to even things out and constantly correct mishaps, I was aghast. And almost bald!

I called my mother at work in a panic. "I've gone and done it," I cried. "I can never leave the house again. I'm a monster!" When she got home and saw me, her eyes popped out of her head. She stared in silence and covered her mouth with one hand. "Oh, my God, what did you do?" she finally said, horrified. She grabbed my hand and yanked me up the stairs to her office—the bathroom. I sat on the toilet seat and she tried to correct the errors of my ways. Out came eye shadow and pencil. She managed to draw in my brows well enough that I could go to school Monday without be-ing mocked severely.

I was warned that overplucking may be hazardous to your face. Hair doesn't always grow back. Luckily mine did. Though it took a few months, during which time I was so self-conscious I took to wearing hats on most days. When they grew back, my mother pre-sented me with my own Tweezerman, hoping I wouldn't make the same mistake twice. I was warned about dropping Tweezerman, as it dulls the points (when they dull, however, you can send it back and the company will sharpen it). From that day on, I have been a brow fanatic.

I still run to the bathroom to remove unwanted errant hairs as soon as I see them pop up. I inherited many of my mom's rou-tines, right down to the felt bag. I have the magnifying mirror and even a heat lamp that emits the kind of fluorescent light that makes it really easy to see every minor and teeny little pore. I sometimes get stuck in my bathroom for forty minutes at a time, examining my brows and trimming the hairs with nail scissors. Over the years I have learned not to overpluck, a struggle against my obsessive nature.

Raising a Brow

The first step to fashionable beauty is the creation of a beautiful face, which means eyebrows, eyebrows, eyebrows!

Brows are perhaps the most important part of the fashionista regimen. Fashionistas swear by their Tweezerman tweezers. There are two basic kinds—the slanted and the pointy; we prefer pointy, but when traveling, do not put them in your carry-on, lest the airport metal-detector cops confiscate them . . . and there is nothing worse than being out of town sans tweezers! The shape of the fashionista brows are always perfectly arched, not flat, not straight. *Never* mono. A few examples:

• The uptown girl—A rounded, softly pretty arch that is closest to the natural shape.

• The earthy chick—Grown out slightly fuller, but still shaped. Just not superarched. (No stray hairs, please.)

• The flaming gay—Male fashionistas tweeze and trim their brows but make it look as if they don't by leaving a few stray hairs. Perfectly tweezed male brows are too queeny!

• The bitch—Severe arch. For those who prefer a power look, try the full-on upside-down V.

• The neurotic—The neurotic's brows are too thin—sometimes the more she plucks, the more she has to! Put those tweezers away!

The Shape of Your Brow Should Be Dictated by the Shape of Your Face. Follow These Guidelines

If you have . . .

• A round face—Consider a high, peaked, slightly full brow à la Brooke Shields, to counter the fullness of your face.

• A square face—By all means, do not pluck eyebrows in a straight line. Try a gently sloping arch with a peak in the middle.

• An oval face—Don't make too high an arch. Gently sloped without peaking in the middle is the best.

• A heart-shaped face—Keep your eyebrows delicate and light; don't grow them in too heavily or use too much brow makeup to darken. It will overwhelm your face.

How to Fill in Your Eyebrows

Eyebrow shade, whether it's specifically made as eyebrow filler or as eye shadow, should only be half of a shade darker than your hair. Use a thin, angled makeup brush and eyebrow powder instead of a pencil. This creates a softer line. Dab it on lightly from the inner brow to the outside. If you press hard and draw like you would with a pencil, the line will be too pronounced and unnatural.

PUT ON A LITTLE MAKEUP, MAKEUP, WE'RE GONNA HAVE A GOOD TIME, GOOD TIME

The Michael Jackson Makeover

✳ MELISSA ✳

My favorite friend my senior year in college was Matt, a blond varsity swimmer from Chicago who had dropped off the team in order to spend his nights at sweaty nightclubs in Chelsea, dressed only in Daisy Dukes and a white tank top. He was hilariously, outlandishly queer. Matt lived dangerously and with much gusto. He and his boyfriend, Garret, spent their junior year abroad in Paris. They arrived at the airport hungover, wearing trench coats, with a boom box on each shoulder, blasting house music at full volume. The French didn't have a chance. Matt and I perfected the art of hanging out and doing absolutely nothing. We bonded over vodka and cigarettes, entertaining ourselves with stories from our childhoods.

One night we were hanging out as usual in my crappy dormitory room, wearing three sweaters each, since the university had yet to fix the heating. (We must have looked like winos crowded around the ashtray.) We were on our fifth cocktail, and I had just finished telling Mark his favorite story—about how my family had lived in high style in Manila.

Matt just thrilled at the word *chauffeur*. He rolled it around on his tongue, savoring it. His parents were divorced, and his mother bought all their clothes from thrift stores and once served them canned turkey for Thanksgiving; hence, he loved all things glamorous.

"What are we going to do now?" Matt asked, stubbing out his cigarette.

"Dunno."

It was ten o'clock on a Saturday night and we hadn't even left my room. All the other kids were asleep or flirting with members of the opposite sex. Matt's boyfriend, Garret, was in the library studying for finals. Since we were flat broke, Matt and I had to steal a bottle of vodka from a suite on the fifth floor, which we filled with water before returning to make it look like nothing happened.

"I know! I have a brilliant idea," Matt said. "I'll give you a makeover!" He told me he loved applying makeup to women's faces, and that he would be honored if I let him work his magic on me. I thrilled to the idea and immediately brought out my hefty makeup bag.

I closed my eyes and felt Matt's soft hands fluffing, blending, brushing my face. "I think we're going to do you as a diva!" he promised, one cigarette hanging off his lip. An hour later he handed me the mirror.

The fact that I didn't scream was a testament to how much I valued our friendship. I didn't look like Diana Ross, more like Michael Jackson! My eyes were grotesquely encased in a green glitter shadow, my eyebrows exaggerated for primo Bride of Frankenstein effect, and my lips were bloodied a candy red. I was hideous.

"I . . . I . . . I love it!" I said.

"Well, we certainly can't stay here with you looking like that!" Matt said.

Oh, yes, we can.

Instead of arguing, I gulped and changed my clothes, and Matt and I hit the popular college bar down the street. A guy I had a crush on took one look at me and turned away without saying hello. When Garret met up with us later, he gave me a sympathetic look.

"Matt give you a makeover?" he whispered.

"Do you think I did this to myself?" I asked.

We never told Matt that he wasn't going to be the next Kevin Aucoin. Some things are better kept between friends.

I Must Look Really Bad Without Makeup!
✳ KAREN ✳

Some people are genetically predisposed to pure natural beauty. They don't need blush, foundation, mascara, lipstick. Clear complexions don't require expensive facial cleansers, exfoliation formulas, and skin regimens. They can roll out of bed and be good to go. I am not one of those girls, which is sometimes a problem because I don't really love wearing makeup unless I'm going to an event or doing something special, be it a work meeting or a date with my man.

I have dark circles under my eyes, permanent sun spots in the form of dark rings, an uneven skin tone, not to mention constant breakouts around the chin region. Because I work from home, I don't have to make myself up that regularly. I get to stay in sweats, skip a shower from time to time, and wear zit cream on my face all day long if I need to. I don't always think about how I look when I'm doing neighborhood errands. If I need to pick up paper for my printer or soy cheese from the health food store, I run out as is—hair atop of my head, pink splotches of drying lotion on my face and all.

I am an extremist. So when I'm not made up, I'm *really* not made up. But when I am, I go all-out. I have as much makeup as a professional artist, including specific camouflage for under my eyes, as well as a cream for the aforementioned sunspots, four shades of eyebrow filler to go with whatever color hair I'm sporting that season, over a hundred lip glosses, Bobbi Brown's leather case of all the right brushes, two kinds of eyelash curlers (one I use for just the edges when I want an angular catlike look). I have cream shadow, powder shadow, and a million tricks up my sleeve. I use red lipstick as blush in emergencies, Kiehl's lip balm as gloss for any lipstick, and when I want my eyes to really pop, I apply liner on the inside of the lid—on the top (a little something I picked up from makeup artist Sue Devitt)!

I hate to think that I look really different when I'm made up versus when I'm not. But I must. I practically live at Cones, a yummy sorbet shop on Bleecker Street, where it's illegal to get a small cup with more than one flavor, but because I'm such a regular customer, the owner allows me to break the rules.

I went there after a nice dinner once and asked for my usual—raspberry and pineapple. The same guy who gives me special treatment every single day looked me in the eye and said, "Sorry, one flavor for the small cup. . . . Can't you read the sign?"

I pleaded, "It's me. It's Karen." He refused to believe me.

"Take the lipstick off and put your hair up. Let me see," he ordered. I had no idea that I was so unrecognizable. I pulled my hair back and wiped off my lipstick. The old man apologized and told me I cleaned up nice. Call me crazy, but I'm not really sure it's a compliment.

Lip Service: Take Care of Those Puckerers

- Clean lips with an exfoliating scrub.

- Pat with foundation or a specific lip-prep lotion.

- If you use lip liner, do not line the lips, but fill in entirely. Dark liner surrounding lighter lipstick is very unchic.

- Vary your lipstick color. If you are always wearing browns, try a rich red, a pale sheer, or vice versa. You will be surprised how much a little change lights up your face. Don't get stuck in a rut. In fact, mix and match your colors to create something new.

- To prevent lipstick from smearing on your teeth, after you apply it, stick your finger in your mouth, wrap your lips around it, and slowly pull it out of your mouth. A ring of lipstick will remain on your finger—the very lipstick that would have eventually landed on your teeth. Do this twice to make sure you get it all.

Tip: Lighter colors make the lips appear bigger. Dark lipsticks make lips look smaller and thinner.

The Color Chart

Red. Blue-red. Orange-red. Plum. Pink. Glossy. Matte. Golden. There are so many color choices to play with (and so little time). What every fashionista needs to know is how to match what's on her lips to what's on her body. There is nothing worse than wearing a lovely coral cocktail dress with a dark wine-colored lip gloss. Below is a color chart that displays the right shade of lipstick to complement the color of your clothes.

IF YOU'RE WEARING . . .	YOUR LIPSTICK COLOR SHOULD BE . . .
Red	Pale pink
Black and/or white	Anything goes
Brown	Red, coral, or pink, but not hot pink
Coral or orange	A pure red with gold gloss over it
Blue	Pinks or blue-reds
Gold or khaki green	Something natural and earthy

Makeup Lessons

Unlike those who are comfortable walking around with a naked face, fashionistas adore being made up by makeup artists. Don't be shy about popping into a counter for a quick touch up before a party, or scheduling a session with a master. Whether you're going to an event where an ex-boyfriend is sure to be in attendance, or you need to be made up for a special occasion like your wedding, it's time to call in the professionals. Some tips from senior makeup artists Brent Ries and Allison McGraine from the Sue Devitt Studio:

• Less is more. Technique is more important than piling on product.

• When applying any product from eye shadow to blush to foundation, blend correctly for precise application.

• Invest in a good set of brushes. Throw away the little applicators that come in the eyeshadow compacts. The basic brushes are powder, blush, and three different eye brushes, one for the base of the lid, one for shading the crease, and one for lining.

- Liquid foundation is the best. With powder foundation you are constantly adding product to your skin. This creates a cakey look.

- Never leave the house without mascara. Curl lashes before applying mascara.

- Bronzer is a must, but don't go overboard. That just-got-back-from-Aruba look in the middle of December is cheesy. Start with a light hand—you can always go darker if need be.

- Line your upper eyelid to create a cleaner, softer eyeliner look.

- Hide dark circles with a pearly yellow cover-up.

- Buy cheap lip gloss from the drugstore, but expensive eye shadow. The ones from the drugstore don't have enough pigment and won't last as long.

- Cover blemishes but don't try to disguise them.

LOCK 'N' ROLL
The Love Affair
✳ MELISSA ✳

My first love when I was a working woman in Manhattan was a guy named Julien Farell. Julien was a doe-eyed Frenchman with a soft caress and a yummy accent. He was the type who always had time for me. We had a very intimate relationship. He was my hairdresser.

He worked at the newly opened Frederik Fekkai salon on the penthouse floor of Bergdorf Goodman. He called me "Meh-leee-sah!" and plied me with apple shampoo and $25 texturizer. The texturizer was part of my signature scent—boyfriends would say, "Mmmm . . . what is that smell in your hair!" Julien cost me $90, then $110, later $250 (with color), or even $480 (with many products) a month. I couldn't resist his suggestions, his strict maintenance regimen, and seeing him every three weeks. Julien taught me that one must never look like one just had a haircut; one's hair should always keep its fabulous shape.

Hairdressers are very seductive people. The marriage between fashionista and hairstylist is one that is often consummated. A close friend had a torrid affair with her stylist, but alas, when it was over, she could no longer get her hair cut at his salon. Julien and I, however, were on strictly platonic, hair-centered terms.

But alas, the affair had to end at some point. They always do.

The news came via a newspaper clipping. The *New York Times* reported that stylists at the Fekkai salon made six-figure salaries. I blanched. Here I was, playing grande madame to Julien, and the bastard was actually making more than I was! It struck me then: I couldn't afford this. It was the equivalent of a monthly car payment—for my hair. After three years at the Fekkai salon, I walked out of its gleaming brass doors forever. But I'll always remember Julien fondly.

Curly Girl, All the Way
✳ KAREN ✳

Like most girls who have curly hair, I have spent much of my time battling the twists and turns of the locks that sprout uncontrollably from my scalp. For most of my life, I fought a nasty case of triangle head, a condition whereby your hair is flat on top and bursting out on the sides such that it resembles the shape of a triangle. I cursed my curls. So unruly were they that before my very first job interview, after college, at Condé Nast, an older, wiser fashionista instructed me to get my hair straightened. "You'll look much more put-together," she advised. I did, but I wasn't happy about it. I never felt like straight hair suited me. I had a curly-girl personality. My hair needed to be wild and adventurous. I just needed to learn how to manage it.

In 1997, a publicist I knew wanted me to try a new salon in Soho, and at the time I was not wed to any one hair person. So I took her up on her offer and stepped inside Devachan. Everything about the place was different from the uptight world of uptown, self-righteous hair salons that I was used to. I was greeted with a champagne flute of sparkling water. When you get your hair washed, you lie down on an ergonomically correct massage table and you get a twenty-minute rubdown.

Lorraine Massey, the owner, a blonde with tight corkscrew curls, sat me down to talk about my hair for ample time. "You've got to embrace your curls and nurture them like a garden," she said in a soothing British accent. She went on to talk about how curly hair curls because of the hair matrix being fine and devoid of moisture. She began massaging my scalp in a circular motion while asking me what I wanted from life and, hence, my hair. She talked about the circle of curls reflecting emotional cycles. She had a very spiritual approach, which I took to. But more than that, she really seemed to understand my hair and wanted to cut it in a way to get the most out of my curls and enhance my features. It was the first time a stylist didn't cut my hair and blow it poker-straight, turning me into whatever Jennifer Aniston was sporting at that moment.

Her first rule of thumb was banning shampoo. Completely. Apparently, "'pooing," as she says, dries the hair. In the back of her salon, she whipped up a nonlathering formula of all-natural products, which she gave me as a gift. (Note: She's not one of those creepy product pushers who get you to spend a fortune on things . . . and her products barely cost $10 each.) Then she told me that from now on, I was not to rinse my conditioner, but not to use leave-in conditioner because it has chemicals. Use regular conditioner and just leave it in, she said, comparing it to hand lotion. ("You don't put that on your hands and wash it right off, do you?") Also, conditioner acts as a weight, which enables the curls to fall downward, not puff out to the side. She gave me an intense hour-long lesson on styling my hair. The routine goes as follows: Scrunch wet hair with the towel or paper towels, which are thinner and, hence, reach the scalp more easily, from the end to the root, squeezing on the way up. Add a curl-friendly gel, and then, the most important part, comes the next step: Take bobby pins and insert them in such a way that they add lift to the hair. Do this where you want the hair to be fuller. Leave in until the hair dries and then remove. That trick gives the hair body. It's also the only remedy for triangle head I have ever seen work—and last.

Lorraine cut my hair while it was dry and showed me how she cuts the curl in a way that promotes its windy movement, not prevents it. I came home and threw away all of the products that never really worked, including all shampoo. (I haven't "pooed" since!) And I have learned to like my hair over time. From that day forward, it grew longitudinally instead of horizontally. And every time I see Lorraine, who is now the only person I will let cut my hair, I pick up new tricks she thinks of. She is something of a mad curl scientist. She even wrote a book about it. I have sent all of my curly-haired friends to her and they have all said she changed their lives. Just like she has changed mine! The moral of the story is: Find a person who really understands your hair, someone who will give you a cut that fits your face, your life, your personality. Otherwise it's just not worth it. Like a husband, you should never settle for anyone who's second-rate!

Hair Affair

While a fashionista follows each gloriously fickle trend and turn of fashion, her hair should simply flatter her face, regardless of the fact that short may be in one season, straight another, and long and curly the next. Many fashionistas get caught up in major straightening moments, when they think they must have poker-straight 'dos. This usually results in hair irons, which can ultimately lead to hair frying, burning, and drying, and other atrocious mishaps. Learn to accept the limitations of your locks and appreciate what you have been born with.

A signature hairstyle can be your determining look for decades—just look at Anna Wintour and her famous bob, Ali McGraw and her long brunette locks, Gwen Stefani and her platinum shade. Experiment with a few styles, invest in a relationship with a fabulous hairstylist, and canvas friends and family for their honest opinion.

Below, some tried-and-true fashionista hair tricks.

• The two-day blowout—We fashionistas are a vain lot. We spend the grocery budget on perfect blowouts. Make a blowout last for two days by having your stylist spray your hair with a silicone-based lotion or hold. This will help your hair retain its shape for more than one night. At night, sleep in the "sleeping princess" position (on your back, with your hair spread on your pillow) and use a satin pillow that does not absorb moisture, which often leads to waves and curls. Do not toss and turn! Do not attempt to have any nooky! Remember, it's about making that $50 blowout last! Invest in a shower cap.

• The Pucci bandanna—The cure to fashionista bad-hair days is a fabulous printed bandanna or scarf to hide the unruly mess. Oversize sunglasses optional.

• Pre-Raphaelite curls—Invigorate your curls by dampening hair with a spray bottle. Take small pieces of hair and wrap around your finger close to your scalp. Pin each curl to the scalp and let it sit while you're getting ready (fifteen to twenty minutes). Remove pins.

• The low ponytail—A *Vogue*-magazine-girl favorite, this is a sleek, classic, sophisticated look that works well with long, straight, silken hair or hair with subtle waves. A few tendrils outside for wavy-haired girls only.

• The SuperSolano hair dryer—A slightly more expensive dryer than the average Conair, this is the Bentley of hot air. After you attain a style you like, give your hair a shot of cold air from the dryer. Hair is moldable like butter—heat will allow you to shape it and the cold air will keep it in place.

THE NETHER REGIONS
I Have Hair There?
✳ KAREN ✳

I had no idea what I was in for when I first went to J. Sisters, a bikini-waxing Shangri-la on West Fifty-seventh Street named after the Brazilian sisters—Jocely, Jonice, Joyce, Janea, Juracy, Judseia—who own the place (if you notice, all of their names start with the letter *J*). It was the fall of 1998. And for four years I had been hearing all about the J. Sisters, how it was the best wax in town and once you got it, you could never go anywhere else. Fashionistas of all kinds—from Christy Turlington and Naomi Campbell to Gwyneth Paltrow and Patti Hansen—swore by them for their bikini-wax expertise, which resulted in a line of hair hardly thicker than a string bean. In fact, Gwyneth signed her photo, which hangs on the spa's wall, with a note that said, "You changed my life." I had to admit, a wax that could change your life made me curious. While I had always been a Gillette razor kind of girl, in the name of south-of-the-border chic, I made an appointment.

In the waiting room I spotted Jennifer Grey and patiently read through the J. Sisters' press clippings from all of the fashion magazines that gave them star-studded reviews. I had never had a wax before, and to be honest, I was kind of scared. But I took Advil beforehand, as I was told it prevents feelings of extreme pain. The salon is pretty bare-bones. No frills. No fancy chairs. Just a highly embellished ceiling with original ornate prewar moldings. I could hear the ripping and tearing noises oozing from the wax rooms, which were barely big enough to hold the table on which you lay for the procedure. A few "ouches" pierced my ears. Just as I was contemplating bailing, Juracy, who is supposed to be the gentlest of them all, beckoned me into the room.

She told me to take my pants—and undies—off. "But I wore my skimpiest panties for the occasion," I said.

"That's nice. But they go off."

I stripped down and got on the table, asking her to go easy on me. "It's my first time," I confessed. She rubbed me down with powder and promised to take good care. Then she pushed my knees apart and slathered on the wax. I stared at the swirls of the molding on the ceiling and the gilded finishing touches on the chandeliers to keep my mind occupied on something other than the fact that this woman was getting a close-up of my vulva. She started with the sides and the part that sort of hits the crease of the thighs. It hurt! I grabbed her hand and asked her to warn me next time. She took more off, moving closer and closer to the middle of my sacred area of untouched skin. She took almost everything off. And that was only the beginning.

She had me lift my legs and hold my knees so that she could really take a good look. I was so self-conscious—and so exposed. I wondered, *Does this count as a lesbian experience?* She continued waxing downward, making her way to my rear end . . . um . . . the opening, if you know what I mean. And there was another rip. I was a bit grossed-out, actually. "I have hair there?" I asked, shocked and embarrassed about my obviously bestial nature. She nodded. Sensing my mortification, she told me it was okay, "Everyone does." That means you do, too!

She got rid of hairs on the lips and—damn—for a minute there, I was pretty sure she was waxing the little bits that were bor-derline inside of me. It felt so intimate. I never imagined giving someone this close a view of me. I wasn't even sure my (then) boyfriend had even taken that good a look! Once she finished the job—ten to fifteen minutes later—I had to admit . . . I looked pretty darn good. And I was smooth as a baby. The fact that the process was—shall we say—invasive no longer mattered. The re-sults were that fabulous. I've been going back religiously ever since.

Let It Rip: The All-important Bikini Wax

It's something every fashionista must do, even if the only person to see it is Jean-Claude, her toy poodle. Fashionistas don't like anything to be messy, even (or especially!) the area south of the border. In the world of hair removal, more is more! Choose a style that's worthy of your Cosabella thongs.

- The Triangle—A seventies throwback.
- The Racing Stripe (a.k.a. the Playboy)—A long strip favored by porno stars and sexy soccer moms alike.
- The Dictator—A square shape reminiscent of a famous tyrant's mustache.
- The Brazilian—Any of the above shapes with a little extra taken off, such as the area from the pubis to the tush. Worth the pain.
- The Logo—When the Gucci ads showed a model with a big G down there, it sparked a trend from Beverly Hills to Madison Avenue. Karen has gotten the letter "T" for her boyfriend, Todd.
- Themed Trim—Heart-shaped for Valentine's Day, a star for Christmas, the addition of Swarovski crystals (just use false eyelash glue), or a little glitter for a wedding. Dye it if you dare or the occasion permits. Green for St. Patrick's Day.

How to Survive a Brazilian

We've all been there, clutching the tissue paper and screaming for mercy. But it doesn't have to be torture.

- Never schedule a wax when you are PMS-ing; the skin is more sensitive during that time of the month.
- Take a painkiller an hour before your appointment. Many of us pop Advil before a Brazilian, but some of us save that Vicodin pill the doctor prescribed for our wisdom-teeth removal.

- Get a topical anesthetic. Just be careful that it stays on the outside only.

- Request the gentle wax for sensitive skin.

- Stop shaving between waxes. The more you shave, the harder and more brittle your hair will become—leading to very painful experiences.

Warning: The Brazilian removes hair underneath the vaginal lips as well as on its surface. It is extremely hurtful. If you cannot stand it, just stick with the basic and forget about flying down to Rio.

Suggestion: After the wax, cleanse with an astringent. Yes, it will sting. But it will help prevent unwanted whiteheads and ingrown hairs.

FASHIONISTA FILES:
THE COLLECTION BY ORLY
Designing Our Own Nail Polish Line
✻ MELISSA AND KAREN ✻

One of our favorite pastimes is getting our nails done together. "Wanna get a mani-pedi?" Karen will ask, which is short for, "Do you want to spend three hours in a salon, get our nails done, and riffle through *US Weekly* and *Vogue* together?" It's a quintessential fashionista bonding moment, combining all of our favorite activities—pampering, virtual shopping, and gossip.

Our only complaint is that we can never find the right nail colors. We always want to be "edgy" and fashion-forward, but the trend for blue (or black, or purple, or gold-dusted) nails seems so . . . adolescent. It's just not "us" anymore. More often than not, we reach for our perennial red or black-red or pale pink classics. But we can never find just the perfect fashionista red—not too orange, not too blue, not too pale, not too dark. Or the perfect pale pink—not too yellowy, not too white, not too bubblegum.

So when the nice people at Orly asked us to design a line that would appeal to fashionistas, we jumped at the chance. We decided that since fashionistas wear only reds and pinks, our collection would have only six colors, from the darkest, blackest red to the most whisper-soft pink. Plus, each color would be named after the type of fashionista we envisioned wearing it. This way it would be easy to mix and match colors, since most fashionistas do a light manicure with a dark pedicure (except for Karen, who only wears dark red nails).

Follow our chart to figure out your nail polish needs!

Fashionista	Nail Color
Wicked Witch	Vampy, dark red
Quirky	Offbeat burgundy
Fairy Godmother	The classic "perfect" red
Pop Tart	Hot-pink fuchsia
Sisters	Girly sweet pink
Mummy	Sheerest pale pink

So pick up the Fashionista Color Collection from Orly—as a fashionista, you'll find all the basic hues you'll ever need for your fingers and toes!

Designing the collection with Stel and Carole from Orly

> ## Nailed
>
> A fashionista's most relaxing moment is at the nail salon. Fashionistas never go out without a proper polish job (although short, bitten nails with chipped red polish does work for tough girls who cultivate the sexy, punk Pat Benetar vibe). Fashionista nails are square in shape (round is too matronly). And they often like to curl up at home with a good book and thick layers of cream on their feet (covered by plastic wrap and cotton socks) to ensure soft soles.

PUTTING ON THE RITZ
Botox for All!
✳ **KAREN** ✳

Warning: Botox is a controversial procedure, and although it's FDA approved, just because some fashionistas are sick in the head and get it the second they see a furrow in their skin doesn't mean you should, too! If you do want it, however, host a Botox party. It's all the rage!

For a fashionista, a dermatologist friend is as golden an accessory as a Birkin. Mine is Dr. Steven Victor, a silver-haired, stately-looking man who has a prestigious client list of the city's biggest fashionistas, socialites, and celebs. As a doctor, he is precise, scrupulous, and cutting-edge, offering a menu of the most experimental procedures from Europe. This is the man who melts fat with ultrasound. And he's also totally cool, the type who frequents trendy, hip restaurants, keeps up on the scandalous gossip, and gets invitations to all the A-list parties. All of my friends see him—and adore him. In order to kill two birds with one stone—get in our necessary procedures from the good MD and hang out—I organized a Botox party for six at his Upper East Side office off of Madison Avenue.

Punch & Judy, a chill tapas and wine bar on the Lower East Side, and one of my favorite haunts, catered the affair with mini smoked-salmon sandwiches, beef carpaccio on toast points, foie gras, and more. Between bites of prosciutto-wrapped asparagus, we all consulted Dr. V about what we needed.

"I just had Botox last week," one guest said. "But I didn't get it between my brows and there is a furrow there. Can you fix that?" Of course he could! Beth wanted Botox, too, but she was petrified, as she was super needle-phobic. Marjorie wanted microdermabrasion, a hard-core exfoliation treatment that practically sands off the top layer of dead skin cells and helps to even out the skin tone, as well as a laser to rid her of broken capillaries on her cheek. Stacey had the doctor examine her postbaby stretch marks. Nicole just wanted an overall checkup and someone to deal with a little problem she'd been having. "I know this sounds crazy, because I'm not overweight, but I have . . . I don't want to call it a double chin . . . but this," she said, "it's just extra face." Dr. Victor hadn't the heart to tell her that "extra face" was a double chin.

As for me, Dr. V suggested a small hit of Botox (hardly wrinkled, I was open to it in the name of prevention . . . you can never start too young!), a laser to take care of my sunspots (damn them!), and while I was at it, a rosacea facial to combat redness. (I needed more than I bargained for!)

Everyone's treatments went without a hitch. Until Beth! Her nerves were on edge over her needle fear. While the actual Botox shot, the puncturing of the skin with the toxin that freezes the muscles that cause wrinkles, wasn't a big deal . . . the thought of it was. Afterward she had a full-on panic attack. She started sweating. She turned pale. Her lips actually got blue. "I need to lie down; I need to lie down," she said, her limbs shaking.

She wasn't allowed to. After Botox, you can't lie down for up to four hours; otherwise the Botox will potentially travel to a different part of the face . . . and the last thing you want is to paralyze (even if it lasts only four to six months), say, your right eye! Dr. V put the chair back a little and held a cold compress on her forehead and neck. "I need sugar. I feel faint," she went on. "Does any-one have candy or orange juice?" She was woozy.

One guest ran to her bag. "I went to Bergdorf Goodman for lunch and took the petit fours we didn't eat," she said, placing a pile of mini cookies and biscotti on Beth's lap.

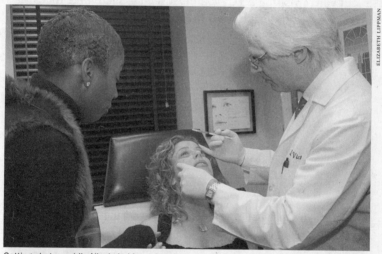

Getting shot up while Nicole holds my hand

Doctors and dining! Last dibs on food from Punch & Judy before parting!

"I'm gonna vomit," Beth said. "No cookies! Just candy."

The nurse brought out the smelling salts and the scene went on for about fifteen minutes. We banned the photographer from the room! What's a fashionista party without the drama? Soon after, everything was fine—and the girls were all booking appointments for six months down the line.

If you're visiting NYC, you must see Dr. Victor. He rocks, and his office is at 30 East Seventy-sixth Street, off Madison Avenue.

The Luxe Life

Fashionistas have very stressful lives, all that running in heels, trying to get ahead of the credit card bills. A day or a weekend at a spa—and a quick trip to the dermatologist—rejuvenates our senses (and skin). Below is a list of remedies for the fatigued fashionista.

• Hot-stone massage—Hot lava rocks are massaged into your body for a grounding, relaxing, soothing effect.

• Oxygenating facial—A normal facial with huge boosts of oxygen, through products, to the skin in order to make it appear younger. Apparently skin loses oxygen every year of your life after puberty.

• Reflexology—The practice of stimulating certain nerve points in the foot in order to affect other parts of the body, from back injuries to the digestive system. Also, it just feels good after a day in stilettos. Don't wear heels for the rest of the day after. In fact, you should even get someone to carry you home.

• Restalyne—An injectable filler for frown lines. For advanced and older fashionistas only, please. Fashionista podiatrists, like Dr. Suzanne Levine in NYC, shoot up the balls of the feet with Restalyne and collagen to add cushion to make wearing heels more comfy. God bless.

- Botox injections in the armpits—Prevents sweating (excuse us, perspiration), which will save you money on dry cleaning, my friend.

- Laser treatments—Fashionistas love all sorts of lasers— plumping up the collagen on your face, getting rid of scars and stretch marks, zapping sunspots—plus you get to wear those cool glasses. Also, any new age-defying treatment will do.

- Cellulite massages—Hard-core massage treatments that are supposed to break up your fat.

- Colon therapy—Nothing like a high colonic to rid you of the toxic perils of white flour and Diet Coke!

- A good night's sleep—That means bedding with a high thread count (anything less than three hundred is not acceptable; Frette sheets are preferable), an eye pillow, a Tempur-Pedic mattress (the best money can buy), and Threadcountzzz pajamas, made of cotton with a thread count of eight hundred! Fact: Sleep deprivation leads to stress, aging skin, and weight gain.

FIT FASHIONISTAS
Starving in Style
KAREN
✳ Day 1 ✳

I am on an airplane, debating whether I should eat the meal the flight attendant places on my tray table: lasagna, salad (only half-wilted!), roll (not *that* stale!), and some kind of dessert that resembles a white square with a red dot on top (strawberry shortcake, I'm told). Under normal circumstances, I'd pass. But I am on my way to We Care, a holistic detox health spa in Desert Hot Springs, California, where I will be fasting on a careful prescription of juices, supplements, teas, and water, getting daily colonics, and indulging in luxurious spa treatments to stimulate my lymph system, rid my body of dried skin, and take care of stress knots. I'm staying for a week.

This may sound like torture, but for fashionistas it's considered a spiritual, even vital experience that is said to replenish the body, mind, and soul. The body accumulates toxins and carcinogens, not to mention preservatives and chemicals from processed foods, and you must unburden yourself of them. Some experts, however, do not agree, and think that fasting and colonics are not that great for you. Whatever the case, We Care has garnered a cultlike following of high-profile Hollywood types—agents, studio heads, and celebs like Ben Affleck, Matt Damon, Liv Tyler, Alicia Silverstone, super-model Gisele Bundchen, and Courtney Love—who think of the desert destination as a bona fide refuge, at $2,000 (and up) per week. The weight loss is not supposed to be the point, but it sure is an added plus, and one of the reasons I decided to check in.

So I opt for the plane food. My last supper—even though I was instructed to eat only fruits and vegetables for three days before arriving. I arrive at four o'clock and Annie, a petite yogi with cropped spiky hair, a dark tan, and the kind of upbeat energy that belies her seventy-something age, orients me to the program. I am given a baggie of meticulously labeled pills—acidophilus, which I'm to take after each colonic, digestive enzymes (two each morning and two in the P.M.), power green (a food supplement that has the same benefits as vegetables and algae and other nutrients), and fiber pills—along with teas (blood, liver, and heart purifiers) and minerals for taking a detox bath (I'm told to take two during my stay).

Then she explains the drink plan: As much water as possible, a teaspoon of Kyo-Green (a green powder to mix with water in order to get the kind of vitamins and minerals you'd find in greens), two detox drinks daily (a fiber-packed beverage that tastes like dirt but helps stimulate the digestive tract), a pure vegetable juice for energy (part carrot juice, part greens), and pureed vegetable soup (to be had in the evening as "dinner").

It is overwhelming. "So much to remember," I say. The thing about We Care is that it's not one of those luxury places where someone makes drinks for you and brings you what you need. It's bare-bones, very do-it-yourself, to keep you aware of what you're putting in your body. Not eating is very hard work! Deprivation is so extravagant!

I am here not more than one hour and I'm already hungry. "It's mind over matter," says Simona, who is giving me my first colonic of the trip.

Postcolonic, I have the acidophilus and the soup. Some We Carers—a fashion publicist, a Hollywood agent, the former VP of a major television network, a bank CEO—lounge around in the "common area" (a living room with cushy sofas and a gaggle of magazines) and talk about their days.

Talk shifts to—what else—food.

"I'm craving Chinese food in the worst way," whines a hungry woman wearing a bathrobe so big, it's swimming on her lithe frame.

"Oh, don't get me started on food. I'm dying for something to eat," chirps her friend, who pauses for a moment and then looks on the bright side. "But this is the good soup. It's better than last night's."

"The trick is to have it early. By the end of the night, it's watered-down, bottom-of-the-barrel stock," says an athletic-looking, gray-haired, six-foot-tall, two-hundred-pound man who's been here for three weeks (three weeks!).

After the soup, which, admittedly, is pretty damn good, I hit the sack. I'm jet-lagged.

✳ DAY 2 ✳

SIX A.M.: I swear, I'm already thinner. My day begins with a teaspoon of castor oil, which is good to take an hour before a colonic.

TEN A.M.: Colonic.

ELEVEN A.M.: I pop an acidophilus, take a nap, drink my Kyo-Green mixture.

NOON: Yoga class and the detox drink (yuck).

TWO P.M.: Sink into the massage table for an eighty-minute rub-down to stimulate the lymphatic system. When I emerge from the pampering session, I feel like Jell-O. I'm dying for a burger—and I don't even eat red meat!

✳ DAY 3 ✳

EIGHT A.M.: I jump out of bed too quickly. I feel faint and light-headed. But my wooziness goes away when I catch a glimpse of my hip bone in the mirror. I have always dreamed of having a hip bone I could see (not the loftiest of ambitions, but at least I can admit it).

TEN A.M.: Surging with energy, I take a two-mile walk in the desert and, for the first time in months, feel truly relaxed. It's delightful. My colonic, however, is rough. Nothing is coming out.

ELEVEN A.M.: I take a nutrition class with Susannah, We Care's founder, who speaks knowledgeably about the dangers of Nu-traSweet (switch to stevia, an all-natural substance, she recom-mends) and teaches us how to make the perfect smoothie. I'm so inspired, I buy the $400 Vita-Mix blender (and I've never cooked or made anything other than salad in my adult life).

TWO P.M.: Three people tell me I look thin (!). And when I call Mel, she is shocked. "I haven't heard you this mellow . . . ever!" Just when I think I can't feel more lucidly calm, I slip into a hot detox bath for thirty minutes and then get a deep-tissue massage. Ah, life here is good. Even though I miss cupcakes.

✳ DAY 4 ✳

FIVE A.M.: Headaches, shivers, chills. I do not feel good. "This usu-ally happens at this time," Rory, We Care's manager, a blue-eyed Tom Cruise type with bulging biceps, tells me later.

TEN A.M.: Rory makes me a small smoothie with soy milk and In-tegris, which levels the blood sugar, to revive me. It works. I am so clearheaded that I rush to my room and work for three solid hours.

FOUR P.M.: Nap time.

SEVEN P.M.: Watch *Maid in Manhattan,* a rental. But I barely make it through five minutes before falling asleep. All of this relaxation is really tiresome!

✳ DAY 5 ✳

TEN A.M.: I am skinny! And starving. I mean, *starving.* I put on the TV and find myself salivating over a dog food commercial. Dog food! It looked just like a Fig Newton!

ONE P.M.: My "body facial" appointment, a two-hour treatment involving mud wraps, coffee-bean exfoliation, and a massage. But the real reason I signed up for it—it comes with a smoothie, a large mango-flavored smoothie. And right now I would do anything for something with more substance.

✳ DAY 6 ✳

NOON: For lunch I have digestive enzymes, acidophilus, Kyo-Green, carrot-greens juice. Later I do my detox drink, power green supplements, and another detox drink. More than twenty glasses of water later, I am feeling alive, well, and fabulous. My skin looks good. My hair feels soft. The bags under my eyes are gone. I may be ready for a nice piece of salmon, but at the same time this not-eating is really working for me—mentally and physically. I plow through work at warp speed.

ONE P.M.: During a trip to the outlet malls, I get my reward. Gucci dress, size two, baby! I probably shouldn't have bought it, because I'm sure I'll gain the weight back as soon as I start eating regularly again, but I couldn't resist.

✳ DAY 7 ✳

TEN A.M.: The last day. I'm seven pounds lighter, which is a lot for me, considering I'm barely five feet tall. I pack and get dressed. I have been waiting for this moment since I arrived: Time to put on my jeans. My butt is tiny! My legs look longer and leaner. My inner thighs are not even touching. But more important, I feel— psychologically—strong, alive, healthy, and well. Plus I am as clean as a whistle.

TEN-THIRTY A.M.: Annie walks me through break-the-fast rules— fruit and veggies only for three days; then introduce protein slowly. I swear off white flour forever (something I've done countless times before, but at this moment I'm serious) and plan to switch to healthier grains. Before hugging my new We Care mates good-bye, I bite into an apple. It is the best apple I've ever had.

The Edina Effect
✳ MELISSA ✳

I hate to exercise. There's nothing that strikes me as more boring than slogging your way through a workout. I was the type of kid who was always picked last in kickball and practically failed gym. Whenever friends and I played tag, I was always "it." For years I was blessed with a healthy metabolism. I could eat whatever I wanted, but I never gained weight. My nickname was "Skinny Annie" (my middle name is Ann). But all good things come to an end, and when I hit my twenties I realized I'd have to join a health club or embrace the roll of pudge around my waist.

As in fashion, I was drawn to the trendiest workouts. First up: Rollerblading. Two of my friends were really good at it, and I envied how they whizzed down the Central Park loop without missing a beat. I enrolled in classes at the Learning Annex, and a few weeks later I joined them. The bastards left me to fend for myself. I didn't so much roll as not-walk. I was 'blading at such a glacial pace that picnickers laughed at me.

"Yo, look at that girl! Go, mama! Go, mama! You can do it!" one cheered, snickering.

"That's so pathetic," another one stage-whispered.

But I was determined to be a 'blader, knee and elbow pads and all. The most harrowing experience was when I decided to blade from my apartment twenty blocks to the health club. I fell several times on the sidewalk, executing a perfect ass-slide down Bleecker Street. Cars honked. People pointed. But no one helped me up. (I was also wearing very trendy polka-dot bike shorts at the time.)

That was it. The blades rusted in my closet. I tried it all: step class, hip-hop dance class, African tribal dance beats, anything to make losing weight more fun. I've done yoga, I've owned a scooter, and I've had several trainers who tried to whip me into shape. One told me, "You are what you eat," after I told him I'd had a sandwich from Blimpie.

These days I slog through my workout on the elliptical trainer—half an hour four times a week. My brother, the track-and-field champion, has told me I really need to lift weights and get muscle definition. Maybe one day . . .

GETTING INTO YOUR SKINNY JEANS

We all have two kinds of jeans—our everyday jeans and our skinny ones, which we can wear only every few years, if we're lucky. Fashionistas are, like all women, obsessed with thinness. You may think fashionistas don't eat. Well, some don't, which we don't recommend, save for a trip to We Care every year. But they do watch what they put into their mouths and stick to exercise regimens, even if it's nothing more than walking through the outlet mall (four hours later, you'll feel the burn). These are our secrets.

• Weight Watchers, the old-school system where you equate food to points, is big with the Condé Nast girls who jaunt to meetings during their lunch breaks.

• The South Beach Diet, a best-selling book with a diet that Bill and Hillary Clinton—who are not fashionistas—both swear by. We haven't really tried the diet, but the premise is Atkins meets Sugar Busters. You'll be sick of ricotta cheese in no time.

• Atkins. No carbs. No way. No how. Put the pretzels down!

• The Zone delivery. A delivery service of three meals and two snacks a day that are balanced a certain way to provide the right ratio of proteins, carbs, and fats. Danger: Oftentimes, followers eat the meals and still go out for dinner after and wind up gaining weight (we won't mention any names, Karen!).

• Love. Falling in love is always a good way to slim down, because food just becomes less appealing and it's very hard to eat with those butterflies in your stomach. But be warned: Once you're in love and comfortable with your new man, pounds tend to pile up because you suddenly find yourself indulging in more dessert and forgoing the gym to spend extra hours in bed with your honey.

• Digestive enzymes from the health food store, which promote digestion, which speeds up the metabolism. Don't eat without taking two with water.

• Green tea. Up to forty-eight cups a day will give you a large dose of an ingredient called EGCG, which boosts the metabolism and, hence, weight loss. But that doesn't mean you can eat all the brownies you want.

• Yoga. No matter what kind of yoga you practice—Ashtanga, Bikram, Vinyasa, Anusara, disco (to the *Satuday Night Fever* soundtrack), doggie (that's yoga with your pet), couples (with your partner), aqua (in the pool), or any other hybrid—it's a great conversation topic with Gwynnie, Madonna, and the fashion editors at all the magazines. Fashionistas may travel to class in their leather pants and Manolos, but once barefoot on the sticky mat, they let go of the superficial and nurture their souls . . . for at least a little while. Just avoid the Gucci mat and the Marc Jacobs mat bag. We understand their appeal, but you'll be mocked in the yoga studio, frankly.

• Pilates. A great way to elongate and stretch your muscles; the supermodels love it.

• Ballet. Uptown ladies love ballet class, followed by a proper tea at the Four Seasons hotel before an evening at the theater.

• Boot camp. Fashionistas are so in control of their lives that being pushed around and forced to run like a crazy person, go a few rounds with the heavy bag, and do some serious push-ups is a nice change of pace.

- Saunas and steam rooms. These are essential.

- Tell your driver to park a few blocks from any destination. This will force you to walk and, consequently, add muscle to your calves.

- Shop in a rush. A mad dash to try on a dozen outfits while on a time crunch will give your abs a workout.

CHAPTER 6

Talking the Talk:
Gorge! Genius! *J'adore!*
Words to Live By!

Like any community of people whose members share many beliefs, world views, values, and recognized patterns of behavior, fashionistas communicate in a language all their own. Utilizing turns of phrase that are full of campy fun, our linguistic habits and insider lexicon enforce a feeling of intimacy, providing the important function of including or excluding others from the (luxury) fabric of our existence. By embracing the fashionista vernacular, you are embracing the entire lifestyle, celebrating a larger—and *très* chic—outlook on the world.

Our words are more forceful, emotive, and interesting versions of everyday terms. For us, language is a way of expressing our milieu, experiences, inspirations, and desires. It's a verbal form of a design, if you will. Like punks, ravers, bikers, and pagans, we are a subculture codified by our own particular brand of jargon and slang. Our expressions—and the way in which we pronounce them—define us, individuate us, and enhance our glamorous purpose and interests. Whether intelligently discussing technical fashion terms, which may sound like crazy, indecipherable convo to nonfashionistas, or paramount issues like cuff lengths, dress silhouettes, and the many, many different kinds of handbags, we speak our minds, with fashionable style.

We have developed and perfected our native tongue over time. Like a couture gown, our native tongue is a constant work in progress that has been perfected over time. Our communication patterns are the result of a long, involved history that flourished from our ancestry, the forefathers and -mothers of design, and the great icons and muses that have shaped our culture. This chapter is your key to talking the talk, learning buzzwords and proper lingo for all kinds of caps, capes, jackets, jumpers, tartans, pockets, shawls, waistlines, scarves, and seams. It is also an introduction to the stylish personalities who have shaped us—important designers from the past and the women who've inspired them (and fashionistas of all kinds). Just follow the guidelines below and you'll be a savvy, fashionable conversationalist, able to go round for round with Anna Wintour (editor in chief of *Vogue* and perhaps the ultimate fashionista) in no time.

WHAT THE HELL ARE THEY TALKING ABOUT?

Faking It!

✳ KAREN ✳

It was a typical Wednesday afternoon on the first day of spring in Nolita, a boho-chic neighborhood on the fringe of Little Italy and adjacent to Soho in New York City. The sun sprinkled on my shoulders as I pranced down Elizabeth Street, almost slipping on a small trail of doggie poop, which I'm sure was deposited by a toy Yorkie and his doting mommy, who was probably too exhausted after a day of modeling to clean it up. The hip downtown fashion girls—a pack of fashionistas with dyed dark hair, chandelier earrings, retro Pumas, bee-stung glossed lips, skinny arms toting large amounts of shopping bags and the occasional bright orange Hermès Birkin— gallivanted in and out of Tracey Feith, Jane Mayle, and all the requisite shopping destinations that are worth calling in sick from work to visit. Street vendors peddled fruit. And Ciao Bella unveiled their newest flavor of sorbet—"cosmopolitan" (no ID required to taste).

Life was sweet.

I stopped by a swank boutique to look for art books, which are sometimes the best fashion purchase (no matter what you look like, they're always flattering). As I flipped through gorgeously bound, newly released reads, I noticed that *David Bowie* (!) was standing next to me. I have always been obsessed and in love with him. I was dying. How to get him to notice me and talk? I wondered as I glanced at a book on the work of artist Tom Friedman. Suddenly, magic in my ears. The delightful British, throaty voice of David Bowie, Ziggy Stardust himself, purred in my auditory canal. "Is that the new Tom Friedman?" he politely asked. I wanted to jump up and down and shout "You're David Bowie! You're David Bowie! I love you!" But I played it cool.

"It *is* the new Tom Friedman. You know, he has an exhibit at the New Museum on Broadway right now," I said calmly, trying to impress him with my knowledge (thank God I had just read a piece on the artist in the *New Yorker* and was abreast of the situation). David got all excited. "Really? He's brilliant. Is the exhibit good, do you know?" he asked. I hadn't seen the show, but I didn't want my conversation with my idol to end just yet. Before I knew it, lies poured from my mouth (as if I had no control!): "Oh, it's genius," I screeched. "I just saw it. You must go!"

David smiled and eagerly nodded. "I definitely will."

There was a moment of silence. Was that it? I wondered. Was our love affair over? Then he spoke again, "His work is just so . . . pre-Memphis."

Pre-Memphis? I had no clue what the hell he was talking about. But I agreed. "You know, I never thought of it that way. But it really is. It's also very ironic and postmodern," I cooed as if I were some kind of seasoned art critic. He agreed—my sign to continue. "They have the toothpaste paintings and the pencil-shaving sculptures on display. Oh, and the toothpick piece is amazing in person," I boasted, thinking, *Thank the Lord I read that article in the magazine! Otherwise, I'd have no way to fudge a conversation along.* Ten minutes later, David and I shook hands and parted ways. We both bought the new Tom Friedman, which remains on display on my glass-and-chrome bookshelf, which is very Bauhaus (see Chapter Seven for Bauhaus reference in the art section).

Meanwhile, I stressed over what *pre-Memphis* meant for months. Did it have something to do with Elvis? Was it a reference to Graceland? What if he was just screwing with my head? I had no clue. I asked everyone I knew and came up blank. Months later I was still on a rampage to find out what this whole pre-Memphis thing was about. And an architect friend knew! Apparently, Memphis was a design movement in the early eighties in Italy, marked by bold shapes and colors, a reaction against minimalism. Memphis furnishings were fanciful, bright, wild, biomorphic in shape. Sort of like Tom Friedman's. But as David Bowie pointed out, Tom's work seems ever so slightly *before* Memphis (at least, that's what I told myself).

A few weeks later, I was at a friend's house and everyone was complimenting a sculpture in their apartment and I pretentiously remarked, "It's so pre-Memphis," just to see what kind of reaction I'd get out of my new favorite word. Everyone smiled and agreed.

Then someone piped up, "It's also kind of ironic."

Another joined in: "And postmodern, don't you think?"

I could only laugh to myself.

SOMETHING TO BUZZ ABOUT

A fashionista must be able to wield proper lexicon as smoothly as James Bond. The point of fashionista chitchat is to come off smart, informed, and fab, whether you know what you're talking about or not. Below, the best buzzwords and how to use them in a sentence.

• **Allan Schwartz** (v.): The act of totally knocking something off, copying it to a T. The phrase is inspired by designer Allen B. Schwartz, of ABS fame, who, after every major award ceremony (Oscars, Golden Globes), successfully rips off the best dresses worn by the brightest stars and then sells them in his boutiques a week later for one-sixteenth of the price. (For example: "Darling, are you wearing Versace or are you Allen Schwartzing?" Some may even just use "Schwartzing" for short; fashionistas hate wasting their breath using multisyllabic words.) Can also be applied to "Steve Madden," the once-imprisoned (tax evasion or fraud or something like that) shoe designer who knocks off whatever Prada and Miu Miu do.

• **Beyond** (adv., adj.): So much, used as an adverb to describe a verb. (For example: "I miss you beyond.") Also used as an adjective to stand for *gorge*. (For example: "That micromini sweater dress with lace is beyond.")

• **Birkin** (n., v.): A style of Hermès handbag that starts at a price of $4,000. The large, soft leather tote is named after actress Jane Birkin, and there are four-year-long waiting lists at Hermès stores around the world. Every fashionista's aspiration. (For example: "Daddy got me a Birkin for my birthday.") It can also be used as a verb, as in, "I just Birkined." Meaning: "I bought a Birkin."

• **Book** (n.): In the magazine world, book is a term that means *magazine*. (For example: "That piece on thigh-high boots in the front of the book was beyond.")

• **Collection** (n.): A body of work. The most common fashionista term for a season of clothing from a designer. (For example: "Halston is no longer doing regular RTW collections, but rather, couture fittings only.")

• **Couture** (adj.): People misuse this word often and throw it around casually in order to describe something that's major, but really it is a French word that describes original styles that are immaculately sewn, tailored, and expensive. Haute couture literally means "high sewing." And true couture clothing is not sold off the rack. Heavens, no! It is handmade—hours of manpower behind it—in an *atelier* (French for studio). Couture designers (Gaultier, John Galliano, Christian Lacroix, to name a few) show their collections twice a year—in the spring and in the fall/winter. A couture gown might cost upward of $100,000. (For example: "It took Lulu eight months of fittings to get her couture dress, but it is so major and beyond, it was worth it.")

• **D-list** (n., adj.): Far from the dean's list, it's actually a person or group of people who are in no way noteworthy. They cannot help you with your career. They often crash parties. They have no significant job and they tend to social-climb in search of the limelight. (For example: "Why would you go to a party in *that* part of town? It's so D-list!")

• **Edgy** (adj.): Modern, slightly off-kilter, forward, or futuristic, and razor-sharp in aesthetic or attitude—in the best possible way. Fashionistas use it to describe designers, outfits, interior design, DJs, CDs, films, or haircuts they can't quite explain, but appreciate. (For example: "I don't know what happened to Moby. He used to be so edgy.")

• **Fashion credits** (n.): Information about who designs what. Typically written in a small font and seen on the pages of a fashion magazine where fashion is being modeled, be it a full-on spread or in a celebrity shoot. (For example: "I am dying for those motocross leather pants, but I forgot to read the fashion credits to see who makes them.")

• **Full Gooch** (n.): Short for full Gucci outfit, head to toe. (For example: Girl 1: "I don't think she looks good tonight." Girl 2: "But she's in full Gooch!" Girl 1: "She is? Huh. Well, in that case she looks hot.")

• **Genius** (adj.): In fashion-speak, genius has nothing to do with one's level of intelligence. Instead, it is meant to describe something (an article of clothing, an earring, a newspaper report about rare goats in the Himalayas that yield a new kind of cashmere) in a positive—nay, incredible!—light. (For example: "The ruffles of that skirt are kind of genius.")

• **Gorge** (adj.): Short for gorgeous. (For example: "That Michael Kors dress! Gorge!") Fashionistas like to speak in short, fragmented words (it allows them to save their energy for other, more important things, like shopping), so you could also say "fab" for fabulous or "to die" instead of "to die for."

- **Hipster** (n.): A low-rise pair of pants (For example: "My hipsters give me plumber's crack when I bend down, but aren't they genius?"); also, one who closely follows the trends, keeps an accurate mental Rolodex of pop-culture references, and tends to wear all black. (For example: "Those cigarette-smoking hipsters at the bar think they're all that.")

- **Ironic** (adj.): The dictionary will report that the word means to express something different from and often opposite to its literal meaning, or an expression marked by a deliberate contrast between apparent and intended meaning. But fashionistas use it in the same vein as they do *postmodern*—to fudge their way through conversations and come off sounding intellectual, savvy, hyperaware. (For example: "What? You don't like my flat shoes? But they're so ironic!" See also, "postmodern.")

- *J'adore* (v.): French for *I love it* or *I love you*. (For example: "Did you see her Birkin? *J'adore!*") Note: Fashionistas love to use random French phrases, such as *très* instead of *very*, for no reason at all (i.e., "That boy is *très* cute. *J'adore!*").

- **JV, varsity** (n, adj): Used to describe or connote beginner and advanced fashionista style. JV is short for *junior varsity*. Varsity is when you are willing to push all the limits and flirt with the danger of looking serious style. (For example: "That outfit she's got on is so JV, but I dig the varsity accessories.")

- **Limo-to-lobby/lobby-to-limo** (adj.): A way to describe gorge garments and/or shoes that are not practical for anything other than show, meaning they would not be comfortable for anything other than getting out of a limo and going to the lobby (or restaurant, party, venue) and vice versa. (For example: "I got the sickest new shoes. I can't really walk in them, but they're made for sitting anyway. They're so lobby-to-limo.")

- **Line** (n.): Collection.

• **Major** (adj.): Beyond! Said with attitude and zeal, it is a way to express something so great, there is not even a word for it. (For example: "She wears Chanel heels to yoga. That is major!" or "Have you had the toro tartare at Nobu? It's major!")

• **Metrosexual** (n.): A way to describe straight men who are in touch with their feminine side, as evidenced by the care they put into grooming and dressing. They can use *Manolos* in a sentence. They tend to get manicures, expensive haircuts, and pricey beauty products. Also described as *fauxmosexuals*. (For example: "Ugh. My date went on and on about his cuticles and his new Gucci shoes. I'm sick of metrosexuals. Where are the real men?")

• **Model's own** (n.): Something fashion-related that belongs to the model. A phrase often relegated to fashion credits. It means that the model was wearing something that the stylist really liked; hence, it wound up in the pages of the magazine. Consumers, sadly, are not left with an inkling of where to find one just like it. (For example: "Silk ruffled butterfly dress with lattice lacing up the

J'adore Juicy!

side and corset hook-and-eye closures, $5,400, Dolce & Gabbana. Hat, $50, Kangol. Boots, model's own.")

- **Monograms** (n.): Initializing something by way of embroidery, engraving, or some kind of permanent mark. (For example: "We both have monogrammed Juicy sweats. They're major!")

- **MPW** (n): An acronym for manicure, pedicure, and wax. (For example: "Are you going for a full day of beauty?" "No, just an MPW.") Worth a note: We like to refer to manicure and pedicure as a "mani-pedi."

- **Muse** (n.): One who inspires a designer. She is stylish, chic, sophisticated, intelligent, artistic, and sometimes even on the payroll to do such meaningful tasks as change four, five, six times a day and make major announcements such as "I like red." A very good job to have, but not one likely to be listed in the classifieds. Muses are usually starlets, models, royalty, and social mavens. (For example: "Sofia Coppola has it all. She's such a sick filmmaker and she's Marc Jacobs's muse! So who cares if things didn't last with Spike Jones!")

- **OTT** (adj.): An acronym for *over the top* and used to describe things that are slightly outrageous. It can be a good thing, like high boots with a micromini vintage sweater dress adorned with lace and your grandmother's cameo, or it can be a bad thing, such as wearing way too many trends in one outfit, like a leopard trench coat with a leopard skirt, fishnets, thigh-high boots, a silky camisole, a leopard scarf, and a large hat. (For example: "Did you notice Halle Berry's perky breasts in the movie *Monster's Ball*? They're OTT." illustrates a positive use of the word. If we referred to a porn star's implants, we would be using the negative implication.)

- **Piece** (n.): Something you're working on, such as a drawing, a sculpture made of sugar cubes at a restaurant, an article, a play, a screenplay, or any kind of art (doodles on your jeans, a paper for your social studies class). A good word to throw around when you want to project an aura of creativity. It also makes for an excellent excuse when you don't want to do something (like go on a date with the loser your mother set you up with). (For example: "I would love to see you tonight, John, really, but I've been working on a piece and I'm on a roll. Maybe another time.")

- **Pink-collar job** (n.): You've heard of blue-collar jobs and white-collar jobs. Well, pink-collar jobs are those in the fashion industry. (For example: "Paul just landed the ultimate pink-collar job—head of PR for Ralph Lauren Men.")

- **Postmodern** (adj.): While the word correctly denotes artistic, literary, or architectural movements that challenge modernist principles, either by pushing them to extremes or by bringing back more traditional styles, fashionistas tend to use the term to refer to *any* new film, show, song, book, building, or piece of art (furniture, paintings, lightbulbs, shoes). The best use of the word comes into play during conversations relating to pop culture. Throw it out there when you have nothing else to say. (For example: "Oh, yes, I saw the new Madonna video. It's so postmodern.")
  At Shopsin's, a dive restaurant where fashionistas splurge on PB&J French toast sandwiches, there are "postmodern pancakes" on the menu, which are pancakes made with chopped-up other pancakes in the middle. Also see "ironic."

- **Product placement** (n.): The art of getting a product (a piece of clothing, a Diet Coke, Advil) seen in a high-profile way—say, in the background of a fashion spread, on film and television, or even at parties. There are people whose job is just to get products seen, but unless they're working for a top film-production studio, they won't make much money. (For example: "Did you see the Nokia phone in the *Charlie's Angels* movie? Talk about genius product placement!")

- **Showroom** (n.): A place of business where designers show their collections for PR and/or sales purposes. In Manhattan, the Garment District, an area of Midtown in the Thirties and Forties on or off Seventh Avenue, is where most of the showrooms are located. (To use in a sentence, try this: "I'm so glad she has a showroom in Soho. I'm sick of traveling to Midtown and Seventh Avenue.")

- **So 1995** (or any other date) (adj.): Used to describe something that is referential of a past season and, therefore, "over." But then isn't saying something is "*so* 1995," *so* 1995?

- **So good** (adj.): A synonym for *gorge*. It should never be used to describe food, only clothes and accessories. (For example, "Where did you get that ruched white shirt you wore yesterday? It was so good.")

- **So very John Galliano** (adj.): Something the designer himself likes to say when something epitomizes his work, which he once described as "something incredibly refined with something savage." (For example: "Saying it's 'so very John Galliano' is so very John Galliano.")

- **Stylist** (n.): Extreme fashionistas. They are in charge of assembling outfits for actors for film and television, as well as dressing models and celebrities for magazine fashion shoots, ad campaigns, glamorous parties, and everyday life. Prop stylists do the same but focus on furniture, knickknacks, and other related props for rooms, and background scenes. (For example: "You look so hot tonight. Who is your stylist?")

- **Walker** (n.): A gay man who accompanies a woman for the evening, typically for an event. Walkers make excellent dates. (For example: "Truman Capote was the perennial walker for high-society babes back in the day.")

TECHNICAL EXPERTISE

In addition to casual phrases, per above, it's vital to be fluent in scientific terminology of fashion. We recommend investing in *The Fairchild Dictionary of Fashion*. In the meantime, memorize these:

- **A-line:** Shape that starts narrow and flares away from the body in the form of the letter A. Originated by Christian Dior in 1955.

- **Asymmetrical:** Not symmetrical. Like that New Wave haircut you sported in tenth grade, where your bangs were long on one side and your head was shaved on the other. Typically applied to hem lengths and sleeves. Fashionistas love skirts and tops that are asymmetrical. Think one-shouldered tops and flirty dresses that skim the knee on one leg and the ankle on the other.

- **Bouffant**: Full-skirted dress shape whereby the bodice is fitted and the skirt is ruffled, poofy, or full. Can also be used to describe a big, OTT hairstyle, in vogue in the middle of the twentieth century.

- **Cape**: Style of outerwear that's sleeveless. The fabric is cut in a full circle. There are usually arm slits and an opening in the front. Capelet is a petite cape that looks great over evening gowns or a tank and jeans.

- **Chandelier earrings**: Large earrings that drape much like crystal chandeliers. A fashionista favorite, right up there with the hoop and door-knocker shapes. For the record, stiletto earrings hang straight down, mimicking a long skinny stiletto heel.

- **Charlotte**: A type of hat that has a very dramatic and large brim with lace ruffling around the edge. Very demure, feminine, country club, and—not surprisingly—the type of thing the character Charlotte would wear on HBO's *Sex and the City*.

- **Chignon**: An elegant hairstyle whereby a knot or bun sits at the nape of the neck or high on the head.

- **Clutch**: Not the small vertical thing that resides next to the gas pedal of a five-speed automobile. It's a sophisticated handbag style with no straps. Looks like an oversize wallet. An extra-long clutch is called an "envelope clutch" because it is reminiscent of an envelope.

- **Cowl**: A collar style involving fabric that drapes in a circular style.

- **Cut on the bias**: Originally made famous by Madame Gres, legendary French couture designer from the thirties. Cutting against the grain, rather than on the seams, so the garment moves easily, accentuates a woman's curves, and has, as John Galliano once said, the effect of making a dress become "like oily water, running through your fingers." A very flattering style for anyone size zero to sixteen.

• **Edwardian:** A style of clothing (fitted frock or suit coats, which are double-breasted, stiff-collared, and knee-length) that refers to the period between 1901 to 1910, when Edward VII was the king of England. Modern designers use fabrics such as denim to update the Edwardian frock coat.

• **Empire waist:** Named after the Napoleonic Empire's Queen Josephine, who liked her dress to have a tight bustline and a free-flowing body. Essentially a shapeless frock that's popular during pregnancy and looks good only on those with pixieish frames. Unless you look like Gwynnie, don't try this at home!

• **Fedora:** Hat with medium-size brim and a high crown with a crease that travels from front to back. Fabulous with suits and masculine yet sexy looks. A chic way to mask a bad-hair day.

• **Felt:** Not the past tense of *feel*. A kind of fabric made by packing wool and hair fibers together by way of heat and steam. A very comfortable and soft textile that works well as slippers, pants, and even rugs. (During one of the photo shoots for this book, Jean-Claude, our Dachshund puppy model, made a number two on Karen's felt rug. She was not pleased.)

• **Fisherman knit:** Chunky hand-knit sweater, typically in natural earth tones, with cables and fancy stitching. Be warned: It pulls easily.

• **Funnel neck:** An oversize collar that stands straight up and away from the face and may or may not have buttons, hook-and-eye closures, or zippers. Great for blocking wind or hiding from an ex you spot walking across the street with someone new. That bastard! How dare he get over you!

• **Gladiator sandal:** A flat sandal that has crossing straps that hold the sole to the foot and one wide strap around the ankle (may also lace up the calf). Great for very tall or slim-legged women in the summertime.

- **Jersey:** Not the smelly area south of New York (Karen's from there!), but a clingy knitted, flat fabric that is great for dresses.

- **Mandarin collar:** A short collar that stands up to only an inch or so above the collarbone. Unless they're Chinese, we do not like seeing men wear shirts with Mandarin collars.

- **Maxi:** While typically used to describe a coat that is ankle-length, it can also be used to describe a skirt length (also to the ankle).

- **Peplum:** Anything that flares from the bodice (waist). Can be found attached to a belt and on jackets and button-down shirts (very 1950s Dior).

- **Petticoat:** Not a coat that gossips with other coats, but a ruffled-up crinoline skirt that is worn underneath another skirt in order to provide a bouncy, full effect. Originally worn in the sixteenth century. Fashionistas wear them as is—with tank tops, denim jackets, and heels.

- **Poor-boy sweater:** Ribbed pull-on knit sweater with a crew or turtleneck. Very Faye Dunaway in *Bonnie and Clyde* (see Chapter Seven anecdote by Karen).

- **RTW:** Acronym for ready-to-wear, which are garments that are made so that they're ready to wear. Do not rent the Robert Altman film of the same title. It is a very poor illustration of the fashion industry and a disappointment to cinema and fashion aficionados.

- **Ruching:** Drapery wherein the fabric is folded many times over to add layering and visual interest. It is actually created by sewing through the center of pleating. Looks like a ruffled ripple effect. Ruching down the center of a top (between cleavage) is a good way to help enhance your waistline—or make it look like you have one.

- **Schmata:** Yiddish word for *rag,* often used to describe a yucky piece of clothing. "What are you wearing that schmata for?"

- **Shantung:** Silk textile with irregular strips of fabric emerging from the surface. Often mimicked in rayon and cotton.

- **Shawl:** A wrap, larger than a scarf, that drapes over the shoulders in a pretty, dramatic, old-world fashion. Very big in India.

- **Sheath dress:** Straight fitted dress that hugs the body just so. Jackie O wore many. Not to be confused with the shift dress, which, while straight, hangs away from the body.

- **Shirtdress:** A dress that looks a lot like a long button-down shirt. Often made sexy by pairing it with knee-high boots and a smart fedora.

- **Shortie:** Contrary to hip-hop slang, in which *shortie* typically means *hot girl,* it is actually a cropped, boxy jacket style originally popular in the thirties.

- **Tartan:** A plaid fabric. Worth a note: Different styles of plaids represent clans of Scottish heritage. Burberry has files of such tartans, and one can custom-order a kilt of kinship.

- **Trompe l'oeil:** Pronounced "trump loy," it actually means *fool the eye* and refers to a garment—pants, top, dress, coat—that has the image of buttons, a tie, a pearl necklace, or some kind of detail that isn't actually there. Mel's favorite T-shirt is a *trompe l'oeil* Chloe that appears to have a collar, buttons, and tie.

- **Victorian:** A romantic style of blouse with ruffles, puffed sleeves, lace trim, and sometimes corsetlike lacing, named after the period from 1837 to 1901, when Queen Victoria was in charge. Refer to Merchant Ivory mainstays, like *Sense and Sensibility* and *A Room with a View.*

- **Yarmulke:** A little hat worn by Jewish men. The Orthodox wear it all day, while others only for religious ceremonies. Karen's parents had red-and-purple leather "yarmies," as they're often nicknamed, for her bat mitzvah.

- **Zoot suit:** Men's style of suit from the forties, marked by a high waist, pleated pants that were tapered at the ankle, and an extra-long coat with wide lapels. Good for swing dancing and costume parties. Also looks cool with a pocket watch.

SOPHISTICATED ACCENTS!

Now that you have your vocabulary skills, we must work on these tongue-twisting pronunciations. Without the proper inflections and intonations, you will, regardless of what you say, look very JV (a nightmare for a fashionista). Your lessons, below.

• French designers whose names end with "on" should be pronounced as "uhhh," as in "Louis Vuittuuuhhhh." "Martine Sitbuu-uhhh." Warning: Don't try this with "French Connectiuuuhhh"!

• French words that end in "ier" are pronounced "eee-ay" with a strong *a* sound. For example, *atelier* is not "ateleer" or "atel-l-eerrr," but rather "ah-tell-eee-ay."

• Issey Miyake is said like this: "i-(soft *i* as in "it")-say mee-yah-ke." Not Issey as in the sound that rhymes with *sissy.*

• Versace: "Verr-sah-chie," not "Ver-says" or "Ver-say-sss." Refer to the poignant scene in the fashionista favorite bad film of all time, *Showgirls,* when Elizabeth Berkeley mispronounces the name of the prestigious Italian designer label. Of course, her character is meant to, which is the whole irony of the scene. But still.

• The design label Loewe is not "low," but rather, "low-ev-ay."

• Designer Moschino is pronounced "mo-ski-no," not "mo-shee-no."

• Hermès is not "her-meeez." It's "air-mez" with a hard s*i* that sounds like a z.

• Gaultier is "go-tee-ay." Not "gaul-teer."

• Italian words with "gn" in them (example: Zegna) are pronounced like the Spanish "nyuh" sound, as in "ñ." So Zegna is said like this: "zen-yuh."

• Byblos is "bee-blow-s."

• Gianfranco Ferré is said with a heavy accent over the last *e* such that it sounds like "ferr-ay."

• Etro is pronounced "ay-tro."

- Cesare Paciotti, the shoe designer, is said like this: "chay-sah-ray pah-chee-oh-tee."

- Nicolas Ghesquière is "Nee-ko-lah Ges-queer."

- Manolo Blahnik is often mispronounced, and one should be punished severely for that! The proper way is "muh-no-low blah-nick."

- Francophiling mainstream American products is totally acceptable, especially when done with a touch of sarcasm. For example, fashionistas like to pronounce Target as "Tar-zjay" in the French style, to give it an upscale little spin. The second syllable is pronounced in the same way as "Zsa Zsa" Gabor's first name and rhymes with tray.

ICONOGRAPHY
Ode to Tom Ford (Gucci, 1994–2004)
✳ A LETTER FROM YOUR ✳
TWO BIGGEST FANS

Dear Tom,

We are devastated that you're leaving Gucci and YSL. We are not stalkers. But we are obsessed with you. *Obsessed!* You are a genius, with an eye for fashion that will go down in history. When all is said and done, you have contributed more to the industry than any designer. For centuries, people will be talking about your creations, your art form, your all-black über-sleek aesthetic and business sense. You are a living legend, an icon of all icons. And that ad campaign with models who waxed their nether regions in the shape of a G? Good Lord! Fabulous! *J'adore!*

What you have done for the house of Gucci is groundbreaking. You took it from the brink of death and turned it into a multibillion-dollar behemoth, based on your vision of what is sexy and cool. You single-handedly turned the logo Gucci bag from faux pas to must, must, must. And you have had such a serious impact on our wardrobes, hence, our lives. We have become collectors of your pieces and catalog your most influential and noteworthy designs, from marabou shrugs and corset dresses in bloodred to hand-embroidered kimonos with sleeves that skim the floor, crystal-encrusted dresses with plunging necklines, thigh-high studded boots, and snakeskin-print pants.

It was 1995 when we first fell for you. You were just a boy with a dream then. And as Gucci was about to plummet into the obscurity of fashion past, you resurrected the brand name by taking over as creative director and sending stream-lined midnight-blue bootleg velvet pants and liquidy silken turquoise blouses, unbuttoned to the navel, down the run-way, along with patent go-go boots with toggles across the toes. We were smitten. So was everyone, actually. It was a newsmaking moment. "Gucci lives" cooed editors around the world.

We are not sure how we'll handle your departure. We don't know who could possibly fill your square-toed shiny shoes. And we're not sure if we'll ever be able to wear Gucci again. But we will forever treasure our relationship with you—and the blue satin skintight skirts, silver slingback heels, bias-cut dresses, and fringe-trimmed ponchos we wear in your honor. We'll miss you, Tom.

Much love,
M and K

DESIGNER DEITIES

Every fashionista must be familiar with the important designers of yesteryear who have made fashion history. Here's your crash course:

- **Alix Gres (pronounced "Gray")**. The French couturiere, originally a sculptor, began her career in the thirties under the name Alix Barton. During World War II, her business was shut down and she reopened it using her married name, Gres, after the war. Known for her craftsmanship, Grecian jersey gowns with crisscross belts, heavy drapery, bias-cut caftans, and bat-wing sleeves, she approached design as a true artist, focused on craftsmanship, shape, and form. Also known simply as Madame Gres.

- **André Courrèges.** Probably one of the most significant designers of the sixties, this is the man who made the swing coat, the little mod dress, the space-age look, and functional, architectural, simple silhouettes cool. Remembered for his all-white collections, minidresses with squared lines, tunics over skinny pants, flat Nancy Sinatra boots, industrial zippers, knee socks, and giant floral appliqués, he was the quintessential man of the mod cloth. Marc Jacobs's fall/winter 2003 line was very Courrèges, which was often worn by Jackie O.

- **Coco Chanel.** She revolutionized fashion. She began as a milliner in the early 1900s (her shop was financed by her lover) and by the twenties grew to become one of the most important couturieres. She is responsible for introducing jersey to high fashion and is the one who gave birth to the little black dress, sportswear, including short skirts, relaxed silhouettes, boyish flapper dresses, and pants for women (gasp!), a reaction to and probably indictment against the buttoned-up, corseted looks that restricted women's bodies. She was the originator of the Chanel look—quilted bags, lots of pearls and chains, the twinset, the wool suits with highly embellished details, gardenia pins, and slingback pumps. Chanel No. 5 was the first perfume to assume a designer's name. She was ahead of her time, though she closed her shop during World War I and relaunched her business during World War II. She became a very controversial figure due to her high-profile relations with a Nazi officer. She hated all forms of establishment, however. One of five children whose mother died at a young age, Chanel grew up impoverished and made a living at a young age as a cabaret singer before designing clothing, which she did because she couldn't find anything that she really wanted to wear. She was also the mistress of many wealthy men. A true Renaissance woman, she died in her chichi quarters at the Ritz Hotel in Paris. The only way to go.

- **Cristobal Balenciaga.** He got his design start at the ripe age of fourteen, when he made a suit for a rich *marquesa*. It got such rave reviews that the young boy left home to make it on his own in the design world. By the time he was thirty-two, he had his own thriving business in Paris, creating the crème de la crème de couture for the crème de la crème de society. He was known as the "master" for the immaculate way he cut, sewed, fitted, and designed a garment, and is credited with popularizing dramatic gowns, semifit jackets, cocoon coats, balloon shirts, flamenco-inspired evening looks (he was Spanish, after all), and the pillbox hat. Today, design prodigy Nicolas Ghesquière heads up the fashion design house, which was resurrected in the early 2000s.

- **Emilio Pucci.** Born to nobility in Italy in 1914, Pucci was a bon vivant—an Olympic skier, a fighter pilot, a designer, and a politician. He became popular in the sixties and was known as the mod genius, the purveyor of ultragraphic, boldly designed swirling prints that burst with fluorescent color. The jet set loved his clothes—all groovy dresses and little pants—and eventually his label grew to an empire that included leather goods, stationery, accessories, linens, lingerie. His vintage originals are collectibles, and recently his line was reborn under the creative control of Emilio's daughter, who has given new life to his signature art. Did we mention he was also a winemaker?

- **James Galanos.** In the middle of the twentieth century, Galanos became a hit with high-society ladies (who would never lunch!) for his exquisitely detailed, highly constructed evening gowns and cocktail dresses of heavenly silk crepe, divine beading, chiffon coats over luscious silk sheaths, and glorious flowing frocks. Remember the yellow vintage strapless number Renée Zellweger wore to some film premiere—and launched her to instant style icon status? It was a Galanos, purchased at Lily et Cie, as per the Shopping chapter. Nancy Reagan was his most famous client and wore a Galanos gown to her husband's inaugural ball.

- **Ossie Clark.** In the sixties and seventies in the arty experimental scene of London, Ossie was a cult designer, discovered by

British *Vogue* magazine. He designed with his wife, textile artist and muse Celia Birtwell, and together they lived a life as bubbly, party-filled, stylish, and extraordinary as the clothes they created, which were worn by rock stars (Mick Jagger) and models (Twiggy). He was big into snakeskin, cascading luxury fabrics full of life, and charmingly vivid and girly prints, immaculate tailoring, sharp trousers, flowing, loose-fitting coats and ruffled tops, mod A-line dresses and shifts, appliqués, and swinging silhouettes that were flirty and feminine yet strong.

• **Roy Halston Frowick.** Known simply as Halston, this dashing man, a fashion institution in the sixties and seventies, practically created the formula for simple classics, invented American style (cashmere dresses, sweaters over the shoulders, slinky chiffon jersey dresses), studied casual, and sexy gowns and dresses that were often worn at Studio 54, where the designer was known to linger into the late night with Warhol, Liza, Bianca Jagger, and Calvin Klein. A big entertainer, he was also famous for his lavishly cool Manhattan pad and being the ultimate in hosts. In the early eighties he sort of fell out of favor (could have been the line he designed for JCPenney, which is ironic, because today something like that is a successful business strategy and a way of funneling in millions to design houses) and eventually went out of business. The line was relaunched with various designers, including Randolph Duke, and is (at the time of publication) spearheaded by Bradley Bayou, whose dresses make a splash at the Oscars every season. Collect Halston originals from the seventies if possible.

• **Yves Saint Laurent.** The fashion world was aghast when Yves Saint Laurent (pronounced "eves saint luh-rauuhhh") announced his retirement in early 2002. His fashion career began as a seventeen-year-old boy, when he worked for design legend Christian Dior. After four years, he wound up taking over, and by 1961 he branched out and launched his own label, which focused on haute couture (for socialites and starlets) and an RTW collection that blurred the gender lines by bringing pantsuits into the mainstream and introducing the smoking jacket. He was also a staple in the

Studio 54 club scene and famous for his oversize glasses, which he was almost never seen without.

• **Elsa Schiaparelli.** A surrealist in the world of high fashion. She collaborated with Salvador Dalí, Jean Cocteau, and Alberto Giacometti. Elsa was born of Italian nobility. She was an innovator, who, together with Coco Chanel, dominated fashion between the two world wars. Most famous for her trompe l'oeil sweaters and the pink suit Jackie Kennedy wore the day of the assassination. (Most people think it was a Chanel; it was actually a Schiaparelli.) Grandmother to Marisa Berenson, the famous model and Studio 54 party girl.

• **Bonnie Cashin.** Her casual designs helped popularize sportswear and the layered look. Her designs included the "dog leash" skirt, ponchos, and roomy turtlenecks. One of the original designers for Coach, she created the oversize "pocketbooks" that have been knocked off by everyone from Marc Jacobs to Prada to Nine West.

• **Claude Montana.** He was born in 1949 in Paris to a German mother and Catalonian (Spanish) father. At an early age he traveled to London (1971) and began his career by designing papiermâché jewelry encrusted with rhinestones. He made his name by designing sexy leather motorcycle jackets that were must-haves in the 1980s. He designed haute couture for the House of Lanvin from 1990 to 1992, but was booted when his designs were considered too bold for the more traditional Lanvin customer. Montana, who greatly admired Madame Gres (1910–1993) as a couturiere, specialized in strong colors, monochromatic fabrics, and lots of leather and wool. His classic and structural pantsuits feature razor-sharp tailoring and strong silhouettes with dramatic proportions. Our idols, Simon Le Bon and Nick Rhodes of Duran Duran, wore his jackets in the eighties.

• **Norman Norell.** Norman David Levinson, born in Noblesville, Indiana, changed his name to Norman Norell after moving from New York to study fashion illustration at the Parson's School of Design. He worked briefly as a costume designer for the

Astoria Studio of Paramount Pictures at age twenty-two. For the next thirty-one years, Norell led American fashion. In 1960, Norell's name alone appeared on the label when he became the sole owner of his company. Norell became known for his understated simple wool dresses with a high, round neckline, sequined cocktail dresses, and sailor motifs. His classic clothes were worn by his clients, such as actress Greer Garson, with a great devotion to the Norell aesthetic.

HOW A-MUSE-ING
Haute Heroine
✳ KAREN ✳

In the fall of 2003, Liz Collins, an up-and-coming designer who has become famous for doing sexy knits with peekaboo holes and loose stitches fused with tight stitches, crochet lace, body-loving silhouettes, and an eighties rocker-chick kind of punk MO that hangs in the closets of Sarah Jessica Parker, supermodel Devon Aoki, and Mariah Carey (to name a few), sent me an e-mail with a JPEG of a black knit bikini encrusted with Swarovski crystals and a built-in belly chain that wraps not once, not twice, but three times around the midsection. "I thought of you when I made this," she wrote. Gulp. Why would that make her think of *moi?* I could never pull that kind of thing off. "Not with my love handles," I wrote her back.

"It just has such a sexy vibe, and with your crazy hair and fierce personality, I think you're the only person who could pull it off," she replied, adding that the entire inspiration for her collection—a chiffon-heavy line full of Marilyn Monroe–style dresses with tight-knit bodices and graceful royal-blue skirts imprinted with big white stars, crazy superhero capes, micromini knit dresses with webbed sleeves, red knit swimsuits made for jumping over buildings and hopping into the invisible jet—was Wonder Woman. Action-hero chic more intense than kryptonite.

Liz and I first met a few years earlier while I was buying one of her pieces—what she deemed a "pimp daddy" fur-trimmed sweater coat. It was love at first sight. We instantly bonded as I strutted around the boutique in her fabulous creation. "It's so you," she shrieked. And we exchanged e-mail addresses on the spot, vowing to become friends. So, about that bikini. Liz was doing a big art project, in which twenty women she thought embodied the spirit of Wonder Woman would be photographed in one of her designs, hair and makeup artists included. "Just bring your sense of power," she said, asking me to be one of the chosen few. I was flattered, beyond! Me, a muse? Of course I would do it. We set a date. I didn't think about what wearing a knit bikini encrusted with crystals would actually mean at the time I agreed to do the shoot. (It means being photographed in a knit bikini encrusted with crystals!) And when Liz and her crew—makeup artist/pixie goddess Shyanne (that name!) and photographer Monika Merva, a Chelsea-based artist known for her documentary-style work that has been featured in *Nylon, Details, Interview,* and *Surface* (see www.monikamerva.com)—showed up at my apartment with my wardrobe—a teeny, itsy-bitsy black bikini (not even full briefs, mind you, but a skimpy Brazilian kind) and glimmering diamond-like silver crystals, hanging perfectly in a garment bag, I thought I might vomit.

I held it up between my forefinger and thumb, as if there were something horribly wrong with it. "This is what I'm supposed to wear?" I mean, it was the fiercest thing I ever did see. But not for my body! Sadly, I had no choice. The makeup was going on my face (insanely gloppy mascara and smoky, smoky shadow with clear shiny lips), and Monika was thinking about the lighting in my apartment as she threw my white Mongolian fur pillow on the floor (my prop). I swallowed my pride. No time to be shy. I put on the swimsuit, along with black patent knee-high Dolce & Gabbana four-inch-heeled boots. Sha-*zam!* (Luckily, I had just returned from We Care and was a bit slimmer than usual.)

I slithered on the floor, trying to flaunt my best angle (whatever position I could find that would allow for sucking in the gut and camouflaging problem areas with strategic hand placement). "Holy sexpot!" Liz said. Monika stood on a stool to shoot me from above, which tends to make for flattering shots. She did a few rolls in color and a few in grainy black-and-white for a sort of porn-chic mood. Between breaks I jockeyed phone calls (with headset), while sitting at my desk (in a far cry from my usual work attire) and felt very glad that I had yet to eat lunch.

Oops! I forgot the headband!

When it was all said and done, I didn't even want to put my real clothes back on. Between all of the flashes of the camera and Liz loving how the whole thing looked, I felt, I must say, as cliché as it sounds, like Wonder Woman. I stopped being so self-conscious and embraced the moment. So what if my body isn't anything like that of Kate Moss? Who cares if I'll never look like Heidi Klum? The real Wonder Woman, per the 1940s comic (not the television show starring Lynda Carter) was not a skinny Minnie. She was strong. She had meat on her bones. She had biceps, developed quads, and battles with the Duke Mephisto Saturno of Saturn. She kicked butt in knee-high red stiletto boots. She had no time to worry about little things, like how her legs looked in those hot pants. So why should I? I'm Karen Robinovitz, dammit! If only I had the Amazon bullet-deflecting cuffs to match!

THE INFLUENCERS

A muse's whole job is to inspire not just a designer, but the general public. Her every move and natural way is so alluring, so intoxicating, so becoming, so fetching. She's the type of person who stops traffic and makes an entire room stare (in envy, lust, and awe). They are image makers and trendsetters. Meet the women fashionistas emulate the most:

• **Babe Paley.** Born Barbara Cushing in 19_? (who knows . . . a real muse must never reveal her age, darling, but she was considered the ultimate glamour girl from the fifties up until her death, due to cancer, in 1978), she was known simply as "Babe" to her friends. She was not born into high-society money, but her mother groomed her to marry well. She did: first to a Mortimer and then to a Paley, who was the chairman of CBS. Her jet-set life involved a billion-dollar art collection, traveling by yacht, an editor gig at *Vogue* in the forties,

Babe Paley. What a babe!

many, many homes designed by the famous Billy Baldwin, cocktails with best friend Slim Keith (see next page), and a close tie to Truman Capote, who later betrayed her by hardly masking her as a character in one of his biting books about the high life. She wrapped scarves around her purse handles; didn't cover up her gray hair; mixed couture with loads of cheapie jewelry; ensconced herself in sable; donned Bill Blass, Oscar de la Renta, wide-brimmed hats, ruby-red lips; and kept her skin milky pale at all times. As flawlessly beautiful and chic as she was, she was also riddled with insecurity and marital problems. No one, alas, has it all. No matter how perfect their lives seem in pictures.

• **Baby Jane Holzer.** A rich-girl actress type who was probably Andy Warhol's greatest starlet (she was in lots of his underground flicks) and got her nickname from a journalist at *Women's Wear Daily.* Andy did a screen test (a.k.a. short film) of her unwrapping a stick of gum and brushing her teeth (who knew such mundane tasks as oral hygiene could be so damn sexy?). With her huge eyes and even huger flaxen-colored hair, Baby Jane was *the* vixen bombshell of the sixties, who wore go-go boots, microdresses, Pucci, Pucci, Pucci, and hung out with the Rolling Stones, art world wunderkinds, and the social mavens on the old-family-money circuit.

• **Diana "Never mind about the facts; just project an image to the public" Vreeland.** Ah, Diana! Such an eccentric, you were: The fashion editor of *Bazaar* for twenty-five years, editor in chief of *Vogue,* and ambassador to the Metropolitan Museum of Art's Costume Institute, she is perhaps one of the reasons fashion has come to the forefront of our society. She actually believed people who ate white bread had no dreams. Superskinny, with a worn face, clownish nose, and small, squinty eyes, she was considered unattractive, yet the matriarch of chic and style. Couture designers gave her wears for free because on her body they laid perfectly, and she was the ultimate marketing machine for chic, a walking advertisement for any brand name. She called her life neither fact nor fiction, but "faction." And she was a spitfire of fashion words of wisdom. She used to send her entire office important memos with demands like: "more gray," "get models with thicker eyebrows," and "find poor Arabs in Greenwich Village to make belts." Her personality was powerful, strong, magical, smart, intense. And her impact on the fashion front will last forever.

• **Talitha Getty.** The Bali-born top seventies model married oilheir Paul Getty and embraced the glamorous jet-set life, traveling the world, living it up at her palace in Marrakech, and perfecting the nouveau-riche hippie, boho style with everything from patchwork caftans with jeweled necklines and capri pants to YSL. She was beautiful and rich, but damned. She suffered from depression and a nasty drug habit and eventually overdosed in her pool in Marrakech—in a fur coat. The yacht, *Talitha G.,* once owned by the Getty family, remains one of the most decadent in the harbor and is charterable for upward of $100,000 per week.

• **Slim Keith.** Some women are born into their fortunes; others earn them the old-fashioned way: They marry them. Lady Slim

Keith fell into the latter category. Born Nancy Gross in Salinas, California, by the age of twenty-two she had already appeared on the cover of *Harper's Bazaar*. She graced the best-dressed list almost yearly, and was the first private citizen to receive the Neiman Marcus Fashion Award. This award was usually given to designers, or to honor someone who has made an impact on fashion. Her three husbands included Hollywood producer Howard Hawks, Broadway producer Leland Hayward (who showered her with jewels and sable furs), and Sir Kenneth Keith. Her best friends were Babe Paley and Truman Capote. Babe and Slim shared an interest in fashion and a mutual devotion to the same charities, which ensured their lifelong friendship. In the 1970s Slim lost both her best friends. Babe, an inveterate smoker, died of lung cancer; Truman was banished from Slim's life after using her as the main character in his book *Answered Prayers*. Though her name was disguised, anyone who knew her could see in an instant just who "Lady Ina Coolbirth" was. Though he tried several times to beg her forgiveness, Slim never spoke to Truman again.

- **Tina Chow.** Half Japanese, half German-American, she started modeling as a teen (and did so sporadically her entire life), but it wasn't until she moved to New York in the early seventies and became a Warhol-circle regular that she elevated to bold-face status. Chow loved fashion and amassed a legendary collection of vintage clothing. Manolo Blahnik and Antonio Lopez were among her closest friends. But it was her innate skill at pared-down elegance that made her an icon: sleek, clipped hair, minimal makeup, a daily uniform of white T-shirts, black Kenzo trousers, and maybe one of her bamboo-wrapped crystal jewels. As Yves Saint Laurent said, "fashion fades; style is eternal." She married Michael Chow of Mr. Chow's and partied with the Hollywood set—her boyfriends included Richard Gere. Her daughter, China Chow, is also a fashionista.

- **Edie Sedgwick.** During the mid-1960s, Edie Sedgwick was the constant companion of pop artist, sixties icon, and filmmaker Andy Warhol, and played a part in his early success. Edie became famous in New York as one of Andy Warhol's "superstars," dazzling everyone with her beauty, style, glamour, and wealth. "She was a very bright and well-spoken young lady, having a penchant for shopping." Edie purchased everything from only the very best stores in New York, including glamorous clothes, as well as considerable quantities of makeup and those huge, shoulder-dusting earrings she made trendy. She managed to spend a large amount of her family inheritance. The Sedgwick family included a number of relatives who played a part in early American history. Edie helped transform the Factory's reputation into a place to be seen for all New York's wealthy socialites and trendsetters. During the period from 1963 until 1965, Edie was featured in leading magazines such as *Time, Life,* and *Vogue.*

• **Jackie O.** First she was Mrs. Kennedy, in demure Oleg Cassini gowns and white gloves. Her husband declared himself, "the man who accompanied Mrs. Kennedy to Paris." She had a whisper-soft voice and a Vassar degree. Born to the WASP-y Bouvier family (her father, "Black Jack" Bouvier, was a handsome, rich rascal), she was a Miss Porter's (a chi chi boarding school) girl and a style icon. She married Aristotle Onassis, one of the richest men in the world, and her Capri uniform of bandanna, oversize sunglasses, and cutoffs is still worn today. She was an editor at Doubleday and lived the rest of her life with her companion, Maurice Templesman. She lived the adage: First you marry for love, then money, then companionship.

CHAPTER 7

Cocktail Fodder: What to Read, Watch, See, and Do to Chic-up Your Schtick!

Now that you look like a fashionista and you talk like a fashionista (isn't life swell?), it's time to embrace the full lifestyle, which means spiffy invitations to major events, parties, dinners, dances, balls, galas, and charity benefits, and keeping up on hot new trends across the globe. (You'll be able to say things like "Did you know that the return of pigtails as an acceptable hairstyle for adults was brought on by Tokyo Street fashion?") Being a fashionista actually means being able to focus on things other than fashion. A healthy obsession with the work of architect Frank Gehry is a perfect example, as he is responsible for the whimsical cafeteria in the Condé Nast headquarters in Manhattan, the Guggenheim Museum in Bilbao, Spain, and the Walt Disney Concert Hall in Los Angeles. The occasional religious movement (Kabbalah, anyone?) and exotic travel destinations, whether you can afford to go there or not, are also hot topics.

Whether you're at your glamorous best friend's wedding or one of Puff Daddy's OTT birthday extravaganzas, you will need to show people that you've got more in your head than just cotton (or clothes). Welcome to your crash course in fashionista literacy and traditions. That means films, magazines, books, music, and all sorts of dialogue-stimulating things to do and topics to discuss intelligently to a discerning circle of irreverent fashion-following friends and acquaintances.

The thing about fashionistas is that they appreciate fashion as something that's more than just fabric you put on your body to look good. A true fashionista sees fashion as an art form that extends to an appreciation and reflection of high design, popular culture, society, political issues, architecture, ethnicity, and art, all of which conjure specific moods and emotions. Witness Yves Saint Laurent's Mandarin smoking jackets, inspired by a trip to the Far East. Innovation can also be found in Helmut Lang's forward-thinking trench coats, wherein loops were attached to the inner armholes so that the coat could be worn over the shoulder as well as in the traditional manner; that year he also showed jackets with puffed nylon built-in-neck-roll collars—perfect for the fashionista's jet-set lifestyle, an inspired combination of form and function. Then there's Nicholas Ghesquière at Balenciaga, who changed the silhouette by rediscovering the waist and giving women a new way to reimagine their bodies.

While sometimes designers can go too far beyond the acceptable line and into politically questionable taste (French designer Jean Paul Gaultier's 1989 collection that recalled Nazi uniforms—models marched the runway in black combat boots, harnessed coats, felt helmets—and John Galliano's 1997 show for Christian Dior that displayed garments made of deconstructed wire, newspaper tatters, and found objects, inspired by the homeless he used to spot on his morning jog come to mind), fashion at its best does not simply lie in the cut of the garment, but serves as an intelligent, savvy reflection of our times.

In the nineties, a new breed of boutiques began to sell everything from avant-garde designer wares to glossy books about Buddhism and Zen, as well as home accessories and compilation CDs from world-respected DJs; and host gallery-quality art exhibits.

There was a need for the kind of cross-cultural diversity that feeds hard-core shoppers, who care about trends and inspirations that transcend whatever the pant leg of the moment is.

You may be able to impress fellow fashionistas by your knowledge of which designer is now heading up which couture house, but to take your lifestyle one step further, you need to know your pop-culture references, your French techno from your deep house music, your Godard from your Truffaut, your Mies van der Rohe from your Richard Meier, and your Cabo from your Cuba.

THE FASHIONISTA FILM ARCHIVE

Fashionistas thrive on films that showcase fashion, or movies that are overdramatic and laughingly bad—as long as they have style. Below, the essential films with short capsule synopses. We point out the "fashion highlight moment" (FHM) and how to use them in conversation to earn "bonus convo points" (BCP) for each.

Classics from the Attic

1. *Breakfast at Tiffany's*—The end-all to fashionista films. A story of a small-town girl en route to big-city style and glamour, starring Audrey Hepburn, a goddess in classic trench coats, black cocktail dresses, and pigtails while it's raining.

- FHM: When Audrey is digging around the bottom of her bed, looking for her shoe, and cries "Alligator!" Also when she puts on the big black hat with the white scarf.
- BCP: Read Truman Capote's original novel, and bemoan the happy Hollywood ending of the movie. Tell your captivated audience that Capote had wanted Marilyn Monroe to play Holly Golightly. He saw the character as grittier, sexier, and more vulnerable.

2. *My Fair Lady*—The original *Pretty Woman* guttersnipe-to-glamorama transformation story.

- FHM: The black-and-white checkerboard dresses during the Ascot race scene.
- BCP: *My Fair Lady* is inspired by George Bernard Shaw's play *Pygmalion,* which was in turn based on the Greek myth of . . . you guessed it, Pygmalion.

3. *The Graduate*—Erotic story of a young, innocent college grad, played by Dustin Hoffman, who's unsure of his life path, and in his attempt to find himself, he instead finds sensual sex lessons with an older woman named Mrs. Robinson, his mother's friend. Then he falls for Mrs. Robinson's lovely daughter.

- FHM: The bride in her wedding dress on a bus to nowhere.
- BCP: Katharine Ross also starred in another fashionista fave, *The Stepford Wives*. And anytime an older woman is with a younger man, you can refer to the seductress as Mrs. Robinson, making a clever allusion to the classic film.

4. *Rear Window*—A psychological thriller about one man's obsession with his neighbor, who he suspects is a murderer and whom he watches through his apartment's rear window.

- FHM: Two words: Grace Kelly. When the polished, cool beauty pulls a nightie out of her tiny Kelly bag—all she needs for the evening.
- BCP: Jimmy Stewart was the only one of Grace Kelly's costars whom she allegedly did *not* sleep with. And anytime you want to indulge your inner spy (like when the guy you're dating suddenly turns to you and says, "I can't tell you what I'm doing because I don't want to put you or other people in danger"), you can say you're not in the mood to star in your own Hitchcock drama.

5. *Shanghai Express*—A dramatic love and war story that takes place on the Shanghai Express during the Civil War. Stars Marlene Dietrich.

- FHM: Dietrich's bold feather-embellished bolero jacket, fishnet veil, and sleek black leather gloves . . . for the office!
- BCP: Marlene Dietrich is the most famous of the sapphic fashionistas. Yes, girls, she was a lipstick lesbian.

6. *Rosemary's Baby*—A dark, creepy, mysterious, otherworldly Roman Polanski–directed piece, starring Mia Farrow, about a young couple living in Manhattan. Rosemary's husband makes a deal with the devil to get his acting career off the ground—and uses his wife as the pawn.

- FHM: Mia's perfect bone structure, those darling baby-doll dresses, and the first time she reveals her new pixie haircut while having a nervous breakdown. Manic chic!
- BCP: During the film, Mia Farrow's character loses it. Her psychotic episodes seem so real. And that is because they were. Those scenes were filmed during a difficult, tumultuously emotional time for her—when her real-life love, Frank Sinatra, dumped her. Also, he reportedly hated her haircut.

7. *Butterfield 8*—A classic melodramatic love story, adapted for the big screen from John O'Hara's novel about a call girl (Elizabeth Taylor) with a sketchy past ("I was the slut at all times," she purrs) and a wealthy, unhappily married lawyer.

- FHM: Elizabeth Taylor at home in lingerie and high heels, with a cocktail.
- BCP: The film brought Elizabeth her first Oscar—and she didn't even want to take the role in the first place, but had to in order to fulfill her contract with MGM. Her Oscar nod turned her into the first $1-million-per-picture actress, which was what she was paid for her next role as Cleopatra, which bombed.

8. *The Mod Squad*—Three fabulously dressed and shagalicious people get in trouble with the cops, and to save their butts they go undercover to stop crime.

- FHM: This is where Austin Powers got his inspiration. Space-age microdresses with opaque tights and all that was late-sixties cool.
- BCP: Although the fashion is slammin', it really wasn't that great a film. And the Hollywood studios really shouldn't have wasted their money to back the remake, which starred Claire Danes. It was more abominable than the first—and even the style department didn't cut it.

Contemporary Flicks with Elaborate Wardrobes

1. *Clueless*—A frothy coming-of-age tale of love and high school in Beverly Hills, starring a well-dressed Alicia Silverstone as a trendoid teen named Cher.

• FHM: There are many: 1. Cher's two-story automated closet and computer "matching" program. 2. When being held up at gunpoint and asked to lie on the ground, Cher cries, "You don't understand. This is an Alaia. He's, like, a totally important designer!" 3. When she's going on a date in a tight white slip dress and her father yells, "Cher, what is that?" She says, "A dress." Dad says, "Says who?" She whines, "Calvin Klein."

• BCP: The aforementioned Alaia dress was donated to one of those Hollywood-theme chain restaurants. The aforementioned white dress was actually a Vivienne Tam. You can also remark on Alicia's heavy animal-rights activism and the fact that it's the only thing she seems to talk about. Move on to character-assassinate Jennifer Love Hewitt—just for fun.

2. *Unzipped*—Documentary on a season in the life of neurotic Jewish flaming fashionista designer Isaac Mizrahi.

• FHM: The bandannas in his hair, the moment he confesses to his mother that he was obsessed with her daisy shoes when he was a little boy, and supermodel Linda Evangelista whining backstage about having to wear flats and then complaining, "My feet hurt and you don't caaaare. . . ."

• BCP: Astound everyone by telling them *Nanook of the North,* the film on which Isaac Mizrahi based his collection, was not a real documentary, per se. Some scenes (like the one where the Eskimo family eats the seal raw) were deliberately staged.

3. *Pulp Fiction*—Postmodern comic-book hipster fairy tale about drugs and violence.

• FHM: Uma Thurman in a black wig doing "the Batman"—the dance step that originated in 1966—with John Travolta. Also, her flat silver shoes.

- BCP: Show them your "Bad Motherfucker" wallet.

4. *Flashdance*—A rise-to-stardom tale of a hot steel-welding small-town girl who becomes a modern dancer . . . and the man who believed in her all along.

- FHM: When Jennifer Beals rips off her tuxedo jacket and reveals nothing but a slinky halter top, a bow tie, and Playboy bunny–style cuff links, while she seductively sucks meat out of a lobster tail. Thought we'd say that sweatshirt, didn't you?
- BCP: The loft Jennifer Beals lives in was the inspiration for "shabby chic."

5. *Legally Blonde*—Elle Woods, a seemingly stupid blonde with a heart of gold, played by Reese Witherspoon, goes to Harvard Law School to get her man back . . . and finally discovers who she really is.

- FHM: Elle and her Chihuahua, Brewster, in matching outfits; Elle and her marabou feather pen taking notes on a heart-shaped notebook the first day of class; Elle dressing as a Playboy bunny for what she thought was a costume party (and making the best of it when she realizes it was a joke to make her look stupid). Oh, we can go on.
- BCP: The movie was based on Amanda Brown's novel, which wasn't published until two years *after* the movie was a blockbuster! Also, the film that established Reese as a bona fide $12-million-per-picture leading lady.

6. *Down with Love*—An ironic love story/period piece starring Renée Zellweger as the blond bombshell who wreaks social havoc by publishing a culture-shocking book about how women don't need love and can have sex like a man—with no emotional ties. Many twists and turns and hilarious moments ensue.

- FHM: The entire duration of the film! It's styled to perfection, from the set (Renée's "adorable" pink palace of an apartment epitomizes midcentury modern design) to her lady-like dresses and matching coats, hats, and gloves.

• BCP: It was a very underrated film that truly marked a significant time for women in society. It also pays homage to the romantic comedies that Rock Hudson made with Doris Day in the late 1950s and early 1960s—*Pillow Talk, Lover Come Back,* and *Send Me No Flowers.* And that Ewan Mc-Gregor sure is yummy!

Foreign and Indies

Foreign and indie flicks are a favorite of fashionistas because they are usually shown in small, out-of-the-way art cinemas (or art houses, as they're aptly called) in obscure neighborhoods and frequented by a similarly groovy, fashion-minded, pseudo-intellectual crowd.

1. *The Umbrellas of Cherbourg*—Jacques Demy directs a twenty-year-old Catherine Deneuve in a sad-happy French musical.

• FHM: When Catherine as Genevieve sings of her love for a lowly garage mechanic. (Mom was right—it's just as easy to fall in love with a rich man as it is a poor man.)

• BCP: Catherine Deneuve was a muse of Yves Saint Laurent and never missed one of his shows in twenty years.

2. *Breathless* (*À Bout de Souffle*)—Jean-Paul Belmondo and Jean Seberg in the best nouvelle vague film of all time.

• FHM: Jean-Paul's black leather jacket. Jean Seberg's nautical-striped boatneck shirt.

• BCP: Tell everyone how you hated the Richard Gere version, which is a perfect segue for discussing how Travolta was a fool for not taking *American Gigolo* and how he hasn't done a decent project since *Pulp Fiction.* Move on to bash Kevin Costner, who hasn't had a decent picture since . . . who can remember?

3. *Blowup*—Michelangelo Antonioni's film of fashion and murder and the sexy David Hemmings as a camera-clicking lothario.

Grainy, gritty, documentary-like production set in swinging London. Supermodel Veruschka plays herself.

- FHM: Zipping through London in David Hemming's Aston Martin.
- BCP: It's rumored that *Blowup* was based on the life of the late fashionista shutterbug Francesco Scavullo. Also, Vanessa Redgrave was scorchingly fierce. You can sound smart by talking about how doing a British film was a nice departure for the Italian filmmaker, who went on to do *Zabriskie Point,* which featured a soundtrack from Pink Floyd.

4. *La Dolce Vita*—Fellini's tale of dissolution and despair centering on the world of a gossip columnist.

- FHM: Anytime Anouk Aimée and Anita Ekberg appear in a scene.
- BCP: Tell everyone you're writing a modern-adaptation rock opera of *La Dolce Vita* based on the reporters from Page Six.

5. *Party Girl*—Parker Posey as the early-nineties answer to Edie Sedgwick.

- FHM: When she steals a Chanel suit at a party.
- BCP: The film makes reference to the Greek myth of Sisyphus, which is such a postmodern and ironic story. Then you can say that it's a shame that Parker Posey never gets to demonstrate her diversity as a performer. In every film she seems to play the same role, no matter if it's a blockbuster like *You've Got Mail* or a small piece, like *Best in Show.* Then you can imitate Parker's manic-bitch-cheerleader routine from *Dazed and Confused.* ("Fry like bacon, you freshman bitches!")

6. *Hedwig and the Angry Inch*—Rock opera about a transsexual who suffers from a botched sex-change operation and a broken heart.

- FHM: Every scene! Denim hot pants, bustiers, stilettos, glitter lipstick and eyeshadow, and Farrah Fawcett hair that just won't quit. Oh, and we love Hedwig's red paint–splattered fur jacket and when he freaks out on his bandmate, who has the audacity to stupidly put a bra in the dryer.

- BCP: *Hedwig* started as an act John Cameron Mitchell would perform at the notorious gay nightclub Squeezebox. He also wrote and directed the film. You can talk about the difficulties of being a cult indie artist and how it's a shame that Mitchell's work will never achieve the status it truly deserves.

The Pedro Almodóvar Oeuvre

Pedro Almodóvar is the much-celebrated, Academy Award–winning Spanish filmmaking genius, who writes, directs, produces, composes, and sometimes acts. His work, no matter how twisted, loopy, dark, perverse, and sensual, embodies all human emotions and issues everyone can relate to. And he portrays women in a beautiful, powerful light. They are all strong, multileveled, psychologically complicated, semitortured, and fighting some kind of demon and conflict, physically or mentally, that they inevitably surmount. He loves drag queens, gays, alcohol-infused moments of giddy delirium, deviance, flamboyance, and the dark underbelly of society, the mind, and sexuality. His film *All About My Mother* is what got Penélope Cruz the kind of attention that turned her into an international starlet. Plus, we love his big, crazy hair and wacky wardrobe. And he had Antonio Banderas playing gay men long before the actor mainstreamed himself by doing *Philadelphia* with Tom Hanks.

Rent his greatest hits:

- *Tie Me Up! Tie Me Down!*
- *Women on the Verge of a Nervous Breakdown*
- *High Heels*
- *All About My Mother*
- *Live Flesh*
- *Talk to Her*

BCP: Pedro, who left home at sixteen to pursue his dream of filmdom, used to draw X-rated comic books, wrote the memoirs of an imaginary porn star he called Patti di Phusa, and performed in a transvestite punk-rock band in his wild, early teenage years in Madrid.

The Baz Luhrmann Oeuvre

This eccentric Australian film director, known for his quick editing style, postmodernist pop-culture play, and elaborate sets and costume designs (created by his wife, who is, of course, his ultimate muse), is the mastermind behind three joyous fashionista favorites:

• *Strictly Ballroom*—One man and his dream to be the number one ballroom dancer of Australia and the ugly duckling he turned into a dancing swan—who taught him a trick or two. Wacky. FHM: The tiered cancan dresses and major panty flashing.

• *Romeo + Juliet*—The classic Shakespearean love story set in modern-day Los Angeles with a hip-hop sound track. Full of guns and Prada clothing. FHM: Claire Danes in a fluid white gown and angel wings.

• *Moulin Rouge*—The postmodern parade of love and music. The "Elephant Love Medley" alone, which combines U2 with Paul McCartney and Jimmy Sommerville, is sooo good, it's genius! And that "Like a Virgin" number! It's beyond! FHM: Nicole Kidman's eyebrows, which do the best acting in the movie.

Worth a note: Baz turned the classic opera *La Bohème* into a Broadway production in New York City, set in 1950s Paris. Baz's wife created the multimillion-dollar set. The singers, a revolving cast of six leads, were sexy and young (read: not old and overweight). And there were subtitles. David Bowie, Iman, and Adrien Brody were spotted (by us) during one of the show's previews.

BIG-SCREEN FASHION
Bonnie, Clyde, and a Babysitter
✳ KAREN ✳

I was in eighth grade when I was first truly inspired by the power of cinema. *Flashdance* was all the rage. Jennifer Beals provoked an

entire nation to cut up their sweatshirts and bust out the leg warmers. I had already been through my wanna-be-Olivia-Newton-John
phase (even though Mom wouldn't let me take on the vixen-in-
spandex look of the "You're the One That I Want" number). But
those were flash-in-the-pan moments. While the off-the-shoulder
sweatshirt and the vinyl catsuit left an indelible mark on fashion's
greatest hits, the trends those two starlets spurred were just that—
trends. It was fashion, not *style*. But I didn't know any better. Until
one fateful night, when I was sleeping at my friend's house and her
older brother, a long-haired, AC/DC-loving, ripped-jeans-wearing,
mustache-sporting, blond hottie all the girls had a crush on, was
forced to babysit us (it was some sort of punishment for skipping
school).

He wanted nothing to do with us. We hung out in my friend's
room for the most part. But the television blared so loudly from the
living room, along with his random electric guitar riffs, that we had
to see what he was watching. "Go away," he barked as we approached the sofa. "Can't we watch with you?" his sister begged.
Some kind of argument ensued, but he finally agreed to share the
common area of the house as long as we didn't say a single word or
ask one question. The film: *Bonnie and Clyde,* something I'm sure
my parents would have deemed too violent for my young, impres-
sionable mind.

Between scenes from random crime sprees across America's
heartland, I was mesmerized by a retro-looking Faye Dunaway. Her
elegance. Her perfect lips. Her hair. Her tough-girl attitude. Her
poor-boy sweaters, tweed skirts, and berets! Good God, she was
amazing. I wanted to look just like her. The next day I pilfered
cable-knit sweaters and scarves from my mother's closet and paired
them with wool skirts and berets and newsboy caps, thinking I was
all that. I fantasized that my friend's brother was a fedora-wearing
Clyde and that together we robbed 7-Elevens of Fun Dip and Jolly
Ranchers. I wouldn't wear anything unless I could imagine Bonnie
in it. I was fascinated by 1930s fashion and a slightly dangerous,
rebellious, yet glamorous lifestyle that was unlike anything I knew
about in my small suburban town, where the wildest thing I had

ever done was sneak outside at three A.M. with a friend to puff on a cigarette on the front lawn and borrow my mother's clothes from time to time without her permission.

To me, *Bonnie and Clyde* was the epitome of cinematic drama. I didn't even care what the film was about. It just represented such style and excitement, a life I craved. Until I saw *The Breakfast Club*—and started wearing a long brown skirt, riding boots, and a pink T-shirt, and bringing sushi to school every day.

Sid and Nancy *and Me*
✳ MELISSA ✳

The most miserable time of my life was my freshman year in high school. I suppose it couldn't get any worse—in addition to the culture shock of having moved to the United States from the Philippines, I was awkward, overweight, and had terrifically bad hair. I didn't have any friends. There was no hope of a boyfriend. To compensate, I became obsessed with the Sex Pistols.

Three skinny, dirty guys from England in the seventies who sang foulmouthed music, spit on their fans, did too many drugs, and vomited onstage! What was not to love? I was especially enamored of Sid Vicious, the misunderstood heroin addict and bass player. Like Sid, I fancied myself tortured, misunderstood, and very, very angry. Of course, I still made straight As and never even gave my parents a hint of trouble. While some of my cousins were sneaking around, climbing out the window and meeting their boyfriends, I was in bed by eleven, and spent all my free time reading.

When my best friend, Corrine, and I went to a Cure concert (Robert Smith was also tortured and misunderstood), we dyed our hair pink and silver. My dad drove us to the concert and picked us up afterward. We were rebels who relied on parental transportation! Corrine and I eagerly awaited the release of the Gary Oldman movie *Sid and Nancy.* When it came out, we walked the few blocks down to the Fillmore Theater and watched it with rapt attention. I remember the full-zipper pants (the zipper went all the way down Johnny's crotch and up his butt), the plaid pants, the ripped

T-shirts, the studded leather bracelets, the studded belts. I even coveted Sid's hospital gown. It was so cool, hanging off his shoulders. I was infatuated with Nancy Spungen's dyed canary-yellow hair, torn fishnets, and beat-up motorcycle jacket. I remembered the gash of red that passed for her lipstick. It looked like it hurt. I also liked the fact that unlike Sid, she had meat on her bones. She was nowhere near skinny.

I must have seen *Sid and Nancy* five times that month. Every time I felt blue, I escaped to 1970s England, and in my dreams I, too, was a whacked-out speed queen with a zonked-out punk boyfriend. That summer I sent away for the first of many Sex Pistols T-shirts. My favorite was a gory one with Sid's mug that said "Don't just sit there, do something. Kill somebody, kill yourself." I felt dangerous even just *thinking* about wearing it. It felt good.

JOAN AND MELISSA RIVERS NEVER STOOD A CHANCE
The Ultimate Spectator Sport
✳ MELISSA AND KAREN ✳

Nothing's as fun as watching the pre-Oscar red-carpet runway show. It's the Super Bowl of fashion, and true fashionistas never turn down a chance to show off their chops. That is, by playing Guess Who Designed It with a roomful of friends as an audience. During the 2000 Oscars, the two of us held court as the supreme arbiters of style.

J.Lo arrived in a see-through pearl-gray chiffon and satin ball-gown. "Versace," Mel said knowingly.

"Totally," Karen agreed.

She was followed by a beaming Catherine Zeta-Jones in a black beaded number. "It's got to be a Lacroix!" Karen yelped.

"But of course!" Mel nodded.

The next day we found out that la Lopez was actually wearing Chanel, and Mrs. Douglas was in Versace. God knows how many more dresses we got wrong! But it was fun to play Mr. Blackwell as we shared our appreciation for each other's (we thought at the time) innate knowledge of designer styles. Guessing-the-designer is a fashionista pastime most fashionistas indulge in with other fashionistas. Try it! It's fun!

DONATO SARDELLA/WWD

Bjork, the quirky fashionista always carries an egg-shaped purse when wearing a swan.

As for our Oscar 2000 gown-guessing game, we both were certain obscure designer Bernard Wilhelm was responsible for Björk's swan song. We shouted Bernard's name in unison and gave each other high fives in what we thought was a true achievement in the Oscar fashion watch! Especially because Bernard is the type of eccentric designer heralded only in *very small*—and *very varsity*—fashionista circles. "Bernard who? How do you know that!" everyone marveled.

We just shrugged our shoulders and sighed. "Occupational hazard." We wound up being wrong (obscure designer Marjan Pejoski actually designed it), but boy, was the room impressed at the time!

STYLE PAGES!

Do fashionistas read? you may wonder. Well they like to flip through pages, certainly. Books make nice decorative objects, and fashionistas like to collect oversize, glossy coffee-table books about art and design, and off-the-beaten-path, hard-to-find, esoteric magazines.

High Gloss

While *Vogue, W, Elle,* and *Bazaar* (as well as the UK versions of each) are a part of the required monthly fashionista reading agenda, we are also inspired by more offbeat, underground magazines that represent countercultures—an artful world of innovative photography, undiscovered designers, untapped talent of all kinds, as well as serious fashion and trends, which are shown in an ultramodern light with a touch of irony. These magazines—the more esoteric, the better—are great conversation builders and give insiders something even more insider-y to talk about. The titles to read—or sprawl out on the coffee table—include:

• Arty fashion books that are a platform for grassroots talent as well as established bigwigs. Get *V* (the magazine version of *Visionaire*), *Dazed & Confused, Spoon,* and *Big.*

• Bulky magazines that showcase innovative, edgy photographers. Get *Purple, Face, I-D, Arena.*

• For a delicious mix of cultural events, gallery exhibits, insanely cool design, and the latest and greatest products from around the country, buy *City* magazine, *Art Forum* (though the specialty here is obviously art), and *Flaunt,* which is much like an art book in itself.

• Vintage magazines of any kind, especially *Vogue, Bazaar, Playboy,* and *M,* which is the now-defunct men's version of *W* that was published by Fairchild Publications, publisher of *WWD* and *W,* which are now owned by Condé Nast, the behemoth that publishes *Vanity Fair, Vogue, Allure, Self, Glamour, The New Yorker, Lucky,* and more.

• Any funky Japanese or Eastern European magazine, typically found in serious, highbrow fashion outlets like Colette in Paris and avant-garde boutiques all over the world.

• Groovy home-design "books" like *Dwell, Nest,* and *Wallpaper*,* which is known for ultra-art-directed decor shoots styled much like fashion shoots in environments that have been curated to perfection.

Note: We also love our tabloids. Aside from guilty pleasures like *US Weekly* and *Star,* the British mags like *Tatler, Hello!,* and *O.K.!* keep us posted on the fashionistas from across the pond.

SHELF LIFE
From A to B and Back Again
✳ MELISSA ✳

Sometimes I feel like New York is a party that I arrived at too late. I moved here in 1989 and I feel like I missed out on everything. When I moved to the city, Studio 54 was over, Liza was in rehab, and Andy Warhol was already dead. Why else do people move to New York except to worship at the temple of Andy? The man who had his wig cut at the hairstylist's? The man who tape-recorded all his conversations? Who made the Polaroid a must-have at any party?

My favorite book of all time is Bob Colacello's biography of Andy Warhol, *Holy Terror: Andy Warhol Up Close.* While I tried to be one of those people who were able to slog through Andy's bitchy diaries ("Bianca Jagger: major body odor, cab fare to Mudd Club $12"), I was too intimidated by the size of that manuscript. It was a doorstop. I found my copy of Bob's book in a remainder bin, for $2 (the bargain hunter and the Andy fan in me cheered). I brought it home and devoured the whole thing in one sitting. The book's philosophy is one that I still adhere to in life.

For instance, Andy, the perennial celebrity-hound, was always excited whether he was meeting the queen of England or the queens from Fourteenth Street. He treated everyone with the same "gee-aw-shucks" manner. He was starstruck and a social climber. But he never let it get in the way of his fun or his true grit. While he wallowed in the glitzy New York nightlife, he lived with his mother all his life.

Andy was a true fashionista, with a signature look, a flair for self-parody, and a desire to go out every night. I carried that book like the bible it was. It still makes me nostalgic for a New York I never experienced.

BOOKED SOLID!

Here's your guide to giving your library an air of sophistication:

• Any photography book by Helmut Newton or Richard Avedon, two of fashion's old greats. Will add luster to your shelves. It's a classic fashionista must-have. Fake-sign it and say you got it on a shoot.

• *Hotel LaChapelle*—David LaChapelle's seminal photographs of transsexuals, errant teens, and bloody naked models partying. Will make you come off as perhaps a little naughty. You can also say you adore Amanda LePore, his "trannie" muse (she's so pre-Memphis!).

• *Visionaire*—The premiere status fashion book that comes out four times a year and is always accompanied by something gimmicky (i.e., a Louis Vuitton satchel) and guest-edited by famous fashionista icons such as Philippe Starck, furniture designer extraordinaire, Tom Ford, and Karl Lagerfeld, and is full of contributions from the greatest artists, photographers, writers, filmmakers, and creators of the day. Extraordinarily expensive, therefore good. It comes out in limited numbers, so having one will earn you varsity status (don't worry—you can buy one online). Each book is more of an art piece, collectible in its own right, and completely ironic, postmodern, genius, gorge, and beyond. A fashionista favorite: The Vreeland Memos no. 37, a compilation of Diana's memos during her tenure at *Vogue*. Karen gave this to Mel as a present to celebrate this book deal, and the two of us gave it to our fabulous literary agent for her fiftieth birthday.

• A typography design book. Fashionistas really like fonts. When asked, say something like "Graphic qualities of letters can be very inspiring."

• *The Harvard Guide to Shopping*—It will give you a fab pretentious edge. It's important to know that this tome was written by seminal Dutch architect Rem Koolhass, who designed all the new Prada stores and is a creative consultant for Condé Nast.

• Diana Vreeland's autobiography, of course. Who else will tell you "try to be born in Paris if you can arrange it," wild stories about Jack Nicholson (true or false is really not the point), and gossip-drenched tales of models, designers, and the goings-on at *Vogue* magazine, where she was editor in chief. To put it in her vernacular: We really do think she's marvelous.

• Any book that includes Andy Warhol photos. The oversize *Andy Warhol Catalogue Raisonne Volume 01* is the best.

• *Fashion Today*—Collin McDowell's enormous book, part style guide, part historical overview, that takes you from Christian Dior's 1947 collection to the current media-embedded industry that fashion has become and meanders through all of fashion's major trend phases and eras along the way. Also his highly graphic book entitled *Manolo Blahnik* (subject self-explanatory).

• The collected works of Truman Capote, one of America's most masterful writers. The author, who always dressed eccentrically, was controversial in his day (1940s and 1950s) for writing about homosexuality, and through the early eighties, served as a literary It boy, avid glam-life consumer, and party circuit regular. The character Dill in *To Kill a Mockingbird* was actually based on the author's childhood friend. Don't feel pressure to actually read these, but do feel pressure to show them off.

• At least one pretentious collection of pages, like Julien d'Y's *Slipcase,* a slipcase that contains four booklets designed like travel books. It includes Polaroids, poetry, sketches—the hairstylist's way of paying homage to the beauty of women and travel. Each is numbered and signed by Julien, who's tricked out the tresses of Naomi, Kate, Amber, and Linda Evangelista. Limited edition.

• A book that immortalizes Japanimation or graffiti art. Fashionistas like to get inspired from "the street" and all sorts of quirky places.

• *Nota Vene Destination Review*—Typically available by subscription only, it's the indie (authors travel anonymously and accept nothing for free) luxe travel guide to the world's most glamorous cities and the best shops, hotels, and restaurants therein. A hallmark for fashionistas who adore travel, even if it's only in their minds.

• Vintage books about fashion, style, lifestyle, design, architecture. Good places to source such things are estate sales, auction houses like Sotheby's and Christie's, garage sales, and the Internet. In your search, it's perfectly okay to judge a book by its cover—you probably won't really read it anyway.

• *How to Become Famous in Two Weeks or Less*—Written by us! A comic, sly, witty, part memoir, part self-help-infused social commentary depicting the zeitgeist of a culture where anyone can become famous just by being famous. (Sorry! We couldn't resist!)

Chic tip: In a bookstore and can't remember what to get? Pretty much anything published by Taschen and Phaidon, who tend to release the most artful, postmodern (and often ironic) books that, while pricey, evoke the fashionista sensibility.

TURN THE BEAT AROUND
Everyone's Talking About Pop Music
✳ MELISSA AND KAREN ✳

It's official. Fashionistas don't always have the best taste in music in the world. Exhibit A: Here's what we packed for a road trip with our boys.

- Culture Club: *The Greatest Hits*
- ABC: *The Look of Love*
- Clay Aiken: *The Measure of a Man*
- Lionel Richie: *Dancing on the Ceiling*
- Air Supply: *All Out of Love*
- Madonna: *The Immaculate Collection*
- Erasure: *Circus*
- Justin Timberlake: *Justified*

Todd and Mike took one look at our CDs and said, "No way!" There's something about simple pop music that fashionistas gravitate toward. While we profess to love the latest jungle trip-hop or French lounge music in public, in private it's all about Shakira. Top 40 music is happy music. We did the lambada. We dig the Macarena. We live "La Vida Loca." It's the best music to sing along to and to get dressed to. When we put on Britney's "One More Time" or Madonna's "Get into the Groove," we feel ready to meet the world in our crazy outfits and uncomfortable shoes.

In college Mel blasted her Billy Joel collection so loudly that she once found an anonymous rude Post-it note taped to her door, complaining about her lack of musical taste. ("If you persist in playing bad Top 40 tunes, at least have the decency to turn it down!")

No chance.

But we did let our boys off the hook and listened to Coldplay during our trip. Hey, we've learned to compromise.

A List of the Kind of Music That Will Impress Others and Reveal Your Expansive, Worldly Taste

• *Buddha Bar Compilation*—A groovy mix of acid-jazzy lounge-lizard tunes with a touch of hip-hop. Buddha Bar, FYI, is a trendy Parisian lounge where Kate Moss downed many a complimentary glass of champagne. Good for cocktails at home and smoking fags out the window while writing in your journal.

• *Café del Mar*—A series of sultry, downtempo, jazz-infused tunes from Ibiza, a favorite fashionista travel destination and the home of fashionista Jade Jagger.

• *Costes la Suite*—Mixed by Stephane Pompougnac, acclaimed French DJ: Hotel Costes is a five-star French hotel patronized by celebrities and royalty. A smart selection for hanging up a new piece of art you just bought. Get any CD mixed by Pompougnac.

• *Room Service, the Standard Hotel Lounge Compilation*—A chilled synthesized cocktail of horns, midnight soul, jazz fusion, and lazy drum and bass. The Standard is Andre Balazs's hip Los Angeles hotel. And the CD is conducive to hot makeout sessions.

• ABBA—Seventies disco lite at its finest. The best thing to come out of Sweden since meatballs. Play it when depressed and you need to connect with your inner dancing queen.

• Junior Vasquez remixes—A favorite of flaming fashionistas and drag queens who did lots of drugs and partied at the Limelight in the eighties and Sound Factory in the nineties. Cue it up with your flaming fashionista friends who like to indulge in drugs that start with the letter X.

• Aimee Mann—Dreamy, sad, girly melodies for when fashionistas feel the need for more "earnest" music. Used during Yves Saint Laurent's fall 2000 runway show. Good for contemplating unrequited love ("Save me").

• Peaches—British pop-tart punk rocker who sings naughty lyrics, introduced to fashionistas during Luella Bartley's runway for spring/summer 2000. Perfect for moments when you need a dose of female empowerment—or to kick some butt. Also, very invigorating music to listen to when you're cleaning out your closet.

• *Best of Blondie*—"The Tide Is High" reminds fashionistas of their hoary collegiate days when they were prefab (prefabulous). A nostalgic choice that works well when getting all dressed up (even if you have no place to go).

• Air—Sexy French techno. Used in Sofia Coppola's *Virgin Suicides* sound track. Especially good during sensual sessions of fashionista sex, which may not be that sensual at all (fold and hang the clothes, please, before the action begins).

• Tones on Tail—Fashionistas who grew up in the suburbs as misunderstood goths favor this Bauhaus offshoot. To be played after worshiping the Wicca goddesses of the night.

• The Smiths—Fashionistas who grew up in the suburbs as misunderstood geeks favored Morrissey's claim of celibacy to camouflage their own not-quite-out-of-the-closet status. A wise choice to listen to while cutting or dying your own hair.

- The Sex Pistols—Anarchy is sooo good. Johnny Rotten is major. But does the music have to be so loud and ugly? Only play when you want to break something.

- David Bowie, the earlier years—A mainstay for any record collection. Some things never ch-ch-ch-change.

- *Hedwig and the Angry Inch* sound track—See film. The two of us have had many dancing-around-the-apartment, belting-out-a-song moments, with John Cameron Mitchell, who starred in the original play and the movie.

Note: Always look for compilation CDs from top boutique-chic hotels (you can get those online at the hotel Web sites) and high-profile stores around the world. Imported CDs are most impressive, even if you're standing in front of your mirror and dancing by yourself. Another important fashionista musical accessory: a friend who's a DJ. If you don't have one, get one. This person will make you great CDs to enhance your repertoire.

THE GALLERINA VERSUS THE FASHIONISTA
Gucci Shoes or a Painting? Such Decisions!
❊ KAREN ❊

If there's anything fashionistas like as much as clothes and fashion, it's art that references clothes and fashion. There seems to be a budding trend in the fashion industry of insiders giving up the latest Balenciaga in favor of a painting, a photograph, a lithograph, or some kind of art piece that will endure for more than a season. I have always loved museums and big-name galleries where the work starts at $100,000, and it was only in the last few years that I realized there was a world of emerging artists whose creations are actually affordable. So it was sort of ironic when I bought my first real piece of art in the fall of 1999.

I was in Paris for Fashion Week for work and falling in love with many, many things I could not afford to buy (no wonder it's the city of romance): suede Dior gowns, Chloe blousons, Chanel logo boots, and one particular Dries Van Noten sequined gold skirt and dramatic pink silk short-sleeved top with an oversize asymmetrical tie. Strolling through Onward, my favorite store on St. Germain in the Sixth District, the Parisian equivalent to Greenwich Village, for what must have been the one hundredth time, I noticed something new: an art exhibit called "Beautiful People" by a fashion illustrator named Miguel.

Each piece was an affected study of long-limbed lovelies wearing modern-day collections from the current fall season. There was Chloe, a vapid-looking blonde, sitting in an empty loft space wearing Chanel. Dandy was a gay man, decked in Prada, leaning against a purple Cappellini sofa. Ginger, the journalist, wore fishnets and red plaid Vivienne Westwood, looking up as if in thought, while smoking a cigarette in a dark, dingy bar. Baby was a pouty blond bombshell in black-and-white houndstooth Galliano against a bubblegum pink backdrop. Three Viktor & Rolf American-flag-button-down-shirt-wearing women cruised the countryside driving a Cadillac convertible. The details were inexplicably fashionista. A champagne bottle wearing a red-patent Gaultier lace-up corset, the perfect red tag on the bum of Levi's jeans, a big-haired tall woman donning a Gucci animal-print fur coat with a leather tie in a living room full of Minotti Italian furniture.

I was in love with all of them. Especially Marisa, an ethnic woman with a fierce snarl, an elegant chignon, a long black cigarette, toenails perfectly painted in Chanel's Vamp, slender fingers, smoky eyes, and the Dries Van Noten ensemble I so desperately wanted. She was $500. Only $400, really, because I was able to get the VAT (European for tax) back at a later date. That's a fraction of the price of the Dries outfit, which I would have, undoubtedly, gotten sick of anyway. I thought about her for days, imagining her against the brick wall of my apartment.

Marisa flew home with me and I look at her every day, thinking, *God! It's so much better to buy something like art, which appreciates in value and lasts a lifetime, instead of a skirt or top or pair of shoes that I'll either trash or get sick of very, very quickly.* (Usually it takes no more than three wearings.) Yes, I still get my fashion fix, as proven by a recent trip to the YSL outlet in Palm Springs, California, where I picked up a sharp jacket that ties with a grosgrain ribbon, a fishnet-sleeve-and-satin black top, and a sophisticated sweater with a square neckline and necktie, but I didn't get the heavily stitched corset, black leather pointy shoes with leather ankle straps, and winter coat that I wanted because I thought, *Hmmm . . . that money might be better spent on something more substantial, like a figurative painting, reminiscent of a sexy old-school movie, from Don Doe . . . or a porcelain sculpture of a revolver by Brooklyn up-and-comer Susan Graham . . . or a graphic Lisa Ruyter painting of an acidic social crowd smoking and sipping cocktails in equally acidic hues. . . .*

Art. It may just be the new little black dress. And call me crazy, but somehow buying it seems a lot less superficial.

ART OFTEN REFERENCED IN FASHION

• **Pop Art.** During 1950s and 1960s, it's a movement that references consumer culture and everyday life in a graphic, colorful, almost cartoonlike style. Leading artists: Andy Warhol (most known for Campbell's soup paintings and blocks of famous people with different background colors), Roy Lichtenstein (oversize comic book–like paintings), Keith Haring (all common things like hearts and simple drawings of colorful people, surrounded by sprouting lines meant to represent energy), and Robert Rauschenberg (magazine photos of current events turned into silk-screen prints, overlapped with paintbrush strokes).

• **Bauhaus.** A modernist school of thought founded in 1919 in Weimar, Germany, by Walter Gropius, it integrates expressionist art with fields of architecture and design and was insistent upon being accessible to all socioeconomic brackets. Later, it was led by architect Ludwig Mies van der Rohe, who's known for clean, sleek homes with stark glass that blend internal and external environments. Also, Mies van der Rohe is the creator of the ubiquitous Barcelona chairs. Bauhaus work is simple, functional, and often involves industrial material like steel, chrome, glass, and concrete. If something is affordable and clean, even utilitarian, proudly declare its Bauhaus roots.

- **Expressionism.** To portray a subject matter in an emotionally charged way in which the artist sees it, rather than the way it is commonly seen. Leading artists: Wassily Kandinsky (1905–1940s), known for abstract intersecting shapes and sharp colors; and Jackson Pollock, known for splatter paint, which has often shown up on runway dresses (though he is considered to be among the abstract expressionist movement, whereby artists between the forties and sixties expressed themselves strictly through use of color and form).

- **Neoplasticism.** A Dutch movement marked by Piet Mondrian, famous for rigid abstract shapes, horizontal and vertical lines, and a limited color palette. Yves Saint Laurent brought Mondrian's work into mainstream fashion by referencing it in a series of mod dresses in 1965. L'Oréal knocked it off, too, for an ad campaign. You know, the graphic one with yellow, red, and black squares? Side note: Can also be used to describe plastic-surgery addicts who look *très* plastic.

- **Minimalism.** A style of art that's stripped down to its most basic form and shape. Leading artists: Ellsworth Kelly and Frank Stella, known for rectangular stripes and hard-core geometry. In the fashion world, minimalism is about basic shapes, stark colors, and clean modernism. Donna Karan and Calvin Klein specialize in this form.

- **Arts 'n' Crafts.** Similar to grade-school class, this is all about celebrating individual craftsmanship, which came about as a backlash reaction against the industrial revolution in Britain in the late nineteenth century. Textiles, stained glass, wallpaper, and things that have that "handmade at home" feeling were prevalent. Designers like Parkinson reflect this sensibility, as do raw-edged pieces, handmade unique fabrics, and patchwork.

THE CULTURATI
Feel Like Making Art
✳ KAREN ✳

At a swank party at the Paramount Hotel in Manhattan, I met Michael COLAVITO Hoiland, a long-haired photographer and painter with intense dark eyes. I had heard of him before, as he was shooting a big book for the NBA, using light infusion and abstract paintings in the work. He has done work commercially for Tiffany & Co., Sony, H.Stern, and the Gap. But in the art community, a discerning, often precarious place where haughty attitude reigns and critics shoot scathing comments like snipers, he is respected and admired—a feat for any artist.

His pieces, ironically, are the epitome of postmodernism. Imagine an enormous silhouette of a woman. You can't make out her face. But you can tell she has a certain kind of haircut and just how her nose is shaped. You can make out her body, her shape, her size. But instead of the creamy tone of her skin, her figure is filled with a sea of Gauguin-like heavy brushstrokes, a gorgeous wash of colors from an original painting or linear arrangements of rich hues. Serious art, his large pieces sell for over $100,000.

When you look at his creations, especially when they're blown up to thirty feet long, you can't help but be aroused. The women in the shots are sexy, portrayed in such a beautiful light. It's not about T & A, gratuitous body parts, but rather the form and composition of a figure and how it relates to its space. His pieces are also intriguing. It's hard to tell what his medium actually is. Is it a portrait? Is it a painting? It's like, as hard as you try, you can't quite figure out how he created it. He takes a photo of his paintings or sculptures, which are then fused with his photography. He shoots with an eight-by-ten-view camera—the kind that looks like an accordion—and, like a cartoon, uses it while covered with a black cloth. A purist, he does not use filters, computer images, or any shortcuts in his art, which is created entirely in camera on one original piece of film.

After I had been chatting with him for a few minutes, he asked if I would ever sit for him. I was floored. A typical female who often struggles with self-esteem issues about her looks, I thought, *What are you, on crack? What could* you *possibly see in* me? I blew him off, I have to admit. I figured it was the champagne talking. He pursued me for months. Well, actually, his girlfriend, who knew me through a mutual friend, did. "Michael really wants to shoot you," she kept saying. I still didn't quite believe he remembered me clearly. Had he, he certainly wouldn't want to shoot me! Not with these thighs and the belly that tends to protrude a little too much for my liking.

Finally, Michael and I sat down for lunch. He whipped out boxes of eight-by-ten chromes, original negatives of his work. They were breathtaking. Modern and yet classical, sexy without trying too hard. The women who posed for him were nude, but you could see nothing more than the outline of their bodies. After my trip to We Care, when I was feeling pretty darn good in my skin (and my jeans), I threw caution to the wind and scheduled a session with Michael, whose work was currently being considered by the Guggenheim. I figured, if anything, posing for him would be an excellent self-esteem boost.

I went to his studio, a stark space with big windows and nothing but enormous paintings, blowups of his painting/photography pieces, sculptures, and one crazy old-fashioned-looking supersized camera. There was a white backdrop waiting just for me. "Now what?" I said, wondering what I should do, knowing full well that the first thing I needed to do was disrobe for his camera. He, luckily, is very respectful, far from a gawking guy who uses art as a means to pick up chicks. He made concerted efforts to look only at my eyes as we spoke. And he talked lovingly about his girlfriend, probably his way of easing my mind.

When I stripped down, I was a nervous wreck. *What if he looks at me and thinks,* "Naah . . . too fat," *and asks me to leave?* All of the typical insecurities that go hand in hand with being naked with a man came to mind. *Ugh, my stretch marks. My hips are too big. Could this be considered cheating on my boyfriend?* I wondered. At the same time, I really wanted to be there, to be a part of his art and something that lasts a lifetime and has deeper meaning than a great red jersey dress from the Celine cruise collection (even though I really want a great red jersey Celine dress from the cruise collection!).

I moved around on the cold white backdrop, thinking about what would be the most flattering position, wondering what in the hell I was doing naked in a studio in the first place. "Don't move. Stay just like that." I was trying to figure out how to pose and he caught me between postures—while I was on my hands and knees, wondering what to do. "Look down. Move your left hand a few inches to the right. Put your fingers closer together. And shift that left leg back a little farther." I listened to his instructions and the way he talked to himself as he buzzed around the camera, making sure everything was set and in order. "Michael, don't lose this shot. Put this on eleven. No ten. Change the light. Catch that shadow. Get her feet in frame," he mumbled to himself. And then he said, "Final focus." From the corner of my eye I caught him inserting a large black cartridge (film for his art) in the camera before he took a snap. We did a similar version of the same pose. And two others. The whole thing lasted thirty minutes, during which time he made not a single comment about anything other than the fact that the shots would be gorgeous. I didn't even have time to feel all of my neuroses about being undressed in front of a man I didn't really know.

The short moments of being there, however, were great for my (often fragile) ego. "Beautiful. Great. Just like that. Oh, my God, that's amazing and gorgeous," he'd say as he looked into his lens (which he had to do while standing on a chair and flipping his head upside down because the camera inverts the image).

Soon after, he sent me on my way. "That's it?" I asked. "Shouldn't I do more?"

He apparently got everything he needed. I walked away, thinking, *I knew it! I knew it! I knew I would be a bad model.* I thought for sure I was a failure. Hours later he called me, freaking out, screaming into the phone, "You have to come to the studio right now and see this. It's so hot. I can't believe how hot it is. I mean, I can't even take it. If an artist is only as good as his last piece, then I'm fucking amazing," he yelled into the phone.

"It's good?" I asked sheepishly.

"It's ridiculous! It's the best work I've done," he said.

I threw on my Uggs and hopped in a taxi to head to the studio. I had to see. I was petrified, though, that I'd take one look and want to hurl. I am my own worst critic. I am the type who looks in the mirror and sees the zits or blemishes before anything else. I would gladly tell you everything that I haven't accomplished over what I have. And while I was in Michael's studio, staring at the eight-by-ten negative, looking at my figure, I didn't see a trace of stretch marks, the thighs I don't like, and the tummy I wish were flatter. You can't really make out any part of my body or my face, which are colored by his painting in oranges, blues, yellows, greens, and another one with graphic lines that are kind of sixties mod.

I wasn't sure whether to laugh or cry. There I was—a piece of art. The composition was so magnificent, I couldn't believe that he caught that with just a few snaps of the camera. I was the girl who looked so languid and curvaceous at once. "I knew you'd be perfect," he told me. "We just made some serious art together." It was an overwhelmingly powerful moment. Tears streamed down my face. I was touched that someone saw this kind of beauty in my energy and captured it on film . . . where it remains forever without a hint of fear that it will someday feel dated, old, or out of style.

That's the beauty of art. It lasts a lifetime and gets better with age. And having the piece (Michael actually gave me a blowup, which now hangs in my boyfriend's apartment) is a constant reminder that some things are greater than fashion.

MODERN-ART DARLINGS TO CASUALLY NAME-DROP

• **Matthew Barney.** Not only is he Björk's husband (can you imagine what hanging out with them would be like?), but he is perhaps one of the most important contemporary artists. His media are painting, drawing, sculpture, photography, and film, which he morphs together in an offbeat and unconventional fashion. His installation "Cremaster Cycle" (1994–2002), named after the muscle of a man's body that flexes upon ejaculation, is an epic, dreamy, surreal, complex work consisting of five 35mm films rife with anatomical, sexually reproductive allusions, building construction,

Sometimes the best art requires no fashion at all.

color, murder, dentistry (!), nineteenth-century Budapest, metaphors of birth, death, and the cycles of nature, not to mention a mosh pit or two.

• **Cecily Brown.** A British glamour-girl painter who shows at the Gagosian Gallery (the Gucci of galleries) and is known for semiabstract, often erotic, wildly colorful paintings that focus on narcissism and human bodies. She often gets more attention for her hotness than her art, and the truth is, she is hot, but her art is hotter.

• **Sophie Matisse.** The great granddaughter of Henri Matisse and the stepgranddaughter of Marcel Duchamp; her work is surreal and vivid. It must run in the family.

• **Damian Hirst.** A British bad-boy shock-art prodigy whose body of work includes pickled sheep, an installation of a pharmacy with stuff on the floor, a wall hanging with meticulously placed pills, a shark in a tank of formaldehyde, dissected animals. A janitor actually threw away a large part of one of his exhibits while cleaning because he thought it was garbage. He also has remarkably cool works that look like those splatter-paint things you spun in circles and played with as a child. He was once spotted in a drunken stupor, stealing furniture from the Soho Grand Hotel—it was plastered all over the gossip columns.

• **Michael COLAVITO Hoiland.** Yes, that's how he spells his name. He likes to capitalize on the Colavito part. Maybe because it sounds so Italian and arty. His art is a modern blend of exotic photography and serious paintings that are reminiscent of old masters of the postimpressionist period, in addition to sculptures, geometric linear creations made with wire and glass, and wild fluorescent light infusions that he blends with his photographs, as well.

• Anyone emerging from the Saatchi Gallery in London, a forty-thousand-square-foot space dedicated to promoting young British contemporary artists. Run by advertising mogul Charles Saatchi, who got a lot of heat for showcasing an artist who put elephant dung on a painting of the Virgin Mary in a much-talked-about exhibit called "Sensations."

• Anyone you like who really affects you. There are no rules as to what's right and wrong in art. Just trust your taste. Claim it's all chic, postmodern, ironic, and pre-Memphis and you'll be fine!

Note: Architects are also a good source of conversation. Admire buildings, modern homes, and sculptures, and consider learning about midcentury icon Richard Neutra, known for his simple, clean "case study" homes (Tom Ford owns a Neutra house), in addition to Richard Meier, one of the premier architects of today and the man behind the Getty Museum in Los Angeles, many trendy restaurants, and two sky-rises in Manhattan where Nicole Kidman, Calvin Klein, and Martha Stewart have all bought.

FASHION GODS
Sign of the Times
✳ MELISSA ✳

Like many other fashionistas before me, I have to admit that I believe in astrology. I got hooked into the cult by two gay friends, who pressed *Linda Goodman's Sun Signs* on me, and it became my bible. I quoted from it, and even gave "readings" to others who weren't indoctrinated into it. I read my horoscope carefully, and always try to follow its advice to the letter. I'm very superstitious.

Maybe it comes from being Filipina. We Filipinos have many superstitions that we adhere to in our daily lives. For instance, if you have a black-and-blue mark on any part of the body without knowing how it was caused, it means that a spirit has touched you. To find a moth in your house means that a spirit is present. To keep spirits away from your home, you should hang a piece of garlic and salt on the windowsill. Filipinos believe that spirits called *"aswangs"* can possess a person and cause illness. Many Filipinos blame spirits for making people sick, and they sometimes depend on faith healers to cure the person, rather than calling a medical doctor. One method of curing aches and pains is called *"hilot,"* a way of massaging certain parts of the body to take away the pain.

Back to astrology. For my twenty-fifth birthday, my sister, who knew how faithful I was to this New Age religion, bought me a session with a professional astrologer, who charted my future. Mrs. Bienvenides predicted that my future husband would be a Sagittarius and that I would meet him later that year. Two months later I met Mike. It wasn't until I realized I was head over heels in love with him (*He's the one!* every cell in my body screamed) that I remembered Mrs. B's prediction.

"What's your sign?" I asked, like a cheesy seventies swinger.

"Uh . . . Sagittarius?"

We were married six years later.

Kabbalah Chic
✳ KAREN ✳

Whether we believe in God or not, religion and spirituality definitely play an important role in the fashionista lifestyle. Whether we're Jewish, Catholic, Muslim, or atheist, we have deep-seated practices and beliefs that keep most of us grounded and in touch with realities far more powerful than the urban warrior aesthetic of a Balenciaga jumpsuit. Some of us meditate, frequent Zen temples, and go to gospel brunches. We are interested in purifying our bodies, minds, and souls—so much so that it's considered chic to embark on a silent retreat in the mountains, where, like monks, you're forbidden to talk for days at a time in order to really be in your body and feel whatever it is that comes up as a result of twenty-four/seven meditation, including leg cramps more painful than spending an entire day in four-inch heels. Not every fashionista does yoga, but every fashionista has gone through a henna-art phase and has the utmost respect for Gandhi (although that whole nonviolence thing doesn't hold any weight at a sample sale). So, you see, it's very important for us to develop our more soulful side.

That is where kabbalah comes in. Madonna and Demi Moore popularized the ancient study of Jewish mysticism by singing its praises in interviews. Madonna even hosted a party as "Esther" (her Hebrew name) for the release of a kabbalah book in the spring of 2003. Testing the lessons of kabbalah is said to make your life better and help you embrace the wisdom in your heart. It's "the science of the soul and the physics of fulfillment," said a psychic-loving, astrology-obsessed, palm-reading, PR fashionista girlfriend, who urged me to come to an open house at the Kabbalah Center. Intrigued, I went. (I have a weakness for all things of this ilk, including tarot cards, channelers, clairvoyants, and such.)

A rabbi discussed the roots of unhappiness and the fact that all things are a result of planting a seed and allowing it to grow over time (for instance, you and your boyfriend didn't suddenly start fighting and break up; a seed for unhappiness was planted early on and nourished well before the problems sprouted up), how everything is connected on a deeper level, and that the meaning of life is not in the pursuit of material objects, but rather in positive spiritual energy.

Kabbalah is very trendy, as evidenced by the fact that the center hired a PR person to get kabbalah press and the woman sitting behind me at the open house tapped my shoulder and whispered, "Your bag! Where did you get it? I love!"

"Thanks . . . Chloe . . . It was fate that I found it because they had sold out of them twice," I replied before I got shushed by an older woman with cascading blond curls and a Chanel suit (That suit! *Love!*). The room was filled with shiksa (Yiddish for non-Jewish women!) fashion editors I work with, socialites, models, and celebrities I have written about, as well as high-profile moguls in the media and financial industries.

It was quite a sight—everyone in their Louboutin heels (can't miss those red soles, not even in a temple of worship); carrying their logo-covered bags; flipping their immaculately coiffed hair, talking about the taming of the ego, being nonjudgmental, letting go of personal attachments and insecurity, and things that really matter in life. I realized I was actually judging people by their appearances, thinking, *Come on . . . you're so caught up with materialism, who are you trying to kid?* before I took note of myself. (I was pretty decked out, I must admit, in a one-shouldered sweater and puckered shoulder jacket from Stella McCartney.) When I caught myself doing the very thing kabbalah is against (judging!), I made a conscious effort to resist such thoughts and take things for what they were at face value: regular (albeit very well dressed) people, open to learning.

I went back a few times in order to absorb more. Mel rolled her eyes at me. "So trendy, you are." She smirked. "I suppose you'll be hanging out with Madonna soon." I dragged her with me to show her it's not a wacky cult, that no one is trying to extort money (well, not unless you include the $26 red string that kabbalists wear on their left wrist to ward off evil glances), and that the life lessons the scriptures provide are useful and beneficial. She kind of liked it, whether she admits it or not. But she didn't come back, crying "Catholic" as her excuse.

Regardless of what she said, I continued to jaunt to the center. I was learning so many great tools with which to navigate life. I was giving up control over things I cannot control, like how people react to me or something I write, and getting jealous over a love letter I found in my boyfriend's desk drawer (something he had gotten from his ex, that little bitch . . . Why he still has it lingering, I don't know, but . . . well . . . I wasn't going to flip out over it, thank you very much). See, I really was learning how to go easier on myself. (I have always been riddled with a guilty personality—in high school, if a teacher said, "Someone cheated," I automatically thought that she thought it was me—and it's safe to say I'm pretty emotional!)

It may sound hokey. In fact, I'm sure it does. Give me a dirty look if you want. I won't feel a thing. Not as long as I have my red string on! Besides, it goes very well with my red-and-black Chloe corset!

SPIRITUAL, HOLISTIC, AND RELIGIOUS PATHS TO CONSIDER EXPLORING

- **Jewish yoga.** That's right. Jewish yoga. For Jews who don't practice yoga for religious reasons, there is a type of yoga geared just for you! Instead of "Om," you chant "Shal*om*!" And the poses are meant to mimic the letters of the Hebrew alphabet and evoke their power and energy. Oy, vey! So meshugh!

- **The Dalai Lama.** The spiritual leader of Tibet who preaches peace and nonviolence. Important to wear authentic ethnic garb and flip-flops when the lama is in town. Also consider jewelry adorned with symbols of Buddhism.

- **Santaría.** A voodoo-ish, Wicca-like syncretistic Caribbean religion, which means "way of the saints" in Spanish. Jennifer Lopez follows it.

• **Regressional therapy.** Whereby you are hypnotized to regress to past lives to heal current phobias, issues, anxiety, etc. Read the book *Many Lives, Many Masters,* by Brian Weiss, MD. A great way to discover how you dressed in your past lives.

• **The chi machine.** A contraption that swings your feet back and forth to get your chi (Chinese for *energy*) flowing through the body. Karen uses it every morning and swears by it. A big trend with LA fashion girls.

• **Zen.** The freedom from suffering, which arises from attachment to desires. Kind of ironic, being that fashionistas love attachment and desire. But we're an ironic, postmodern bunch. Avoid logos, perfume, and using hair products when visiting the monastery.

• **Acupuncture.** The ancient Chinese healing remedy of sticking pins in pressure points to alleviate tension, stress, injuries, and ailments of any kind. Especially good for PMS and Blahnik relief. We also like all kinds of body work, like Rolfing, interconnective tissue massage to realign the fascia, which improves your structure and your mental health (it's true!); shiatsu massages; and energy work like Reiki and polarity therapy, all of which fall under the holistic category.

• **Smudging.** The Native American ritual of burning sage, which cleanses the aura. A good thing to do postbreakup or during tax season, when you realize you can't pay your bills because you've spent all of your liquid income on clothes.

• **Feng shui.** The Chinese art of arranging your space and positioning objects and furniture in a certain way to generate prosperity, abundance, success, health, and love. The southwest corner is your love nook—to find romance, use the color pink (it represents harmony and balance), things in twos (to attract coupledom), flowers (promotes growth), and images that represent romance to you.

• **Burning Man.** A weeklong artistic celebration of freedom, liberation, exploration, and self-discovery on a stretch of desert land in Black Rock City, California (near San Fran). It's considered the religion of expressing art. Not really hippie, but kind of. The one place where it's safe to wear your most outrageous garb. Couture is acceptable (wearable art, man). Heels, however, are not. Desert and stilettos do not mix. It takes place every year at the end of August. See www.burningman.com for details.

- *Ab Fab*. The comical British half-hour sitcom, a riotous spoof on fashionistas who are too old and too fat to do and wear the things they do, which is the very reason we love them. There must be no talking or distractions while the show is on.

- **Spas.** We touched on this in the beauty chapter. Still, it's considered a religious experience for some.

- **Paris.** The holy land for all fashionistas. Make at least one pilgrimage per year and pray toward the Eiffel Tower five times a day.

FLY THE FASHIONISTA SKIES AND TRAVEL IN STYLE

Fashionistas love exotic vacations, taking the entire month of August off if possible, and bringing home mementos to recall their trips: flip-flops from the beaches of Bali, large straw hats from Palm Beach, Florida, jewelry from Ibiza, hangovers from the Ocean Club in the Bahamas. Sadly, Mel hasn't been to any such resorts due to not having her pesky green card—and Karen hasn't gone due to her pesky finances. But still. We know everything about them. Whether you can make the journey or not, this is what you need to understand about how fashionistas travel.

Prepare for Takeoff

- Fashionistas prefer to fly private. If they are unable to charter a plane or hitch a ride on a wealthy friend's jet, they like to upgrade their tickets to first class if possible. Should they be relegated to coach (ugh!), they request the emergency-exit row (it's got more room) and order champagne. Nothing like some bubbly to make you feel like you're living large. Also, use bathrooms in first class, even if you're in the last row of the plane. They're better in the front of the plane. If you get reprimanded, hold up a tampon. They'll let you go.

• Get a vintage Louis Vuitton carry-on to enhance your image. And a matching one for le puppy. (Fanny packs, unless they're logo-encrusted with Gucci's Gs, which should be worn only with a sense of irony, are a no-no.)

• Don't remove your oversize sunglasses until you're actually seated comfortably on the plane.

• Bring cashmere socks so you can take your shoes off and feel cozy.

• Always have a delicious wrap of some kind in your bag. It will double as a blanket so you won't have to use that scratchy, unclean sandpaper the airlines give you.

• Bust out the lavender aromatherapy, which induces relaxation. Spritz a little on your travel pillow (read: the one you bring from home) to make the flight more enjoyable.

• Eye pillows are a must.

• Keep a spritz bottle of Evian for the face. That plane air is so dehydrating. Follow it up with moisturizer.

• Travel with your own food (those plane meals are not acceptable). Pack pretentiously. Think toast points and caviar.

• Have a meditative CD on hand. See music selection for reference.

• Use your cell phone the second the plane lands and begins taxing on the runway.

A-list Destinations
✳ EXOTIC ✳

• The Four Seasons Hotel in Maui, Hawaii (the jet set are famous for ordering their nannies to stake out the cabanas at three A.M.). Hottest season: Christmas/New Year's.

- The Ile de France, a posh hotel in St. Barths, in close proximity to the Hermès and Cavalli stores.

- Chartering yachts (read: never say "Renting a boat"—that's very déclassé) anywhere in the Caribbean.

- A fabulous designer's villa. Dolce & Gabbana, Donatella Versace, and Valentino all have them (those Italians really know how to live). Try very hard to get invited. And bring us if you do!

❋ THE GOOD OLD USA ❋

- Aspen in the winter. Check into the Hotel Jerome (Jack Nicholson does).

- The Raffles L'Ermitage hotel in Beverly Hills. Fashionistas love the business cards the hotel provides for all its guests, with a personal fax number and your name with "In Residence" before the hotel's address. The spa on the top floor boasts an Egyptian-style courtyard and pool with a view of the entire city. Jaan, the Asian fusion restaurant, serves tiny plates of exquisite tastes twenty-four hours a day.

- The Hamptons during the summer months. East Hampton and Southampton are the most trendy. Shack up well and complain that it's too trendy.

- Ian Schrager hotels anywhere (the Delano and the Shore Club in Miami; the Mondrian in Los Angeles; the Clift in San Francisco; the Hudson, Paramount, and Royalton in New York City). High-style lobbies, glittery restaurants, tiny rooms with almost no closet space, but still, it's cool to stay there. (Karen once put her parents up at the Hudson Hotel when it first opened in New York and her mother called her and snapped, "There's nowhere to put our clothes! We'll be at the Plaza!" Clearly the Robinovitz parentals don't understand the fashionista way and that there's nothing's wrong with keeping your clothes in neat piles on a desk, near the plasma-screen TV!)

- *W* hotels are also a smart choice in savvy stays. Their customer service is phenomenal, and in some hotel locales they have holistic rooms, where you can choose an aromatherapy scent and have a minibar stocked with organic goods. The LA establishment has huge rooms—all suites—that rule. And the hotel stores make for very good gift shopping for friends back home.

• Hard Rock Hotel & Casino in Las Vegas. They have the best parties—and poolside eye candy. Just make sure to befriend (or, um, tip) the right people in order to secure a cabana by the pool—and a reservation at Nobu, the famous Japanese restaurant, co-owned by DeNiro, on the premises.

✳ EURO ✳

• 3 Rooms, the retro Scandinavian-designed modern B&B attached to the store, 10 Corso Como in Milan (see shopping chapter). With sixties shag rugs and Eames and Arne Jacobsen furnishings, it's a curatorial fashionista fantasy. It looks like it fell right out of the pages of *Wallpaper** (refer to High Gloss section earlier in this chapter).

• Hôtel du Cap, where the stars stay when in Cannes, France. Visit during the film festival and bring glorious gowns for lobby loitering. Look good enough and you'll get an invite to a premiere.

• Hôtel Costes in Paris. Very posh, very old world, very snooty. No need to actually stay there if you own the CD (refer to previously mentioned music section). But you should, at the very least, stop in for a cocktail. To be honest, we prefer shacking up in the Sixth District because it's more low-key and laid-back.

• La Scalinatella, five-star charm at its finest. On the Isle of Capri. You'll thank us as you eat your fresh mozzarella-and-tomato salad by the pool, where Dolce bikinis and heels are required.

• St Martins Lane Hotel in London. See Ian Schrager hotels above.

The Suite Life and Haute Hoteling!

• If your hotel is subpar, put a positive spin on it and call it "charming" or "rustic chic."

- Bring mini travel candles for your room, preferably a designer kind like Matthew Williamson. Donatella Versace brings no fewer than fourteen suitcases when she travels because she likes to be surrounded by her own things.

- Pack slippers.

- To make the room feel like home, fashionistas like to bring photos of their friends, families, and pets and put them on display.

- Steal logo-encrusted things from the hotel room (ashtrays, something from the room-service cart, bathrobes). It may not be legal, but it sure does feel good when you open your closet at home to find a pristine pile of fluffy white Ritz-Carlton towels. To pull it off, call housekeeping upon arriving and say you never got a robe, enough towels, or whatever it is you want.

- Collect matches from the hotel so you can use them when you're at home and strike up conversation about your glamorous trip.

- Complain about an awful stench in your room and you just may get a free upgrade to a suite. It worked for us on numerous occasions (although we were put on a smoking floor at the time and neither of us smoke).

- Immediately befriend the concierge. This person will help hook you up with great reservations and extra-special treatment while you're checked into the hotel. Tip this person well, too.

Roughing It. Sometimes Abstinence Is the Ultimate Indulgence

- The Ashram, a boot camp in Calabasas, California, where you're forced to stay in icky accommodations and hike for miles before eating as little as a melba toast. Cindy Crawford and Julia Roberts have gone. It's great for weight loss.

- The Spirit Rock Meditation Center, a retreat that offers inner peace by telling you to shut up! Guests are forbidden to talk. Karl Lagerfeld once said, "Silence is chic."

• Hotelito Desconocido, a Mexican getaway where there is no electricity or any of the luxuries fashionistas are accustomed to. Here they like to get back to the simple things in life and find their *Little House on the Prairie* roots, and read by candlelight. Though there are working toilets in the rooms.

• Vladi Private Islands, a company that sells and rents islands, offers a $250 survival kit with a two-person tent, fishing rod, hammock, and magnifying glass (the better to start a fire with, my dear).

Fashionistas After Dark: Sequins on Monday, Flannel on Friday

The only reason fashionistas like to go out is so they can dress up. The hour(s) spent getting ready and obsessing over the outfit is always much more enjoyable than a crowded, loud, smoky restaurant where the beautiful waiter/model/actor/writer/diva forgets to hold the pears and Gruyère cheese and puts the aged balsamic vinaigrette directly on your mesclun, Gruyère cheese, and pear salad, instead of on the side, as you had asked.

Fashionistas also favor going out on the nights of the week when everyone else is staying at home watching Must-See TV. They are out on Monday and Tuesday nights, but on weekend nights can be on la sofa, tucking into a pint of Ben & Jerry's and happily watching such secret fashionista favorites as the Sci-Fi Network's *Farscape* and Lifetime, Television for Women (fashionistas never miss an episode of *The Golden Girls*).

In this chapter you'll learn about the nightlife of fashionistas—what they do in their off time, a list of boyfriends every fashionista has in her dating history, and why she must always "not-eat" at the newest restaurant in town.

THE BEST PART OF EVERY EVENING: GETTING READY

Social Schedule and Reality

❋ MELISSA AND KAREN ❋

There's nothing quite like the anticipation of an evening out. Most of the time we will plan our social calendar far in advance. It usually looks something like this:

MONDAY NIGHT: Dinner party with publicists, editors, and architect friends.

TUESDAY NIGHT: Cocktail party to celebrate a new store/product/magazine issue.

WEDNESDAY NIGHT: Opening party at new nightclub/restaurant.

THURSDAY NIGHT: Charity benefit.

We spend the weekend planning, going over our closet, trying on all our clothes, shopping, preparing our outfits (from the shoes to the coat to the jewelry) in advance. We meet at our favorite nail salon to get our special Orly manicures (the classic red for Mel, dark, vampy almost-black for Karen!), chatting, gossiping, and talking about the events we will be attending.

And then it happens . . . all that work . . . all that anxiety and social psyching-up! Here's what really goes down:

MONDAY NIGHT: We arrive in time for dessert.

TUESDAY NIGHT: We sleep in front of the latest reality TV show (take your pick).

WEDNESDAY NIGHT: We drag ourselves out to do a five-minute lap around the room (after two hours of getting ready). Don't worry. We record *The Bachelor*.

THURSDAY NIGHT: We find better things to do with our $200 contribution.

It's just all part of the game. There's nothing fashionistas like more than being invited to everything, having a seemingly packed social calendar, and then blowing it all off to sit in front of the television. After all, in our heads, we've already gone to the party!

How to Get Ready in Style

- Hair—Do you need a blowout? Book an appointment at a salon. Or if you're doing it at home, set aside an appropriate amount of time to deal with your locks.

- Nails—Nothing looks worse than chipped polish and raggedy, bitten nails. Get your butt to a salon and get buffed to a shine!

- Bath—Calgon, take us away! All the pressure of looking good can get to a girl. Soak your troubles in the tub, just like Diane von Furstenberg, who never takes showers. Epsom salt is great for muscle relaxation post–fashionista workouts.

- Music—Cue up something that makes you feel happy.

- Prepare clothes the night before so you're not running around in a frenzy, and arriving way too late.

The Fashionista Saturday Night

A LIST OF ACTIVITIES WE DO ON THE WEEKENDS

- Movies with friends—or solo. It's good to have some personal time.

- *Farscape.* Hello!

- Turn home into a spa—oatmeal facials, coffee-bean exfoliation, anyone?

- Catch up on reading—those *Vogue*s have really piled up.

- By all means, don't go out! Saturday night is for amateurs! Unless, of course, you have a hot date. Then do it up and take no prisoners.

THE ARRIVAL
The Stars Are Here?
✳ MELISSA AND KAREN ✳

Summer 2002.

We had just published our book *How to Become Famous in Two Weeks or Less*. The hard part was over. Now it was time to hit the book-launch parties (the really, really hard part!).

We would get only one chance to make an entrance at each of our events, and we wanted to make a huge impact. In New York, our party was at the Paramount Hotel lobby. We holed up in a private suite, getting manicures and blowouts, and doing television interviews while sipping champagne and hanging out with Lou, our bodyguard, who brought us borrowed rocks from Harry Winston. The phones were incessantly ringing, and our publicist answered it like this: "Famous suite!" Finally, it was an hour after our party had started. Time to join the mayhem. (Mel had to restrain Karen from popping out of our room too early and spoiling our arrival!)

We slowly walked hand in hand down the glass staircase as David Bowie's "Fame" blasted in the speakers. The crowd of seven hundred went wild. Camera flashes were blinding. "Mel, over here! Karen, over here!" We paused at the bottom for some pictures. The

The grand staircase arrival—very fashionably late

blowup board from our book was nowhere to be found, so Heidi, our PR gal, found it and—with her Yorkie, Isaac, in her bag—ducked down and held it up behind us so the book would be seen in all the pics. We were escorted outside before we could give even our parents a proper hello. There, more paparazzi awaited us. We posed with one leg facing forward, held our book for the cameras, and then strangers got in on the action, snapping away, as well. This is what being a rock star feels like! Pretty darn good!

JEFF BROCON

Arriving on our red carpet in Chicago

For our Los Angeles party, we had to get ready (look at our priorities—the getting ready is always high on our list!) across town at Privé, where they were doing our hair and makeup for free. Mel's mother kept calling—"All the stars are here, your party's started, where are you?!" The publicist called. "If you don't get here right now, your press will leave!" she fumed.

We arrived an hour and a half late. All the celebrities (from Jenna from *Survivor* to Paris Hilton) had arrived promptly. They were gone by the time we showed. And we had our assigned book escort, who drove a Ford Escort, drop us off fifty feet from the entrance, so it wouldn't seem like our moms had to drop us off. Once we got there, we knew no one inside, Mel's family notwithstanding.

In Miami we were an hour late, but only because we had to do so many television interviews. It was so humid that by the time we arrived at the party, our hair was flat from the heat. Oy.

For our Chicago party, we donned ball gowns from Escada to wear to our party at the Escada store on Miracle Mile. Mel wore a red beaded number (once worn by Vivica Fox), Karen a brown-and-white-striped sequined zebra. We traveled in style, in a Bentley specially on loan to us for the occasion. We were half an hour late, and greeted by a Joan Rivers impersonator. We were getting the hang of this.

We arrived right on time for our Las Vegas party. The only problem was, we were the only ones there! Sometimes it's even better not to show up!

How to Make an Entrance

Exactly what time is fashionably late?

- When you should be prompt: Weddings, especially when you're in them.

- Fifteen minutes late is acceptable: Dinner with friends, lunch.

- An hour after it started, at least: Fashion parties, gallery openings.

- Two A.M. is prime time: Nightclubs.

- Great excuses for being late: Traffic, Mom called with serious news, badly stubbed your toe scurrying around to get ready, lost ATM card, stuck in elevator, struggled with a mugger (and won).

CHEEK TO CHEEK

Fashionistas always air-kiss each other so much not because they're fond of each other but so they can whisper fresh insults into each other's ears.
—MOSCHINO

The Perils of Air-kissing
✳ MELISSA AND KAREN ✳

We're the types who kiss everyone we know—even vaguely. We kiss our editors, business acquaintances, people we don't even like.

After all, it's just a greeting—and not even a kiss—more like a smack in the air next to someone's cheek. How harmless is that?

Mel bumped into a familiar-looking person on the street once. The person gave her a hearty hello, and she responded automatically. "Helllooo!" she said, trying to cover up for the fact that she couldn't remember his name, and proceeded to give the standard double-kiss greeting. It was only when she walked away that she realized she had just kissed the doorman of her old building.

How to Perfect the Double Air-Kiss

1. Woooooo! The excitement. Mouth open, elbows bent, hands up!

2. Lean in to one side of cheek. It doesn't matter what side to lean toward first; you'll pick subtle cues from the other fashionista on where to go. Must remain at least two inches away from the cheek. Notice the space between us. Hands still remain in the air as if your nails are wet—fresh from a manicure.

3. Lean back, lips remaining slightly puckered.

4. Go in for the second cheek. Remember: An air-kiss is always both cheeks! Sometimes it seems as though you're kissing hair, not air. It's all about gesture anyway.

GOIN' TO THE CHAPEL
White Plastic Versace?
✳ MELISSA ✳

I had a vision for my wedding. White. Plastic. Versace. And knee-high patent leather boots. A drag-queen chorus singing "Here Comes Your Man." But it was the dress that always figured highly in my dreams. Sometimes it was a white shredded-chiffon minidress from Balenciaga (from his naughty Angelic collection) with ankle boots. Other times it was a Helmut Lang tulle cocktail dress with wide spandex strap sandals. Or else an Alexander McQueen white leather corset dress. But the basic idea never changed. My wedding dress would definitely be short. Very short. Very fashiony.

Weeellll . . . things didn't quite happen that way. Mike and I had said that we would have a "cool" wedding. We would buy his groomsmen Prada knockoff suits from H&M (a steal at $150), and I would wear some crazy fashionista outfit. I was all ready to book the drag chorus. Then it hit me. I was really getting married. I would have these pictures for the rest of my life. I thought about my mom's wedding album, and how I loved poring over it and dreaming about how my wedding would be exactly the same as hers. And how she would not understand about the white plastic Versace.

I thought about all the things I would be missing if I bought my wedding dress the same way I bought all my clothes—alone, with no one to cry and tell me I looked beautiful, and none of the great emotional bonding moments that weddings bring. I decided I wanted a more traditional wedding—and I

Mel couldn't resist the princess dress.

wanted the big-hankie moments more than the Helmut Lang off the rack.

My mother and I went to the bridal shop together, and we picked out a beautifully beaded, embroidered, ivory tulle dress that had a big ball-gown Cinderella skirt, completed by a handmade pearl-studded veil. As Mom dabbed her eyes and fluffed up my multiple petticoats, I looked in the mirror and smiled. I could wear Versace any day. I would never be able to wear this princess dress ever again.

I took a page out of Grace Kelly and added a mink stole as my cover-up. (It was October, after all.) And with my J.Lo-style orchid bouquet (the one from her marriage to Chris Judd!), I was set. I had my tiara, my mom's diamond earrings, and, of course, my Christian Louboutin heels (with a blue sole instead of a red one for his wedding collection—and one of my favorite bargains—$40 from $550 at the Barneys warehouse sale).

I walked down the aisle feeling like all of myself.

Bride to Be?
✳ KAREN ✳

I am not engaged. I never have been. And while I've never been one of those girls looking for the rock on her finger, desperate to land a man to take care of her till death do us part, I often fantasize about my wedding. It's not about the man, actually. Not even close. It's about what I'm wearing (surprise, surprise). I love to pretend any designer of my choosing will create my dress, which would definitely be far from brides-y, far from off the rack, but definitely off the hook.

I can't imagine anything about my wedding being traditional. No bridesmaids. No walk down the aisle by my father who "gives me away." That seems so chauvinistic to me. I imagine walking down an aisle with my guy—or by myself, behind my parents. I imagine being wed by some kind of spiritual healer, a shaman, perhaps, atop Machu Picchu. Or maybe a cool interfaith minister, poolside by the Delano Hotel. I would want a rockin' DJ, not a band. I would want great food. But most of all, I want to be sexy.

No tulle. No poof. No big updo. Some days I imagine myself in all-beaded corset-y dresses by McQueen. Other times it's sexpot chic from Tom Ford. Once in a while I'm a twenties flapper girl from Valentino. I want to look back on the pictures and think, *God damn, I was hot.* God knows how I'd afford it. But I'll deal with that later, just like having someone say, "Will you marry me?"

What to Wear as a Fashionista Bride

• City wedding—Sleek, chic, like Caroline Bessette Kennedy's Narciso Rodriguez slip dress. Or try a different color—burgundy or black. Helmut Lang's white taffeta dresses are also a good choice. (Stella Tennant wore one to her wedding.)

- Beach wedding—Fresh flowers and a sarong, or try a short beaded slip dress and bare feet à la Cindy Crawford.
- Traditional wedding—The bigger the better.

What to Wear as a Fashionista Wedding Guest

- City wedding—Cool black, über-sleek, one-shoulder, hot jewels, outstanding cover-up—maybe fur or orange velvet.
- Beach wedding—Cool black. Tropical wear? What's that?
- Traditional wedding—See above. There's nothing traditional about you.

DINING OUT IN STYLE
Restauranting as a Sport
✳ KAREN ✳

Restaurants, for fashionistas, are just as much about being seen as being fed. While we love a good four-star meal and a culinarily exquisite experience, we also love frequenting the latest, newest, hottest, trendiest restaurants around. It's not unusual to hear a fellow fashionista say, "Oh, you have to go to [insert name of restaurant here]. You'll hate it. It's so pretentious." No matter how badly a place is received, if it's hot—usually something that comes with a celebrity type of chef (they're rock stars in New York), a high-profile designer who turned out another Zen-like minimal postmodern space, and a killer location—we need to check it out. Just to say we've been. A hot restaurant, regardless of food quality, is very hard to get into. So being there is a feat in itself.

The first issue is a reservation. They're very hard to get. You usually have to know someone—or know someone who knows someone—to get in. Even then, you may be relegated to the five P.M. or eleven P.M. seating. And God forbid you arrive five minutes late! If you do, your table is as good as gone. Pretty ironic considering that they make you wait for forty minutes before your table is ready anyway. I think it's a control thing. Inside, however, you are sure to spot some A-list fashionistas—a supermodel or two, a B-list celebrity wearing YSL, those who are always written about in gossip columns, fashion girls and their gay best friends. Waiters give you long speeches about how the menu works, as if you were unable to figure it out.

And then you order. Things like foie gras dumplings and grapefruit dipping sauce are menu regulars, as are whole grilled bronzino, the occasional frog-leg situation, and at least two types of tartare. The food is never as big as the price. There is almost always a rest-room doorman, showing you the way to the bathroom, which is often stocked with perfume and Doublemint gum. Everyone around you is acting very smugly fabulous. And it's a joy to be a part of it all. Just to say you've been.

Isn't life delicious?

Do Fashionistas Eat?

Studies have shown that a woman dining on less is a lot more attractive than one who has ordered a three-course meal. That's unfair and wrong, but that's life. So the answer to the question is, Of course we do. In private, we shovel down steaks and cram as many Magnolia cupcakes and pints of Häagen-Dazs as we can handle. But in public, most of us pick at the following foods, in order to raise our attractiveness quotient.

Here's what to order in a restaurant when dining with other fashionistas:

• Flat bottled water—Carbonated water leads to bloating. Skip the Pellegrino.

- Grilled fish—Usually salmon (good for curing wrinkles, says Dr. Nicholas Perricone, celebrity derm) or seared tuna.

- Any kind of salad—The one filled with bacon and avocado and blue cheese dressing is still fashionista-approved. Just request that it be finely chopped. Send it back if it isn't. You almost want to be able to drink it with a straw.

- Dessert—But only with the caveat, "I haven't eaten anything sweet in three weeks (months/years)!" Dessert is usually consumed ravenously by a pack of hungry fashionistas.

The Gin Revolution
❋ MELISSA AND KAREN ❋

For years, fashionistas relied on Cosmopolitans and Dirty Martinis, but how many can a girl (or guy) drink without getting sick of them (read: not sick *from* them!)? Exactly. That is why the modern-day fashionista sips gin, darling, like they did once upon a time. Damrak, the oldest gin recipe out there, is our brand of choice. It's smooth, refreshing, crisp, and it mixes well with lemonade, tonic, or nothing but olives, martini-style. Bottoms up!

Stop Your Whining! How to Deal with Champagne Hangovers

- Take aspirin, not Advil.

- Drink one glass of water for every glass of bubbly.

- Stay home, snuggle on the Cappellini sofa in your cashmere robe. Cancel all your morning appointments and ask your man to give you a foot massage.

- Treat yourself to a yummy, greasy brunch. The best cure!

THE FASHIONISTA DATING HISTORY
You're Just Like Cher in Clueless
✳ MELISSA ✳

I was twenty-two years old and my boyfriend at the time, Sasha, was ten years older. I thought he was really cool; he thought I was really cute—you know how these things go. He was a writer, too—an aspiring playwright, who worked nights at an investment bank as a word processor. I had a day job, too—as a computer programmer—and had written an unpublished novel on the side. But somehow he never saw me as a writer, just as a shopper.

It's easy to get categorized and labeled and put in a nice, easy package when you're a fashionista. People don't see beyond the blowout, the well-chosen outfit, the expensive shoes. What you get is what you see, and to him I looked like some trendy, fashion-obsessed chick, which, of course, I am. But just because I was fashion-crazed and knew to rotate my conditioners daily didn't mean that was all there was to me. Why is it always smart versus beautiful? Or fashion versus intellect? Why can't a girl have both? I was becoming increasingly annoyed by his condescending treatment.

Especially when he suggested a career as "costume designer" for me. Now, there's nothing I respect more than designers of any stripe, and costume designer for a film would be a great fantasy job—but it wasn't my dream. I swallowed my irritation when he said "You're just like Cher in *Clueless.*" I had loved the film, and, of course, empathized with Alicia Silverstone's Cher. But I hadn't grown up in Beverly Hills, spending Daddy's credit cards. I loved to shop; did that make me a ditz? I decided it was time to show my true colors.

Sasha was obsessed with games—board games, like Scrabble, Trivial Pursuit, and Risk, as well as puzzles and crosswords. He equated winning with superior intelligence, which is such a silly way to live. Everybody knows whoever makes the most money always wins. (I'm *kidding!*) We often played Jeopardy on his computer. I'm a very competitive person, but had been suppressing my gamer's instincts. One night we played Gestures with some of his friends. "Oh, look how cute; she even laughs like a doll," said one of the frumpy women in the group, all wanna-be writers who took themselves too seriously and probably had reindeer sweaters in the back of their closets. It was enough to set my (very whitened) teeth on edge.

The next day, Sasha brought out the Jeopardy and I beat him handily. (My dad's ambition for me is to go on TV, meet Alex Trebek, and win the championship.) He was stumped, and wanted to play something else. He had one of those handheld puzzle things, kind of like a Rubik's Cube, where you have to fit all the pieces together by moving in only one direction. "Ha!" he said. "I did it in seventy-five moves! Let's see you try." I took the game from him and returned it after a second. "Fourteen moves," I said flatly. His eyes widened, and he started to panic. We played Scrabble, Monopoly, and Trivial Pursuit. I beat him at every game. (I can be quite ferocious when I'm angry.) When we played Risk and I marched into Russia and claimed all his territories, he waved the white flag. I had destroyed him and his ego. I wasn't happy about it, but I was sick of being treated like some featherheaded "little squirrel" from *A Doll's House*.

I never heard from him again. Good riddance.

You Wear Such Silly Clothes
✳ KAREN ✳

In January of 2003 I met a guy. Not just any guy, but a gorgeous, smart, successful, tall, athletic guy with a chiseled face, aqua-blue eyes, and a full head of thick brown hair. Our first date was amazing. He even brought a digital camera to document it and told me he wanted to capture all of our great moments. He held my hand, told me I was beautiful, kissed me for hours, and shared his wine by passing it from his mouth to mine. It was all so terribly romantic. We began to spend every day together for the next two months.

He brought me flowers, sent me sexy text messages on my phone, and treated me like I was special.

My friends liked him. And I thought, just maybe, he could be "the one." We got along so beautifully. We appreciated the same kinds of food, skiing, home design, and architecture. We went to museums, spent entire days going around Manhattan to look at the most famous buildings and show each other our favorite blocks. He even brought up getting a loft and living together—in the not-so-distant future. He was so dreamy.

For Valentine's Day, he took me to his winter home in Utah for a week. I couldn't wait to be away with him. And I packed so well—my Christian Dior green-and-orange sweater and Rock & Republic jeans to be worn with Uggs, the fox-fur chubby for Juicy sweats, and two supersexy outfits for the big nights he had planned. I wanted to look like a cute little ski bunny. Sadly, that was when things started falling apart.

My first sign was when we planned a party at his house for his friend's birthday. I helped him devise a fun menu of small PB&J sandwiches, cupcakes (Duncan Hines), shot glasses of mac-and-cheese, and s'mores. As we cooked and scurried around his kitchen—a huge kitchen with three stainless-steel fridges, a Viking stove, and limestone counters—he noticed that after I washed my hands, I shook them out as I walked across the room. "Um, we do not shake our hands out over the floor and ruin the marble. We use the towels in the top drawer," he scolded as if I were some three-year-old. I made a mental note of his behavior (possible warning signal) and continued. Insult number two came next. As I poured the cupcake batter into the pan, he yelled, "That is not how you do it. Use a different spoon. You'll make a mess." Okay. I figured messes could be cleaned, but I'd use a different spoon. Before I knew it, everything I did was wrong. Apparently I couldn't even light the candles correctly. ("Use a lighter, not matches," he reprimanded.) My perfect man turned into the most awful control freak.

I went to shower in order to take a break. When I emerged from the bathroom, wearing low-waisted shiny black Stella Mc-

Cartney pants and a one-shouldered wine-colored top and big hoop earrings, he gave me a double take. I thought for sure a compliment was coming.

"What are you wearing? You look like a tramp," he said.

A tramp? "This shirt is hot. It's Calvin Klein."

"God, you're such a label whore. You wouldn't know good design if it bit you on the ass," he said.

I told him he was being passive-aggressive and that that was no way to talk to a lady. And he told me to change. Screw that. No man tells me how to dress! I gave him the benefit of the doubt, however, and figured he was nervous or stressed about work and the party that was about to begin. The next night he took me to a big benefit for the opening of some public library designed by a famous architect. I put on a ruched black Chanel dress from a sample sale and he looked me up and down and barked, "What are you wearing? This is Utah. You don't need to be so dolled up. And that dress is so hoochie-mama."

It was a classic Chanel, anything but hoochie. I said, "It must be lost on you, and I love it." I wore it anyway and got a dozen compliments from women I didn't know.

The next day he lost it on me. "You wear such silly clothes. You look ridiculous," he said when I put on jeans and a long-sleeved black T-shirt that I had cut into a V-neck. Could I have been more basic? "Why do you have to cut your tops to reveal your breasts?" he asked. First of all, the cut was nowhere near my breasts, and second of all, I'll cut what I want to cut! "Don't you have any respect for your clothes? You just cut them," he barked.

The next two days, things got worse. Every minute of the day I was told my jeans were too tight (ironic, considering he told me he thought I had a good ass), my slit-sleeved shirt was impractical (okay, so what if it kept dipping into the garlic-butter sauce of my king salmon?), and the lingerie I had bought specifically to surprise him was "dumb."

That was the last straw. I packed my silly clothes, took a cab to the airport, and went back to New York, where my style was much more appreciated.

The Five Guys Fashionistas Date Before They Settle Down

- The troubled artist—Because your friends will respect you for it. You love going to see his work at a gallery or on a stage, where he's performing. And he will treat you like you're his muse. Be warned: He's whiny.

- The gift-giving finance guy—Because lavishing you with luxury is part of his self-esteem. Be warned: He can be truly wretched and boring. You're definitely dating for dollars here. And don't think he's rewarding just you with gifts. He goes to strip bars on his lunch break.

- The gorgeous model—Just so you can say you did. Complain about his self-involvedness.

- The totally inappropriate guy—He's a bartender; you make seven figures. He's your plumber or your gardener, but truly hot. You can't imagine marrying him, but some of us do.

- The tattooed bad boy—They walk on the wild side. Live a little.

9

Money! Financing Your Fashionista Habit and Battling (or Preventing!) Bankruptcy

Fashionistas love to accumulate things: vintage cameos, the same pair of shoes in every color, jeans of almost identical hue, and six-figure credit card debt chief among them. Even the thriftiest fashionista cannot escape it. Fashionista assets are Balenciaga dresses, a very special Bruce vest, and Vivienne Westwood corsets (vintage!). When you consider the positive feelings that shopping and buying something new evokes, it can become easy to overlook things—like phone bills, taxes, the money you owe your best friend who loaned you a few hundred bucks when you were short—for the sake of getting the instant fix of fashion. We don't own apartments, cars, or vacation homes. We don't have 401(k)s or IRAs, and there's a good chance we'll probably spend our retirements as little old ladies who live in their (very expensive) shoes—or maybe just the boxes, which, of course, we always save.

Fashion may very well give you an instant high. But it can also be a harsh reality check, a means to confront some of your mental demons, especially the ones that revolve around money. It's easy to feel like a failure when you can't afford something. Money, in our society, tends to represent a measure of success. While the truth of success has nothing to do with dollar signs, we are still victims of a materialistic culture caught up in the throes of competition, one-upmanship, and "which handbag did you get this season?" pettiness. In the fashion industry, such pressures are hard to avoid.

In fact, being in the fashion industry really warps the mind. After years of writing about the decadence of $5,000 jackets, $2,500 cocktail dresses, and $1,200 evening wraps, career fashionistas, many of whom get 30 percent discounts from designer stores and have the privilege of receiving free gifts from designers and ordering things wholesale from showrooms, begin to see things that are still astronomically priced, like $1,000 dresses or sweaters, as affordable. Cheap even. We have witnessed many a fashionista picking up a pair of $295 shoes and cheering, "They're practically free! I'll take two!" just because they're used to paying more like $500 for one pair. It's not something to be proud of, this crazy sense of monetary value or lack thereof.

This chapter was not easy for us to write. We have both struggled (and continue to struggle) with money issues, especially in the fashion department. We've fielded calls from creditors, walked twenty blocks because we could afford to go only so far in a taxi ("Greene Street and Prince, please, but I only have six dollars, so you'll have to stop the cab when you get to five dollars"), and had zero dollars in the bank. Just because this life has "worked" for us does not mean we recommend it. In fact, we *don't*! We beseech fellow fashionistas to take it easy out there! The biggest tip we can provide is this: Never say, "I'm poor"; say, "I'm broke" instead. Remember: Broke is temporary. Poor is forever! Just like a bad sense of style.

The following pages will give you the inside scoop on ascertaining your financial situation (there are many different levels of sickness), financial tricks to get you through the fiscal fashion year, making money off of old clothes, dealing with your weakness, and balancing your checkbook—and your style needs. Not to mention a few skeletons from our closets that we're not exactly proud of, but maybe you can learn from our mistakes!

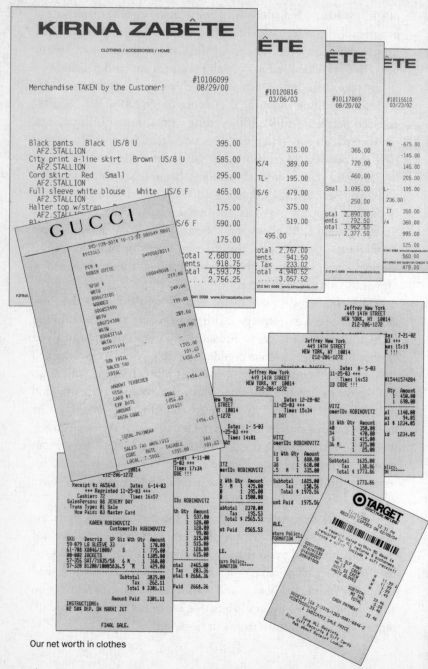

Our net worth in clothes

AWARENESS: ADMITTING YOU HAVE A PROBLEM IS HALF THE BATTLE

You Charge Me $150 per Hour and Call This Advice?

✳ KAREN ✳

I was recently complaining to my therapist about the fact that I have no money. I wasn't even sure how I'd pay her at the end of the month. It was one of those awful moments in life when I felt totally out of control, unsure how to handle my predicament and the fact that what I have in clothing, I lack in the bank.

I had twelve dollars to my name, and no one would ever have suspected it by the way I looked—like a million bucks. "I need to learn how to budget," I told her, feeling truly helpless and doomed. "I spend way too much money. I never take public transportation. I go out to dinner every night. It's bad," I continued, trying to blame my situation on something other than my fashion addiction.

"I don't think the problem is that," my therapist said. "I think it may have something to do with your *shopping*." My shopping? What? She started talking to me about learning to control myself. (Control?)

Then she looked at me from her brown leather reclining chair, her clog-clad feet perched perfectly on the ottoman, and proposed a probable solution: "I think you should consider limiting yourself to a certain amount of money each season and try to stay within that budget." After a bit of a pause, she said, "Say, for example, three thousand dollars for spring." Three thousand dollars! I looked at her in all seriousness and started cackling. Cackling! I recognize that for most people, $3,000 per season is an absurd amount of clothing, but for a fashionista who is powerless over enticingly pretty new trends and the latest version of the trench coat and who fancies things like $800 handbags and $500 shoes, $3,000 doesn't get you much.

I scanned my outfit and quickly did some math. "I'm *wearing* three thousand dollars!" I said. The breakdown: $725 Balenciaga white jeans, $680 Gaultier shredded-leather biker top, $600 Pierre Hardy ankle boots, $300 Dean Harris gold hoop earrings, $900 Balenciaga handbag.

I was laughing, yes. But I was also mortified. *What has happened to me?* I thought. Where did my integrity go? I am no TFB (trust-fund baby). I do okay for myself, but I do not make *that* much money (in fact, some months I can barely pay my $300 cell phone bill). I have no right to be wearing these things, and yet I feel like I cannot survive without them. It was such a reality check. It was the first time that I really looked at myself and said, "I am a fashionista and I need help!"

Money to Burn
✳ MELISSA ✳

1996—I was broke. I had $45 in my wallet, $2 in my savings account, and $1 in my checking account. I had no credit cards, no bank cards, no department-store cards, and my debt was in the high five-figure range. Yet my tax returns insisted I should be an affluent member of society—someone who needs to put money in a condo, set up a tax shelter, invest in mutual funds, and generally be leading the good life.

Instead, I owned a closetful of designer clothes I hardly wore, an apartmentful of furniture for people I'll never entertain, and absolutely nothing to show for the hundreds of thousands of dollars I've made except for multiple taxi receipts, torn dinner chits, club invitations, souvenir champagne corks, and maybe a Polaroid of me, drunk and completely decked out, smiling garishly into the flashing lights.

I was a debtor, and an insatiable one. At twenty-six, I hadn't met a credit card I couldn't charge to its maximum limit. Overdraft was my middle name. So was Over-the-limit. And Overspend. Of the fourteen credit cards I used to wield, ranging from the tacky (A&S) to the sublime (Bergdorf Goodman), not one of them has ever been paid on time . . . to be honest, not many were *paid*, period. Same goes at one time or another for rent, electricity, and phone bills. Because of my shopping habits, I've been almost evicted twice, threatened with arrest once, and was banned from opening a bank account in the state of New York.

Of my post-tax-and-401(k)-withholding income every two weeks, 95 percent was spent in the first *two* days upon joyous deliverance of such sum by direct deposit into my checking account. I was a pauper until the cycle begins itself again. When I found myself broke—which was often—I even resorted to turning in gift certificates for cash, Christmas presents for cash, Valentine's Day presents for cash, selling jewelry for cash, and even the clothing off my back for cash. My life was a roller-coaster ride of feast or famine—dinner at the Four Seasons one evening, canned vegetables the next. I was never able to live within my means.

I had absolutely no idea what my "means" were. To find out, I was constantly adding and subtracting, multiplying and dividing, costs and expenses—not to balance my checkbook, of course, but to calculate how much I could spend before I had to starve. This was a necessary pastime of mine—calculating money. Everywhere in my apartment and in my office cubicle—on scraps of paper, on the backs of envelopes, laundry tickets, business cards, Post-its, scribbled in the pages of my Filofax, my sketchbook, my journal—marched a column of figures that calculated how much I had in my bank account, and exactly how much, after all the bills were paid and the rent was due and the food was bought—how much *exactly*—there was to *burn*.

Most of the time the answer was "not nearly enough," which was why I was in trouble. Because even with my meticulous calculations, I never quite paid off the obligatory bills, and instead threw it away on superfluous trivialities—a $900 Helmut Lang jacket, say, while the electric company threatened final disconnection, or else a $200 dinner the month I couldn't pay the rent. To be homeless but cultured, poor but dressed divinely—it wasn't an ambition; it was my lifestyle.

My one solace was that I was not alone in my heedlessness. There isn't a great history of handling financial responsibility in my family. My grandfather was notorious for the pride he vested in his credit cards. He had about twenty of them, and kept them in an accordion-like cardholder in his wallet, so that he could pull them out and show them to strangers. Which he did. Usually on San Francisco BART trains, on his way to triple-X movie theaters in Oakland. "I'm very rich; I own my own business," he'd tell passengers seated next to him. "Look at my credit cards. Macy's. Saks. Visa Gold."

Even if most of the credit cards had expired or were practically useless from maxed-out credit limits, and my grandfather had never owned a business of any kind, it didn't stop him from thinking he was a rich man. My grandfather had grown up the second child of a wealthy Chinese family in Manila. He bought expensive clothes, and told strangers his father owned the largest movie theaters in Quezon City. He was heavily in debt, perennially on the verge of bankruptcy, and proud of his credit cards.

There's a Filipino proverb that says people who spend a lot of money are "angry" at money—"*galit sa pera.*" They can't stand to have it around. I know too many people who have declared bankruptcy. It's they who came to mind when my phone rang at nine in the morning, with a shrill, piercing urgency that signaled the start of another round of a game I liked to call Dodging the Creditors. To combat this constant aggravation, I learned to answer my phone in Spanish. *"No entiendo, señor. ¿Habla Español?"* If they happened to catch me off guard and answering my phone in English, I developed a sick and perverse delight in telling them my "roommate" Melissa was out of the country, was working late, was never home, was dead. The last one scared me, and I didn't do that again.

Like most debtors, my freefall down the rabbit hole started in college. It was probably a trip to Florida that did it. Not the real trip to South Beach I took my senior year—when three girlfriends and I holed up at the Cordozo Hotel, spent nights making eyes at swarthy waiters in Cuban restaurants, and generally had the liquor-soaked time of our lives, our $500 expenses paid for by our generous parents (mine included). No, not *that* Florida vacation, which ended with me, broke as usual, begging to borrow $25 from my best friend, Jennie, just so I could share a cab ride to our dormitory once we got to New York City.

"What would you do without me?" Jennie had asked. She was amused and a little annoyed, since we'd been down this road before. I didn't know how to answer her. She was the one who had bailed me out the year before when the police—*the police*—called to say they were going to arrest me for a bounced check. Unless I coughed up the $115 I owed Canal Jeans in Soho for a pair of Doc Martens I'd purchased there, it was debtor's prison for me (actually a desk-appearance ticket and a misdemeanor charge). Of course, I didn't have the money. I couldn't return the boots either, since they had been a present to the gay man I loved at the time. So Jennie lent me the money, and I paid her back with the hundred dollars my parents sent me that Thanksgiving so my sister and I could take the train to Washington and spend the holidays with relatives.

I made my sister take the bus instead. It was horrid—bus stations at Thanksgiving are filled with large caravans of military men, poor college kids like us, and the occasional bag lady with a free ticket home. It's doubtful my sister will ever forgive me, although she's had much practice. My sophomore year in college she lent me $900 to pay an overdue American Express bill. My credit history was virgin then: pure, solvent. At the time it seemed important to keep it that way. Aina, who was in high school, and boasted a fat savings account, sent me a MoneyGram plus $50 in cash to help me get through the month. The next month it was my parents who were stuck with the $1,500 AmEx bill. They weren't as understanding.

My life is filled with such free associations—from one person who's bailed me out of a money jam to another and another. I am bound to my friends and family not just by love but by debt. There is no limit to how much I owe them, and I owe some of them quite a lot. Lately I've come to realize how much they have learned to tolerate such shameless selfishness on my part. My reputation precedes me. Sometimes when I call, my friends don't even bother to say "Hello," only "How much?"

But back to Florida. The Florida vacation I *didn't* take. The Florida vacation that started the cash-flow crisis I'm in now. It was my freshman year at college, the first day back from winter break. My roommate at the time was a girl named Madelyn, a prep-school princess with an enormous wardrobe and a fickle temperament. I liked Madelyn, and more important, I wanted her to like me.

"Let's go to Florida," she said one evening while we smoked cigarettes in the hallway and tried to affect cool.

"Sure," I happily agreed. "Spring break?"

"No . . . tomorrow," she suggested, flicking ash everywhere. "Classes don't start for a couple days still. We could jet down, get an awesome tan, and be back for registration. Wouldn't that be fun?" she asked.

"Tomorrow?" I repeated. "But what about the plane tickets? We'd have to pay premium for them. And where would we stay?"

Madelyn shrugged. "I'm sure it wouldn't cost that much," she said. "We could stay at a hotel or something. It'll only be, like, a couple hundred bucks. It's just a weekend," she emphasized.

"Sure, sure." I nodded, already perturbed. I only had a "couple hundred" bucks in my checking account at that point—money that was supposed to take me well into the semester. I'd spent almost my entire savings already, just to keep up with the Madelyns of my life.

We didn't go to Florida. There was no way I'd have enough money or even the nonchalance to pull off that kind of stunt. Madelyn was nice about it: She pretended that it was okay for her to spend the week in a New York blizzard.

But her offhand suggestion was an eye-opener for me. It was the first time I fully comprehended the difference between Madelyn and me, rich versus poor, spontaneous versus anxious. For Madelyn, the world was an exciting place, full of endless possibilities. She could imagine flying off to Miami on a whim, just to get a good tan. For me, excitement meant a dinner downtown. At Benny's Burritos.

I vowed I'd never have to cry poor again, that if I ever found myself in a similar situation, when a friend suggested blowing $200 on a magnum of Korbel, a table at Au Bar, a taxicab uptown, or even to "for God's sake just buy the damn leather gloves"—I wouldn't say no. I would be prepared. I intended to cultivate the seductive characteristics of rich, spoiled American girls. Ringing in my mind was a phrase from Tolstoy's *War and Peace:* "Natasha, the rich girl with everything, was beloved by all. Self-sacrificing Sonya, who had nothing, was barren and forgotten." I didn't want to be Sonya, forever indebted and dependent. All my friends had Natasha's wicked fire, her free spirit, her confident sense of entitlement—all of which I wanted to emulate. So I did. With a little help from my credit cards.

The next year I was armed to the teeth in plastic: MBNA Visa, MBNA Visa Gold, Chase Platinum, AmEx, Citibank Preferred. Too late, though—Madelyn never included me in any of her travel plans again.

Money. At the time I was half afraid and half amazed by the way I earned it—working forty hours a week at a software company, an art history major writing lines of code for customized computer programs. So I got rid of it before it consumed me. Before it defined me. Allowing myself to spend it all carelessly, recklessly, and with a certain wild abandon, leaving me poor and destitute after these manic bouts of spending, afforded me to retain the perverted sense of pride and identity I cultivated by being poor. Once I earned enough to renounce my hero worship of bitchy, thin girls with Daddy's trust funds, I was actually proud of my erstwhile poverty. I didn't want to save money or worry about it and lord it over other people. I found it was much easier to live with the anxiety of being broke than the anxiety of being rich.

It's a misery, nonetheless, and one no amount of shopping sprees and fancy restaurants can solve. I was terribly unhappy. I didn't clean my unpaid apartment for months, and grew accustomed to living in filth. My living room was overrun by laundry bags, empty gin bottles, stacks of unopened bills and glossy magazines. I threw large, raucous parties in my backyard garden, spending several hundred dollars on booze and food to entertain large groups of people who didn't give a shit about me.

Luckily I did find a solution to my problems—both psychological and financial. I fell in love with my now husband. And my father helped me find a credit counselor. I came home one evening and found that Mike had cleaned the bedroom. There had been dust bunnies growing out of the wall like fungi. I realized how unhealthy my life had become. The nine A.M. phone calls, the angry missives from landlords and utility companies, the neurotic additions and subtractions, the bags of laundry in the living room, the dust collecting everywhere. A fog had lifted. I didn't want to be this kind of person. I didn't want to live as if every day were my last. With Mike I saw a future—and a life I wanted to be able to afford and enjoy.

My father helped me get myself back in financial shape. For years he had urged me to do something about my bills—to pay them on time, mostly, and get rid of my credit cards. Finally I took his advice and made an appointment with Consumer Credit Counseling Services. My credit counselor cut up my credit cards, put me on a budget, and reduced my monthly payments to a manageable rate. He even let me keep my $100-a-month dry-cleaning expenses. I also moved from my overpriced West Village alcove studio into a more spacious rent-stabilized one-bedroom on the Upper West Side that I shared with my boyfriend (now my husband).

I was on the program for about five years, and except for several slipups, I managed to pay my bills on time. Although I am still partial to the siren call of fashionable clothes, I pay for my half-price Gucci with cash. I've also reconciled myself to the fact that I am unfashionably bourgeoisie and staunchly middle-class. I am not a socialite.

There are no more credit cards in my wallet. I've even passed on the notion of applying for an account-based credit card (a credit card whose limit is attached to the funds stored in a savings account) that's been offered to me in the mail. The journey has begun.

2003—there is life after fashionista! Don't despair. It took me five years and lots of struggling to get out of crushing consumer debt. But I did it. My husband and I paid for our share of our wedding costs in cash—and that included a two-week vacation at the Princeville Resort in Hawaii. While buying those clothes now might make you feel better, think about what you really want down the line—a great midcentury bungalow in the Hollywood Hills, a vintage BMW, financial independence—and weigh it against the price tag of whatever you're holding in your hand. You might find you don't really want it after all.

Ascertain Your Level of Fashionista Financial Hell!

✳ LEVEL ONE ✳

You're a little bit behind, but you have money coming (of course, when it does arrive, you know exactly where it's going: to the cash register of your favorite store). Your cell phone was shut off only once. You have to charge tomatoes and Diet Coke at the gourmet grocery store, but when you're out with friends you have just enough cash to catch a cab, buy a beverage, and tip the coat check.

Tips:

• Pay double the minimum on the due amount of your credit card when the bill comes.

• Try to arrange professional meetings over lunch or dinner so someone else can expense it and pick up the tab.

• Start to keep a log of all of your expenditures in order to figure out where you can cut back, and create a budget that will allow you to still enjoy fashion to some extent.

• Return clothes if tags remain intact (or if you wore it once, didn't love it, and still have the receipt).

✳ LEVEL TWO ✳

You start to get phone calls from strangers who call themselves "Miss Jones," "Mr. Brown," or some other innocuous name, and leave a 1-800 number. You're eating Special K for dinner (but you've lost two pounds!). You date men you're not interested in because they'll take you to nice restaurants.

Tips:

• Don't call that 800 number back until you have the money, an organized plan you can stick to for paying it back, or a really good excuse (we recommend telling them you've been in Europe for an emergency situation that is too difficult to discuss).

• Give a friend your credit card to hold. You are clearly not to be trusted with it for a while.

• Self-imposed probation: Tell the stores where you do the most damage that you're not allowed to shop for a certain amount of time. Beg them to not take your money. (This doesn't always work.)

• At a drinks date, dramatically dig through your bag and start freaking out about "lost wallet" phobia. Your cocktail partner will pay. Thank him or her profusely and send a sweet note with an IOU card or flowers when you get a shot of cash flow (ultimately, flowering someone will be costlier than a $7 cocktail, but it's all about image).

✳ LEVEL THREE ✳

Matters have become dire. Eviction notices are piling up. Your phone is . . . well, let's just say temporarily out of service. The IRS has put a lien on your paycheck. And even worse, your skin is breaking out from all the stress.

Tips:

• Filing Chapter 11 may be your best option. If you declare bankruptcy, you can't have credit for ten years. But all your debts are forgiven. Seek advice (get on an allowance plan) from a good accountant, preferably one who's friends with the family, so you can get away with free advice.

• Cut up your credit cards, or, at the very least, make your limit far less than whatever it currently is.

- Change many things about your life. Forbid yourself to even step into stores, and if you take walks, make sure you travel a path that will enable you to avoid any kind of temptation.

- Get thee to rehab, or at the very least, Debtor's Anonymous meetings.

- If you don't have a boyfriend, find one (fast!) and move in with him (nothing like a little impulsive behavior to make life more exciting).

- Change your name and move to Nebraska (no one would ever think of looking for you *there*!).

INSUFFICIENT FUNDS!?
Oops, I Did It Again!
❋ KAREN ❋

Tax season, 2003. No different from tax seasons 2002, 2001, 2000, and 1999 . . . I have to pay an undisclosed amount to the government, and for the seventh year in a row I am in dire straits. Not only can I not pay my taxes right now, but I can't even take out $40 from the bank because my account is depleted, kaput, empty. I have no money, even if I'm wearing a fortune.

I have this little problem called "living off the gross." As a freelancer, taxes are not taken out of my paychecks, and as a fashionista I am prone to impulsive behavior, living in the moment, and shopping rather than saving for: a.) a rainy day, and b.) to pay the IRS (those wretched people!). Full disclosure: One-third of my income is spent on fashion.

I struggle with my fashion desires on many emotional levels. While I love, love, love it as an art, I feel pressure in my industry to look a certain way, wear certain things, and also a deeper sense of insecurity, not feeling good enough as I am, a result of far too many childhood wounds and psychological meshugahs. Buying fills a void, albeit temporarily. Dressing well has been a way for me to overcompensate in some ways. Not that it makes it okay. But it is an issue that has caused me much angst.

I am aware when I'm shopping as a means to treat myself to something nice and when I am doing it to escape, deny, or cope with one of life's hurdles. Like a bad drunk, sometimes the more I shop, the more I feel like I need to shop. Afterward I'm left with a nasty hangover—a sense of emptiness and guilt—not to mention things that I wear a few times and get sick of.

The truth about my net worth: I have no liquid assets, other than Nicolas Ghesquière's greatest hits from the previous fall and a feathered Gucci dress so precious, I'm afraid to even wear it. Full of shame, I feel like I have nowhere to turn. I am in a dark hole. And I need to pull myself up by my (very expensive) bootstraps and emerge.

The process feels so overwhelming. Frightening, even. That is probably why, in the past, it has been easier for me to remain in denial and continue on my unhealthy path instead of dealing. My whole life I have been relying on old behaviors that may not work, but feed some part of my soul—even if for only a moment. Although such cycles actually make things worse, they're easy to nourish.

This year, however, I decide it needs to be different. This year, I have to make a change. My actions are no longer making me happy. In fact, they're making me miserable. I spent nearly half of my life battling an eating disorder, which I conquered in 1999. But the shopping, in so many ways, is the exact same problem as what was behind the body image and control issues that led me to bulimia. I basically took one addiction and replaced it with another. It's time to grab the Mombasa YSL bag by the horn handle.

I call in my accountant, Michael, for backup. Together we carefully go over every one of my necessary expenses (i.e., cable, phone, electric, etc.), extras (manicure, pedicure, hair, entertainment, etc.), and luxuries (shopping, massages, cab fare, etc.) in order to deduce where I need to cut back (duh!). It is the kind of tear-filled meeting that forces me to take a good, hard look at my flaws and mistakes—never an easy thing to do.

I am still working on it. And I continue to every day. Sometimes I feel like Sisyphus, pushing a giant rock uphill. Once I reach the top, it falls to the bottom again. And I keep pushing it up, chasing it down, pushing it up and chasing it down. Every time I have the urge to shop, I take a step back in order to do something that feels more soothing—a bath, a manicure, yoga, a movie on Lifetime. I leave the house without my wallet when I frequent Soho or an area near a store I can't resist, as a means of prevention. This hasn't always worked . . . some stores have my credit card number on file. (The bastards!)

Mel, the good friend she is, introduced me to Century 21. We both thought, if I had to shop, I'd better at least do it in an affordable place that won't leave me high and dry. In the overcrowded department store, I spent hours marveling at the Lagerfeld, Balenciaga, and Gaultier pieces I had once paid full price for (they were so cheap at Century 21 that it was sickening, even if the stuff was a season old). Although I must admit I missed the personal, intimate environment of a small boutique and the thrill of seeing clothes that weren't aging and picked over.

I went to the cash register with white moleskin Balenciaga pants, an Ungaro ruffled silk blouse, and white four-inch D & G heels, an ensemble that cost a total of $400, $100 less than what the pants would cost retail. As the woman rang me up, I started panicking, thinking of the remorse I'd walk away with, the fact that I still have taxes to pay, bills to deal with, and a savings account to finally start.

"How would you like to pay for that?" the woman asked.

I thought about it for a minute and calmly said, "Actually, I wouldn't." I apologized for the trouble I might have caused and walked away empty-handed. It was the first sign I was on my way to recovery. In the past I would have said, "Who cares, I'll deal with it later," and bought it anyway. I wouldn't have thought twice about putting myself in a bind for the rest of the month or being relegated to eating the canned peas and corn that have been sitting in my cupboard for seven (yes, seven) years.

Mel was shocked. And so proud of me.

I felt such a sense of accomplishment, too, even if it took me a day or two to get over not having the new wares. Not shopping can often be as traumatic as acting out. But nothing good comes easy. And things usually get worse before they improve (kind of like your skin after a deep facial). I am handling my healing the twelve-step way: one day at a time.

I get hard on myself for what seems like failure (a.k.a. when I fall off the wagon and give in to temptation, which was the case at a Spring 2004 trunk show for Luisa Beccaria at Kirna Zabete) from time to time. However, I am confident that it will work out, as all things do. I have successfully killed many demons in my head in my life. This is merely another one on my path.

Just don't ask me about my taxes.

CLOSET BANKER

Forget dinner with your friends—or even buying a bottle of Diet Coke! You can't even take out $20 from the ATM machine. Dealing with your issue is not easy. But here's one solution: Make money off your clothes—and find smart ways to save every dime you can along the way.

• Sell stuff on eBay. All you need is a digital camera and a little bit of motivation.

• Hock all your old gold jewelry—stuff you would never wear, especially if an ex-boyfriend gave it to you. Trade in for Costume National shoes.

• Have a garage sale. Your trash is another girl's treasure.

• Bring old designer duds (or ones you're not hopelessly in love with) to consignment shops. You don't get the money—which is typically way less than what you paid for it, but it all adds up, right?—immediately, but you will as soon as your stuff sells. In New York City, INA is the place where the supermodels relinquish garbage bags of fresh Marc Jacobs, Narciso Rodriguez, and designer samples.

• Return gift certificates for cash.

• Donate unwearables to the Salvation Army or Goodwill; it will be a tax-deductible expense.

• Learn to be skillful when you're dealing with your taxes. If actresses can expense makeup, fashionistas should be able to expense clothes! Pray you don't get audited.

• Befriend the woman who owns your favorite store. After a year, discuss the possibility of layaway . . . and even discounts. Keep it a secret.

• Raid your mom's closet. There must be something you can refurbish.

• Check out novelty fetish shops for shoes. The designers of Preen, a label in London that's highbrow and artsy, get their fierce ankle boots from a cheap little sex store.

• Set a realistic budget, not one that you will cheat on, and one that will allow you to still buy what you want—within reason.

• Skip breakfast. It may be the most important meal of the day, but after one month of not having breakfast you might be able to save enough for a really great pair of chandelier earrings!

• Cut and color your own hair—messy, shaggy looks can be chic. And very Meg Ryan.

CHAPTER 10

Fashion Week!
Seven Days of Heaven

Twice a year, in the cities of New York, Paris, Milan, and London, the fashion flock gather and parade and display their wares. It's known as Fashion Week, and it's when designers show their new collections and fashionistas line up, push, shove, and make their way into crowded venues in order to see the spectacle. "The shows," as they're usually called, are the fashionista equivalent of a rock concert—complete with loud music, dazzling lights, drama, and the chance to cheer on the model du jour. Fashion shows involve months of prep work—from scouting a space with the right image, hiring and fitting the perfect models, designing invitations and just the right guest list, finding the best DJ, retaining a PR firm, raising funds and finding sponsors in some cases, and—forget about it—handling the seating assignments, which might just involve more creative energy than it took the designer to come up with a line to push, market, and sell. As hot as the action is on the runway, however, it doesn't quite compare to the action in the seats.

The most interesting thing about Fashion Week is not the sneak peek of what we will be wearing in six months, when the model's fifteen-inch car-wash skirt hits the department stores at a more palatable twenty-five inches, but to see what we should be wearing *right now.* It's a time when the fashionistas pull out all the stops, flash their style in the most exaggerated way, and show off all of their new purchases. It could be eighty degrees out in September, but that won't stop someone from making an entrance in the latest knee-high boots and heavy wool coat from Marc Jacobs. It is a sea of spectators sizing one another up, giving one another the once-over, the double take, and a good, hard, long look up and down.

Are the *Vogue* editors all in humongous fur hats? Are the *Bazaar* girls running around in striped scarves? Is that the *W* accessories director in pink lizard-skin slingbacks? What about the kooky art kids from *Surface, Paper,* and *Black Book?* Why are they suddenly all wearing glitter-encrusted stretch jeans? The latest trends are all on display—whether they are ponchos or vintage tweed suits or full-length flight suits. Fashion Week is for the advanced fashionistas, the professionals—but there's no reason why an amateur can't join in the fun.

In this chapter we'll give you a no-holds-barred inside look at the phenomenon that is Fashion Week, as well as teach you how to crash fashion shows and dress like you belong, which parties to attend, where to get the best goody bags, whether to take a town car or taxi, and where to find the best champagne in the house. Drink up!

TAKING OFF FOR THE RUNWAYS!
Sneaking out to Set the Style Agenda
✳ MELISSA ✳

During the five years that I regularly covered Fashion Week for several New York newspapers and magazines, I was also working full-time as a computer programmer. Stealth was definitely in order if I wanted to attend the shows. Luckily I was a computer consultant during the heyday of the boom, when totally unnecessary (and very lazy) people like me could command six-figure corporate salaries without batting an eyelash.

Two weeks before Fashion Week I put aside my travel budget. While the shows in New York are mostly set up in the tents in

Bryant Park, several rogue designers like to show off-site, like Marc Jacobs, who always shows at the Lexington Armory, or design darlings from overseas like Alexander McQueen, Nicolas Ghesquière, and Helmut Lang, who prefer to rent airline hangars or former gas stations for their presentations, which are usually better than the most decadent Broadway production.

There are a minimum of eight to ten shows every day during Fashion Week, and some shows are scheduled for the same hour. I checked with my editor about my expense account, looked at my options, and took action as necessary. First off, I had to go to work. I would arrive at the bank wearing my nondescript corporate drag, carrying a garment bag with my Fashion Week outfit. In the bathroom, on would go the zebra-print Dolce & Gabbana jeans, the bejeweled Christian Dior pumps, the ostrich-feather hat.

"Cool shoes" was all my coworkers said whenever they saw me dressed this way. By now they were used to seeing me do the fashion superwoman transformation. I would hail a cab to the tents in Bryant Park or wherever, attend several shows, and get back to the office in time to clock out a full eight-hour day, with no one the wiser. While most of the real fashion editors were holed up at fancy hotels or else running back to the Condé Nast tower to close the next issue, I would return to the drab confines of my gray, carpet-walled cubicle. But perhaps because I saw what life without fashion would be like (bleak, empty, ultimately depressing despite the fat paychecks), I treasured those two weeks a year even more.

Getting There and Getting Noticed

IT'S NOT THE JOURNEY; IT'S THE DESTINATION.
FASHION WEEK TRAVEL AT ITS FINEST

- If you can wrangle the use of a car and driver through work or friends, or have been approved for town car use in a city, give other fashionistas a ride if they lack one. They will remember your generosity—and one night you might find you don't have a car and they do, and they will happily share their limo with you.

• New York, Paris, Milan, and London all have very dependable rail systems. If you're on a budget, take the underground, the metro or the subway, and save yourself the ten dollars it would cost to take a cab. Just don't tell anyone. Public transportation is often frowned upon.

• Investing in a car and driver if you are going to attend several shows in different areas in one day is worth it. While the organizers provide a bus, most high-profile fashionistas never take it. Offer to share the cost and your ride with a friend to save money.

• Get in touch with the PR company whose client is sponsoring Fashion Week and try to get hooked up through them. For years Mercedes was the title sponsor of New York's Fashion Week, and they often provided cars and drivers for the biggest stars in the biz.

• Travel with your bodyguards, à la Anna Wintour. It elevates your image.

• At a high-profile show, escape paparazzi by getting PR flacks to escort you to secret back entranceways. Calvin Klein shows at Milk Studios, glossy lofts on West Fifteenth Street, and VIPs avoid annoying camera action by entering through Jeffrey, the West Fourteenth Street store that is attached to Milk.

CRASHING THE HIGH
Following the Flock
✳ MELISSA ✳

During the fall of 2000 the fashion world anointed its new boy genius, the man who would be its savior, the next John Galliano. The next Gaultier. The next McQueen. His name was Miguel Adrover, and he was the Great Majorcan Hope, a shy thirty-two-year-old who toiled in the East Village and caused an immediate buzz from his lone guerrilla fashion show the last season. The show birthed several key iconic pieces: a mattress coat made out of the late Quentin Crisp's bedding, a deconstructed Burberry trench coat re-made as a dress, a "cap-sleeve" sweater made with real Yankee base-ball caps, and a coat made from vintage Louis Vuitton luggage. Anna Wintour reportedly trampled overturned cars to see the show.

It was understandable, then, that everyone was excited to see what the man would do next. Miguel was now being backed by the Pegasus Group, who sank five million dollars into his enterprise. The funding gave Miguel's atelier the ability to hire a real fashion publicist, Marion Greenberg Inc., a major force to be reckoned with.

Tickets to the show were in such high demand that the news was that if you hadn't merited a hand-delivered invitation (which consisted of a dirty dollar bill with the location and seat assignment stamped on it), you had to make the pilgrimage, plead your case with Marion, and perhaps—only perhaps—you would be deemed worthy to attend. As writers for an indie fashion site, my editor in chief and I made the trek to the showroom to work our magic. It worked. Sort of. My editor got a "standing" denomination. But I left empty-handed.

"And I've known Miguel since he was sewing patches on rag dolls!" my editor fumed. I was even more upset! But there was no way I was going to miss this show. At first we decided we would create our own dollar bill and approximate the orange stamp. But after a few tries with a Sharpie, we ended up with dollar mush. We decided to plot strategy, as intricately and with as much serious-ness as generals going to war. We knew what we were up against. Security at fashion shows is so tight you'd think they were guarding the Pope. Liz Tilberis, the late and great editor in chief of *Bazaar,* was famous for socking the security guards in the nose after they wouldn't let her two assistant fashion editors into a show in Paris.

"We'll just fight our way in," my editor declared. "I'll hold up the bill, and you just run in with me." I pushed up my Helmut

Lang sleeves and agreed. When we arrived at the temple, it looked like all of fashionable New York was in front of the building. It was frightening. We feared death by stomping, which would have been fatal with all those nail-heeled Gucci shoes! Nonetheless, we shouldered on. Around us everyone was waving dollar bills at the clipboard girls. It was such madness that people simply clawed their way inside and the PR chicks gave up trying to control the situation. We were all suffering from fashion mania. It was straight out of WWE!

It was rumored that Anna Wintour had given up trying to get in after two hours. (Anna Wintour rumors are rampant during Fashion Week. What's Anna wearing? What did Anna think of the show? How skinny is she these days?) Lo and behold, I made my way inside. I felt triumphant, sweaty, and a little deranged. My carefully blown-out hair was askew, my sweater was torn, and I think I still had both my shoes, but I wasn't sure. It didn't matter. We found seats! We had to battle two nasty editors from French *Vogue* for them, but we wouldn't give them up. *Ne parlez Français.* We shrugged helplessly.

As for the show . . . What could live up to that kind of expectation? Miguel offered long, drab skirts, djellabas, and a flock of sheep shepherded by models on the runway. One sheep wouldn't go where it was told, and stood on the end, bleating in annoyance. Some of the "models" left turds on the runway. If there was any "fashion genius" going on, it was completely beyond me. But at least I was there to witness the lack of it!

Secret of My Success
❋ KAREN ❋

From 1994 to 1997 I worked as a peon at Fairchild Publications, the powerhouse media company that publishes *Women's Wear Daily* (a.k.a. the fashion bible) and *W* magazine. While my days were spent doing the remedial, low-end tasks for which important people hadn't the time—handing out mail, carrying flowers from the messenger center to some big editor's desk, occasionally returning a few hundred thousand dollars' worth of diamonds to Tiffany, and fetching coffee for the powers that be—I thought myself lucky to be in an environment where such vital fashion news was being reported. Every minute I was exposed to glorious racks of clothing rolling through the office, detailed conversations and faxes about the production of photo shoots (the best way to learn is by eavesdropping), and what life is like on a crazy deadline schedule. It seemed like such a dream. I couldn't wait to move up the ranks and be more than just a gofer. This was the place where Calvin Klein got his start.

The fashionistas lurking inside the fluorescent-lit loftlike space had a commanding presence. They almost always wore black. Every day I overheard watercooler convo about who was wearing what ("Did you see that Miu Miu fur? What about Bridget's skirt? It's Galliano!"), but as a newbie on the circuit I was too intimidated to speak up. Instead I watched carefully and learned a lot about dressing and style. It was the first time I was exposed to superhigh pointy-toed stilettos—with jeans! And I relished the look, promptly adopting it with my own spin. The aura of the place was always fast-paced, slightly insane, and stylish. And during Fashion Week it was the same, only much more so.

No one was in the office during showtime. It was go, go, go. Big editors got car services while the rest were left to their own devices. The crew dressed to the nines. No expense was spared for Fashion Week style. Most people "called in" clothes from big design houses in order to borrow something chic. And everyone would try to give a designer a "nod" by showing up at the collection in something from the designer in question. Wear Oscar to Oscar, Calvin to Calvin, Ralph to Ralph. Change in the cab if you must. I wanted to be a part of the craziness of it all, but there was no way. I was too low on the ladder to merit an invite. Once someone let me have a "standing only" invitation that no one had claimed, but I had too many things to file in order to go.

By my second year at *WWD*, however, I started to know more people. Extra perks were thrown my way from time to time (they must have figured, "Give the dog a bone. . . ." After all, there was only so much begging they could handle). But the perks never came in the form of a fashion show invite. So I took it upon myself to find a way in. One season I dolled myself up like nobody's business, having saved for months to afford wares of a certain caliber from the gleaming Calvin Klein store on Madison Avenue.

I was determined to get into his show, no matter what. I managed to attach myself to a group of what appeared to be important editors (they were all speaking with British accents and wearing wild fedoras and leather Dior suits, which must have meant they were *someone*). I got up the nerve to put on my most pretentious accent and say to one of the women, "Darling, these Manolos are killing my feet. Do you mind if I hold on to you while we make it through this crowd of vulgarians?" She understood—and being the fairy-godmother fashionista from across the pond that she was, she said, "Darling, I do understand. Of course, love." She gave me her arm. With that I tricked the doorkeeper, who assumed I was part of the posse.

My next step was seat scouring. I waited until most of the crowd poured in before I pounced. I figured I'd let the real invitees sit and then grab a seat belonging to an ungrateful no-show. Thirty-five minutes later (these things never start on time), I was perched in the second row (not as good as first, but much better than being in my office, filing). I watched the show in awe. I had never seen such beauty, such flawless makeup, such tall, gorgeous women, such covetable clothes.

And as I walked out, I wasn't thinking about the fact that I'd have to explain my extended lunch break. My low-level status didn't even come to mind. I just felt high, like I had just tasted the good life and I never wanted the flavor to go away. It did, sadly. The second I got back to the office! An editor had spotted me in the second row and reamed me for it, saying that I had no right to be there because I was just an assistant. She wanted to know how I got in and what the hell I was doing there. She threatened to get my ass fired in a snap. I found out later that she was just angry because she was in the fourth row. The horror!

No Invitation? No Problem!

Fashion shows are closed to the public. But with a little guile, a lot of chutzpah, and a great outfit, you too can scam your way past the burly security guards.

• The best way to snag an invitation is to put together press credentials. Write for your college paper, or a small alternative press that doesn't cover fashion, but is well known in town. Convince the editor you're the girl (or guy) for the job. Register for a press pass and wait for the invitations to come to you.

• Seventh on Sixth (the organization that runs the official shows in New York and Los Angeles) has a list of public relations firms that handle the shows. Fax them your credentials (a few clips will help support your case) and they will pass them along to the PR firms so that you are on the invitation list.

• Subscribe to the *Fashion Calendar* ($400 a year) to get the latest news on all happenings. Fashion Calendar Publications, 153 E. Eighty-seventh Street, New York, NY 10128 (212) 289-0420.

• Standing-room tickets are given to students at fashion colleges, like FIT and Parsons. If you're not enrolled there, find a friend who is, and snag invitations from him or her.

• To upgrade a standing-room ticket, simply write in a seat number. Show seating is most commonly a section number, a row number, and a seat number. Sections are usually alphabetical. Try "B-3-5" or "C-7-11." Only the truly brash upgrade all the way to the first-calls rows, like "A-1-10." (A section, first row, seat 10). Once you arrive at your stolen seat, peel off the name of the person whose seat you have swiped. Never give up your seat unless threatened with bodily harm. A furious fashionista is a frightening sight!

> • If you want to sneak a friend into the shows, give your friend your ticket so she can waltz into the show without being stopped. You yourself will check in at the front desk, saying you lost your ticket. You will be given a white paper slip with your seat assignment. There is always an excess of empty seats, so your friend should have no trouble finding one. You can both even upgrade to better seats—all the way to the front row—if you have the nerve!

WHO ARE YOU WEARING?
Close Encounters with a Camera Lens
✳ MELISSA ✳

There's a tenacious type of reporter that covers Fashion Week with a dedication rivaled by no other. I'm speaking, of course, of the Japanese paparazzi. The Japanese paparazzi are a funky-looking group made up of small mustached and bearded men with huge Nikon lenses. They are accompanied by supremely chic bosses in cat-eye glasses, schoolgirl uniforms, and fluorescent-colored running shoes. The Japanese paparazzi cover the clothes of the fashionista attendees with the zeal of war correspondents.

As editors and socialites alight from their cabs and town cars, the Japarazzi swarm, hounding their heels, snapping flashbulbs, and yelling in Japanese. Once the photographers are satisfied they have their shot, the editors tentatively approach to get your name, age, and what designer you are wearing. Unlike Bill Cunningham, the *New York Times*'s Sunday Styles photographer, who uses long-lens cameras and is very discriminate about whom he shoots (in fact, most fashionista wanna-bes walk vainly in front of him several times in outrageous outfits to try to nab his attention), the Japarazzi give everybody love.

Still, the Japanese have their regular "favorites" each season, and one year I was honored to be one of them. In fact, another fashionista pastime is to appear jaded about the Japanese atten-

Fashion show invitations: tickets to the world of style

tion. "Oh, God, they want a picture of me *again*?" fashionistas often say, rolling their eyes as they turn to face the cameras. "Aren't they tired of me by now?"

Every time I arrived at the tents that year, the same crew went in for the kill. Unlike the other fashionistas, who were rewarded with full-length body shots, the Japanese photographers were obsessed with my shoes. In all my years of attending Fashion Week, my face never appeared in *Cutie,* Japanese *Vogue, Ginza,* or any of the Japanese glossies. But my feet have been regular models.

Dressing for the Paparazzi

Putting together a wardrobe for Fashion Week requires quick-change artistry. You might find that the outfit you had imagined for Monday (bomber jacket, satin skirt, ankle-strap heels) might not work by Tuesday, when you realize everyone is working the haute hippie look instead of the slutty secretary scenario. Here are a few tips to get everyone's attention—and admiration.

• Eccentricity is a plus. Indulge in a full-length eye-catching outfit. You will find the most colorfully and outrageously dressed always win the game. We have seen men in checkered four-piece plaid suits, clown shoes, huge Mad Hatter hats, and walking canes get assaulted by the cameras.

• When in doubt, oversize. A three-foot-tall cowboy hat, or six-inch heels, or a Big Bird–yellow floor-length fur coat.

• Vintage touches always turn heads. Marilyn Kirschner, a former editor at *Bazaar,* was rewarded with a full-page spread in the Sunday *Times* for her exquisite vintage outfits. (She always wore on the trend of the moment without paying the price of the moment.)

• Weird always works. The editors of *Paper* attend the shows in blankets, hobo-style coats, vinyl running shoes, and plastic Hermès knockoffs.

- Tote a one-of-a-kind statement, like a bag made of license plates.

- Borrow something from a major designer from the season that is being shown on the runway. It is a privilege allotted to a very proud few. If you can't get one from the season of the runway moment, at least wear something from the current season.

- Put on something new and fabulous, regardless of how seasonal or weather-appropriate it is. This is no time to be shy about your fashion scores.

- A great handbag is key. During Fashion Week, magazines show huge spreads of what people are wearing to the shows and often focus on the front row of handbags littering the floor. Louis Vuitton, Hermès, Balenciaga, Gucci, Fendi, Hogan, and so on. It is also the time when the fake peddlers come out and sell knock-offs nearby. Patricia Field, the stylist for *Sex and the City,* was spotted getting a faux LV Murakami for $20. The seller was chased away by cops!

- Don't read a magazine. You don't want to illustrate your media loyalty to the public. *WWD* staffers are instructed not to read any competitor publication at the shows!

FRONT AND CENTER
David Copperfield, Toni Braxton, Karen Robinovitz!?
✳ KAREN ✳

First you get an invitation. Then you RSVP. Once you get that far, you just sit and wait. Wait for what? Your seating assignment, of course. It's an Adivan moment, riddled with anxiety. Anything can happen between the time you RSVP and the time you get your seat confirmation. In this business you are only as good as the row you're sitting in. The seat, for a fashionista, is a lot like a car for a man going through a midlife crisis. You have to have the best. You have to be front-row. The more high-profile the designer, the more your seat confirms your position, status, and class among other fashionistas. And considering that this is a world focused on image, you can only imagine how heart-wrenching it is to be cursed with a bad spot.

On the town with Liv Tyler during Fashion Week, when all the stars come out

I have to admit, I would love to be a first-row gal at Marc Jacobs or Narciso Rodriguez. I am not. In fact, this season (Spring/Summer 2003), I didn't even get an invitation to those shows (curses!). But I was given spectacular affirmation at the Rosa Cha show. Rosa Cha is a Brazilian swimwear line designed by Amir Slama, who makes shocking bathing suits. Think hardly-there silhouettes, reversible fabrics, treated suede, ruffles, layers of tulle, corseting, lacing, ruching, boning, and as much care as what would go into a highly elaborate Michael Kors gown. It's waterproof art.

And this season's show was destined to be an outsize smash hit. Beyoncé and Jay Z. were in the house. It was sponsored by Ortho Evra, the birth-control-patch company. The models were going to be parading the runway, half-naked with high heels and birth-control patches! The glamorous irony! And the line to get in was absolute mayhem. I was elbowed in the gut twice—and even had the bruise to prove it. I was pushed so hard, my Gucci hat fell off and some fashionista was stepping all over it. When I asked her if she'd mind moving a bit so I could retrieve it, she actually said, "Yes, I do mind." I was like, *Hello! It's fur!*

I was accosted by no less than three doorkeepers, who couldn't find my name on the list (it was, of course, misspelled, as usual).

Front-row glory . . . worth every ounce of pain it took to get there!

A skinny flaming fashionista fell over, and in the process of tipping over he reached out and grabbed whatever he could find to hold him up—my Chloe necklace, which broke on the spot. I thought about leaving, but it was pouring out. And I knew I'd never find a cab. So I sucked it up and finally made my way to my seat. All was forgotten as I was led to my cushy front-row spot, right between David Copperfield and Toni Braxton—and in front of so many of the people who hurt me as I made my way inside!

The View Is Marvelous!
✳ **MELISSA AND KAREN** ✳

Who doesn't love sitting in the front row? The crème de la crème of the fashion world park their butts on this prime real estate. And once you have sat in front, there's no going back.

"Mel, are you going to Alvin's show?" Karen asked.

"I don't know," Mel lamented.

"Why? Isn't he your favorite designer?"

"Yes. But he only gave me *third* row."

Third row! A nightmare! Sitting with nobodies in the cheap seats! In the third row, you wouldn't even be able to see the models' shoes! "That is unacceptable!" Karen said.

"I know. I don't know what to do."

We begged and pleaded and faxed. And we were rewarded. The next day Alvin's publicist hand-delivered two invitations with front-row designations. Of course, on the day of the show we suffered fashion lethargy: the disease that comes from wanting so much to go somewhere, but once the time comes, it seems like your home has never been more comfortable.

It's not who you are, it's where you sit that counts.

"Mel, do you want to go to Alvin's show?" Karen asked.

"I don't feel like it." Mel replied.

"You can't! We have to go!" Karen said. "After the workout we did to that publicist? She'll *kill* us!" In the end, we made our way to Alvin's show. And we noticed that so many people had requested front-row that the show producers had fixed the problem by creating a U-shaped runway, which doubled the amount of front-row seats. Still, it was good to have such a plum spot. A photographer at *W* recognized us and took our photo. See above.

WHO'S WHO AT THE SHOWS AND WHERE THEY SIT

Seating politics is serious business at the shows. Production companies and PR firms work literally twenty-four/seven to get it together, chomping down pizza, sipping Red Bull, and staying up all night to figure out who to seat where (can't put this person next to this person because they hate each other, and—oh, my God!—what about Carine from Paris? At the eleventh hour she hasn't a seat, and that is a major faux pas and grounds for immediate firing). It's very tricky, getting it all right. It is a time of catfights, cutting remarks, painful tears, and dirty politics. Seating charts go back and forth from designer to PR company to fashion show producers until everything is right . . . and even then, things change at the very last second. Editors have stabbed other editors in the back with a ballpoint pen over seats. Luckily, it's usually Montblanc.

Front row	Editors in chief of major magazines (*Vogue, W, Bazaar,* etc.) and their offspring (Anna Wintour's daughter Bee gets front-row every year); fashion and creative directors if they're very A-list; buyers from major department stores (Barneys, Bloomingdale's, Saks, Bendel, etc.); celebrities (Britney Spears, Sarah Jessica Parker); socialites (Nan Kempner, Aerin Lauder); crashers (notice them by their shifty eyes and not-quite-Manolo shoes!).
Second row	Fashion directors/senior fashion editors from national newspapers and major local newspapers (the *New York Times* and the *New York Post*), however, editors in chief and style directors from the *New York Times* get front-row props.
Third row	Regional papers; associate editors; fashion assistants.
Fourth row	Small local papers; small boutique buyers that don't have premier status in the biz; corporate sponsors.
Fifth row	The designers' families.
Standing	FIT students; any of the above if there are more of the first- and second-row people—i.e., Puffy

bumps down the accessories director, who
bumps down the assistant, who bumps down the
regional paper . . . and so it goes. . . .

FASHION WEEK ON THE WEST COAST . . . AN OXYMORON?

Rocking the House

✳ MELISSA ✳

I was skeptical about the whole notion of Los Angeles Fashion Week. I mean, *c'mon*. First of all, there is no such thing as weather in Southern California—it's a breezy, sunny eighty degrees every day, even in the middle of January. When it rained in Silver Lake, it was actually on the news.

"John Smith, caught off guard by the rain," flashed on the television set, as confused Angelinos confronted the cloudy skies. Since there's no opportunity to wear crocodile boots, tweed and fur coats, or even high heels, what passes for high style in La La Land is simple: Juicy sweats, Ugg boots or wedgies, wraparound sunglasses. The men climbing out of Bentleys wear tracksuits instead of Armani.

The first sign that I wasn't in Manhattan anymore (Toto!) was that everyone at the Smashbox Fashion Week (held at the groovy Smashbox Studios in Culver City) was given a free goody bag. Now, in New York only registered members of the press merit the overstuffed freebie. But in LA anyone could walk to a booth marked, helpfully, GIFT BAGS, flash an ID, and waltz off with one. It was very democratic.

The second sign was that there was free booze for everyone. Absolut set up vodka bars, and everyone was milling around drinking. In the Big Apple, the champagne is reserved for those privileged enough to be invited to the Moët & Chandon lounge.

Next, most of the models walking the shows were Hollywood progeny. Kim Stewart (Rod's daughter) and Jake Sumner (Sting's son) at Rock & Republic, Malcolm Ford (Harrison's son) at

2BFREE, and so on and so forth. But what really struck me as purely Los Angeles was the way the crowd responded to the fashion shows. Instead of sitting quietly and clapping tepidly after a presentation, the crowd hooted, stamped their feet, and actually cheered the models on the runways, calling their names.

I was appalled. This was no way to conduct a fashion show! I kept my New York face on and frowned. Then I remembered one of the first fashion shows I attended. It was for a major designer—and this was in 1994—when supermodels still walked the earth. RuPaul was sitting in the front row, and whenever someone walked out who was truly divine (Kate, Naomi, Christy, Helena), she would stand up (all six-six of her) and snap her fingers and yell, "Work it!" The kids in the rafters (where I was standing) loved it. I cheered and hollered along with everybody. The models were stars. The show was fun. It was electric and crazy.

When the models from Rock & Republic slipped on the beer that they were spilling on the runway, a laugh went up, but when one dusted off her butt (not hard, considering the skirt barely covered it!) and continued her walk, the crowd erupted in cheers worthy of an NFL football game. I found myself standing and yelling as loudly as the rest of them. The excitement was contagious.

The Fashionista Poker Face

At fashion shows no one ever smiles. No one cranes her neck to catch a glimpse of the celebrity surrounded by flashbulbs. Everyone is too cool and above it all. Here's how to master the proper show gaze:

- Whatever you do, never clap enthusiastically. Once you reach fashionista icon status, like Polly Mellen (former creative director of *Allure*), feel free to cartwheel down the runway in joy. Otherwise, a tepid two-finger clap will do.

- Keep your face straight. Never show them what you're feel-ing. No gasping. No choking. No rolling eyes. Fashion is a serious business. Show the designer some respect.

- No smiling. No nudging your seatmate. No having fun. (If Derek Jeter is nearby, however, it's okay to ask for an autograph for your boyfriend/husband/son/nephew—or a phone number. Even the editor in chief of *Marie Claire* has done so.)

- Complain. Endlessly. Fashionistas *always* complain about Fashion Week. The tedium of going from show to show, how there is never anything "new" on the runways, how terrible to see all the same people and their attitude *again.* Part of the fun of going to Fashion Week is being privileged enough to complain about hav-ing to cover it, as if someone is forcing us to drink champagne, gobble down canapés, and take cabs all over the city. Right. We know we're ridiculous, but if you're part of the tribe, a jaded atti-tude is par for the course.

FROM THE SIDEWALK TO THE CATWALK
Lessons from a Runway Master
✳ MELISSA AND KAREN ✳

Drew Linehan, a thirty-something flaming fashionista with a razor-sharp wit, short-cropped white hair, pale ice-blue eyes, and fan-tastic Prada shoes, is a casting director for runway shoes. A former antiques dealer, he moved to New York and fell sideways into fash-ion. "I didn't even know this kind of job existed!" he says.

He cast a DKNY men's fashion show as his first job and got hooked immediately. Few can resist the charms of the fashion world—a curse and a blessing at once. After stints at casting pow-erhouse Bureau Betak (the company responsible for the book *Fash-ion Cues by Bureau Betak,* which published the designers' directives to models, like "Glamorous, but not modely!" and "Keep your look deep and intense with your eyes forward directly ahead of you" and "You're at your lodge in Montana. . . . It's chilly . . . but you're wrapped in cashmere!" and "Gentlemen, for the swimsuit finale, please wear your willie down!") and doing shows for the likes of Michael Kors, Drew went on to be a modeling agent at DNA.

"I had to babysit some fourteen-year-olds making ten thousand dollars a day and hear them complain!" he gossips. The models would whine that they were missing the prom or a date—normal teenage lives. "They never realized how special they were. This is a tough, tough industry. If you're working and in demand, you have to be committed," he said.

He was an editor at *Mirabella* and *Marie Claire* before starting his own production company, Trew Productions, where he now casts eight shows in New York, as well as the new LA Fashion Week and Bridal Week. And he also hosts lectures on modeling for a thousand to fifteen hundred wanna-be models at a time, and judged the Miss USA pageant!

In the business, there are four thousand working models and only thirty jobs per day. "We're always looking for perfect shape, perfect skin, perfection. It's an image," he explains, adding that he sees one thousand five hundred wanna-bes a day when he is scouting and finds only twenty-four or so with promise.

One of his funny anecdotes: "I did this designer Atil Kutoglu—some fabulous Turkish designer. I told all the girls he used to work for Helmut Lang so they would walk in his show."

Did he?

"No!" he says gleefully. "But that's the business. You gotta do what you gotta do."

In the name of "doing what you have to do," he gave us catwalk lessons in order to perfect our sidewalk presence. (He did it for Joan Jett; he can certainly do it for us.)

"Modeling is in your head. You're going out there to the most important editors, the most important magazines and newspapers. You've got to sell the clothes—no, you *are* the clothes! You've got to make it work! Make them want you! Make them want to be you!" was tip number one.

Second tip: "Feel the music. Walk to the rhythm. Be one with the beat. *Don't prance*. Be a show pony, but don't look like you're trying to be." Then, pause at the end of the runway, as if you're saying, "Yeah, you want a piece of me," swivel your hips to the side, pivot your feet, and turn around to go back to where you came from. "Leave them wanting more," he said.

Easier said than done!

The Melissa!

The Melissa!

I like to slink, shuffle. As many have pointed out, I can't even walk in the many pairs of four-inch heels I own. I have flat feet and a duck walk (toes pointed out). I strap on my five-inch Saint Laurent heels and look to Drew for guidance. "Can I do the thumb hook?" I ask, looping my thumbs on my belt loops.

"Whatever makes you the most comfortable!" he encourages.

The office in Soho, where we're practicing, is filled with people on the phone. No one is looking at me, but as I begin to make my way across the room, from the racks of clothing to the big bay windows, the atmosphere is suddenly tense. Walking like a model is commanding the room to look at you, to make your presence known. I was struck with stage fright. I couldn't do it.

"Shoulders up. Attitude, attitude," Drew yelled.

After two attempts, he suggested I try it in sneakers! I go again. In Adidas, I'm much more on my game. I pull off the hip swivel. Left, right, I'm on fire. I imagine that the cameras are flashing and I'm dating Leo DiCaprio! I work it! Hooray!

Karen joins me on the "runway" and we high-five each other in the middle, just like we've seen real catwalk mavens do. It's exhilarating. We're actually having fun! This is what modeling is all about.

SARA JAYE WEISS

The Karen!

The Karen!

I actually thought the walk would be easy at first. I'm a flashy kind of girl. I like attention, I admit (must be because of some of the positive affirmation I lacked in childhood). I like to think I have the soul of an actor and that I can become anyone I want if I try real hard. *Wrong!* The second I begin my stride, I crack up. I cannot keep a straight face while my walk is being judged. I don't have the most beautiful saunter to begin with. I drag my heels and tend to put most of my weight on the outer edges of my foot, as evidenced by the way all my shoes are worn down on the outside edge rather than in the center. I swing my arms ungracefully. And I have a bit of a forward shoulder posture, which, I've been told by more than one massage therapist, makes me look older than I am.

"You didn't realize you'd have such a hard case on your hands, huh?" I say to Drew. He tells me to make a concerted effort to lift my feet more. At first I lift them so much, he laughs. "You're not mountain climbing, remember." Three more tries and I nail it. Then we focus on the shoulders. I put my yoga practice to work and do what I do when I'm in triangle pose—I melt my shoulder blades down my back. "Yes, you're taller. I feel it," he encourages. "Now, pretend you're making eyes at the hottest guy across the room," he suggests. I imagine my boyfriend across from me and put on my sexiest stare.

"Bigger steps and you have it," Drew says. The second I take bigger steps, I drag my feet again and the whole walk is lost. "Attitude, attitude. Remember it's all in your head. Everyone wants you. Everyone wants to be you," he says.

Try as I may, I just can't imagine such a thing. And we double air-kiss good-bye. As I leave the office, he shrieks, "That's it!" I wasn't even trying that time—and he says I'm 70 percent there: "That's huge for a civilian!" He told me I have to perfect my attitude more. And I've been working on it ever since.

Walk This Way

- Stride. Walk in time to the music—even if it's just the sound track you hear only in your head.

- Keep your hips loose.

- Don't swing your arms too much. Hooking a thumb into your jeans pocket is acceptable.

- Shoulders back, but not parallel to the floor.

- Don't drag your feet—lift them but not too much. You don't want to bend your knees so high that they hit your chin. Only Gisele can get away with that.

- You are a diva! You are a goddess! Feel the energy of the crowd and let it inspire you.

- End-of-runway poses:

    1. The hip swivel—At the end of the runway, shift weight from one hip to the other. Then pirouette. Make sure your head is the last thing to turn.

    2. The cold shoulder—This is the current favorite by designers. When you begin your pirouette, turn the shoulder first. Then turn your head.

    3. The Tyson—Male models are usually instructed not to stop at the end of the runway, and just to keep walking, slowing down a bit at the end for the cameras, then turning away.

Supermodel, Work!

MODEL WALKS TO EMULATE

- The Gisele!—High knees. The big tromp. Clomp, clomp, clomp like a Clydesdale pony.

- The Carmen!—A little shake. A little jiggle. Lots of sex appeal.

- The Erin!—Sideways head. Very sportswear.

- The Shalom!—Old-school style, full-on swayback. Walking as if you're the backslash key on a computer keyboard.

A FINAL NOTE FROM THE FASHIONISTAS

Now that you can walk the walk, talk the talk, and know how to get others to pay the drink bill if you've "forgotten your wallet at home"—it's time to get out there and live life to the fashionable fullest! Being a fashionista means having a sense of humor and a desire to be outrageous and over-the-top, and never, ever staying home just because you have nothing to wear (unless, of course, the couch has never felt more comfortable). Clean out your closets, take a pair of scissors to your favorite T-shirt, and attack the sales, the thrift shops, and eBay with aplomb. Remember, even if you stumble on your four-inch heels, the fact that you pull yourself up and keep walking is the mark of a true fashionista.

Acknowledgments

We owe so many double-cheek air-kisses to so many chic, stylish people, it's beyond. First of all, Allison Dickens, our genius editor. A bitch-and-swap party in your name is definitely in order—along with a mani-pedi date at Buff in Bergdorf Goodman! And Deborah Schneider, the most sophisticated agent on the planet. You are gorge! Thank you both for giving us a reason to overindulge at shopping malls, outlet stores, sample sales, thrift shops, and many boutiques around the country. Thanks to Elizabeth Lippman, our energetic photographer, who would lie down in the street just to get the shot right. Your shutterbug brilliance rocks—and plus, you look so cute in those hot-pink shoes.

We are so grateful to our dads, Bert de la Cruz and Alan Robinovitz. Thank you for your belief, encouragement, and the occasional clothing stipend. We love you.

Thanks to our siblings, who constantly support us and let us influence what they wear, and their families. Jason Robinovitz (you are very well trained and your Birkin knowledge should be commended), Francis de la Cruz, Steve, Christina, and Nicholas (a most stylish baby!) Green, Mom and Dad Johnston, John, Anji, Tim, Rob, Jenn, and Valerie. Thanks to our extended families, our aunts, uncles, and cousins, who never laughed at our outfits (well, not that loudly, at least)—that means all of the Robinovitzes, Ongs, Torres, Gaisanos, de la Cruzes, and Johnstons out there.

Todd, thank you for letting me Gucci you out. You are such a GQ man. And just as gorgeous dressed up as you are dressed down.

I love you all chic and sleek or biker and tough. Either way, you rock my world.

Thanks to Mike Johnston for always, for everything.

And so much love to everyone who helped make our fashionista lifestyles and our book a reality: Alice Roi, Allison Newman at Frette, Amanda Schuon and everyone at Truth be Told PR, Andrea Victor, Anne Waterman, Avon's amazing spa, everyone at Ballantine, especially Nancy Stevenson, Kim Hovey, Heather Smith, Avideh Bashirrad, Christine Cabello, Bacardi, Basia Irzyk, Bobbi Brown, Bonni Fuller, Brent Rimes, Campari, Caroline Suh (for all those tapered jeans freshman year!), Chrissy D (the British shopping guru . . . sort of), Danna Weiss, Diane von Fustenberg, Douglas Geller, Diana Gosendi, Dr. Victor, Edgardo de la Cruz (otherwise known as "Tito Ed!"), Elisa Jimenez, Gabriel de Guzman, Gina Dinisio, Helaine Schmier, Jaclyn Savar, Jaime Maser, Janice Dickinson, Jasmine Faustino, Jennifer Kim (for always lending a broke fashionista ten or twenty bucks when she needed it), Jen Weinberg, Jeffrey Kalinsky, Juicy Couture (Pam and Gela, we live in our monogrammed sweats!), Heidi Krupp, Karen Thorne, Kelly Cutrone, Kyristine Muldowney, Kim DeMarco, Kirna and Zabete, Laura Baddish, Lauren Weisberg, Leslie Stevens, Libby Callaway (without whom this book would not exist!), Levi's, Michael Kors, Michael Musto, Michael Palladino (you are such a delight), Molly Kim (a.k.a. "Jean-Claude," the Dachshund), Nicole Young, Punch & Judy, Melissa Comito at Fairchild Publications, Pamela Peckerman, Patrick McCarthy, Sam Firer, Shel Pink and everyone at Orly, Sally Narkis (our not-always-reasonable voice of reason and the best shopping partner in crime!), Sara Jaye Weiss, Simon Doonan, Stacy Kaplan, Stacey Mayesh, Steve Eichner, Steven Hall, Sue Devitt, Tammie Walker (for all of the Krispy Kremes that killed our thighs!), Target, Tartare, Teril Turner, Tiffany Dubin, Tristan Ashby, Tyler Rollins, Vegas (the fashionista dog), Volvo, Warren Tricomi, We Care, Whisper PR, Woodbury Commons.

And then there's Phoebe Philo, Stella McCartney, Marc Jacobs, Karl Lagerfeld, Tom Ford, Alexander McQueen, John Galliano, Jean Paul Gaultier, Nicolas Ghesquière, Manolo Blahnik, Jimmy Choo, Christian Louboutin, and all of our favorite designers who have inspired us and helped add glamour, whimsy, and style to our lives.

Mwah! Mwah! *J'adore!*

About the Authors

ELIZABETH LIPPMAN

On Mel (left):
Filigrana earrings,
cashmere sweater
by Tse,
leather-band wool
trousers by Alvin Valley

On Karen (right):
sweater with tie
by Yves Saint Laurent,
jeans by Levi's

Hair: Dennis Gotsopoulos
for Warren-Tricomi Salons
Make-up: Brent Riens
and Allison McGraine
for Sue Devitt Studio
Location: Studio 259

Melissa de la Cruz and **Karen Robinovitz** are the authors of *How to Become Famous in Two Weeks or Less* (Ballantine Books, 2003), which was optioned for development as a major motion picture by Walt Disney Studios and optioned for development as a reality television series by Universal Studios/Reveille Productions.

Melissa is the author of *Cat's Meow* and *The Au Pairs*. Her work has been translated into many languages. She has written for *Marie Claire, Harper's Bazaar, Gotham, Hamptons, Teen Vogue, Glamour, Allure,* the *New York Times,* and *McSweeney's*. Her forthcoming works include the novel *Fresh off the Boat* and her essay "A Model Boyfriend" in the anthology *Sex & Sensibility*. She lives in Los Angeles with her husband.

Karen is a prolific writer who covers fashion, trends, style, celebrities, lifestyles of the rich and fabulous, and sex for *Marie Claire, Harper's Bazaar,* the *New York Post,* and *Elle*. She has contributed to the *New York Times* Style section, *Details, Glamour,* and *In Style*. She is a co-author, with Lara Shriftman and Elizabeth Harrison, of *Fête Accompli! The Ultimate Guide to Creative Entertaining* (Clarkson Potter), being released in 2004. She lives in New York City.

ORLY®

FASHIONISTA FILES
adventures in nail couture